Radiance of Glory

A Forty-day Journey
to Discover Jesus

Lanny K Cook, PhD; D.MIN

Poetry written and provided as noted ~
Clarice D. Cook or **Lanny K. Cook**

Editing provided by Judy Cook - B.A., English; M.A
Literary Review provided by Kathleen Cook – B.A., Communication
Cover Design – Lanny Cook

Denver, Colorado

ISBN: 979-8-9895354-9-1
Library of Congress: 2025911527

Author Contact Information:
Lanny.Cook@LannyCook.com

Long ago God spoke to the fathers by the prophets at different times and in different ways. In these last days, He has spoken to us by His Son. God has appointed Him heir of all things and made the universe through Him. The *Son* is the *radiance of God's glory* and the exact expression of His nature, sustaining all things by His powerful word. After making purification for sins, He sat down at the right hand of the Majesty on high. *Hebrews 1:1-3 HCSB*

Contents

Contents cont....

Also, from the appearance of His waist and upward I saw, as it were, the color of amber with the appearance of fire all around within it; and from the appearance of His waist and downward I saw, as it were, the appearance of fire with brightness all around. Like the appearance of a rainbow in a cloud on a rainy day, so *was* the appearance of the brightness all around it. This *was* the appearance of the likeness of the *glory* of the Lord. Ezekiel 1:27, 28 NKJV

DEDICATED TO:
Gladys P. Williams

Gladys P. Williams, born on May 18, 1901, is Lanny's maternal grandmother. Her deep Christian faith was instilled through the efforts of her parents Peter Hans and Lillie Frees Peterson, who were immigrants to this country from Denmark in the late eighteenth century. Starting at a very young age, she embraced the Gospel of Jesus Christ and allowed her faith to shine brightly onto the lives of her family, including; her husband, Bob, their three children, eight grandchildren, and numerous great-grandchildren. Gladys dedicated her entire life to Jesus, fervently serving Him for nearly a century after accepting Him into her life as a small child. Within the unwavering devotion to her faith, she served as a light and a faithful witness of Jesus Christ for the world to see. Indeed, she was a *good and faithful servant to her Lord and Master.*

"Only one life 'twill soon be past, only what's done for Christ will last." C.T. Studd

I have fought the good fight, I have finished the race, I have kept the faith. Now there is in store for me the crown of righteousness, which the Lord, the righteous Judge, will award to me on that day—and not only to me, but also to all who have longed for his appearing. *2 Timothy 4:7-8 NIV*

Acknowledgement

Therefore, we also, since we are surrounded by so great a cloud of witnesses, let us lay aside every weight, and the sin which so easily ensnares us, and let us run with endurance the race that is set before us, looking unto Jesus, the author and finisher of our faith, who for the joy that was set before Him endured the cross, despising the shame, and has sat down at the right hand of the throne of God. *Hebrews 12:1,2 NKJV*

I grew up in a family blessed by a great cloud of witnesses. From my earliest recollections, the truth of the Gospel was spoken over my life through devoted followers of Jesus. Grandparents, parents, aunts, uncles, and cousins openly shared their faith in meaningful ways. Their lives were a testimony to the love, grace, mercy, and provision of God Almighty. As I became an adult, the challenges and trials of life sent me on a journey of discovery that confirmed my faith. Around every corner, behind every obstacle, and within every daunting challenge, my faith was validated in profound ways. As I was finishing up the final details of this forty-day journey, I received news of the passing of my oldest cousin, Ken who I was particularly close with and admired greatly. He was ten years older than me and he was my hero when I was a child. He became a mighty warrior for the Lord, serving many years ministering as a Gideon, and trying to make sure that both family, friends, and strangers had an opportunity to come into relationship with Jesus. This was his own personal ministry. Because of the admiration I had for Ken, along with the timing in which He entered into his eternal reward, I felt compelled to acknowledge a few loved ones who have gone on before me; those that not only openly and eloquently professed their faith in Jesus Christ, but who followed Him with passion, all the days of their lives.

Kenneth Lee Fender - 1946-2025 (Cousin)
Timothy Eugene Trusty - 1956 -1988 (Cousin)
Donald Eugene Trusty -1932-2017 (Uncle)
Gordon Samuel Cook - 1933-2018 (Father)
Gladys P. Williams - 1901-2003 (Grandmother)

For to me, to live is Christ, to die is gain. *Philippians 1:21 NKJV*

A Message from Lanny!

No single life in the history of mankind has had a greater impact on this world, than Jesus Christ. To millions of followers, He is considered to be many things: Master, Teacher, Savior, Redeemer, Prophet, and the Son of God. Jesus is the Living Word, the Truth, the Light, and Way. He is the long-awaited Messiah, who came as the fulfillment of the entire Old Testament Law. Now is the time to discover for yourself that Jesus truly is who He says He is. But that requires you to set out on a committed quest for the truth. You were born for such a time as this. Your life is about to change forever, as you embark on this forty-day journey to personally encounter Jesus!

The Holy Bible is the best-selling book of all times. It was written over a 1500-year period, on three different continents, in two different languages, by over forty individual authors. These authors were divinely inspired to scribe the words through the power of the Holy Spirit. This scriptural document is divided into two distinct sections, the Old and the New Testaments. The Old Testament, often referred to as the Old Covenant, begins with the Five Books of Moses, or the Torah. All of which were transcribed during the forty years of Israel's wandering in the wilderness before entering the Promised Land. It's followed by the history of Israel, the Judges, her Kings, her rebellion, her repentance; all accompanied with the words of the Prophets involving Israel's call. That purpose was totally defined according to God's plan of salvation for all of humanity. All of which is embodied within the prophetic tapestry of Jesus Christ, the Messiah.

The Bible, in its entirety, is the story of Jesus, the Christ. While it is a book filled with history, mystery, poetry, prophecy, moral guidance, and the good news of the Gospels, which capture the story of Jesus after His birth; it collectively provides the plan for humanity's redemption through God's grace, mercy, and promise. The Bible, dramatically points to the Word (Jesus), that became flesh and dwelt among us. Simply stated, Scripture intricately defines God's appointed desire to bring fallen humanity back into relationship with Himself – for all eternity.

Contained within the sacred pages of the Holy Scripture are hundreds of Messianic prophecies, which provide profound insight concerning the birth, death, resurrection, and Second Coming of the

Lord Jesus Christ. They also include details into the Day of the Lord and His ultimate reign for a thousand years at the end of this Age of Grace. The majority of these prophecies, all inspired by God, were spoken by His appointed prophets, hundreds of years before the birth of Jesus. Words sealed throughout the pages of antiquity vividly proclaim God's plan of salvation to a lost and hurting world. It has been determined that there are more than 300 Messianic prophecies foretelling the events leading to the life, death, and resurrection of Jesus Christ. The odds of one man being able to fill all of these long-proclaimed prophecies are nearly impossible to calculate, let alone comprehend.

Jesus Christ willingly became the Sacrificial Lamb, His blood served as the atonement for the sins of the world. It is only through Him, that you can enter into communion and fellowship with God, the Father. Once inside His Door, you are forever changed---transformed---and your eternal destiny is sealed as your name is written in the *Lamb's Book of Life*. You are then, by the grace of God, ordained for life everlasting with Him---in a world beyond human comprehension. It is written: *"eye hath not seen, nor ear heard, neither have entered into the heart of man, the things which God hath prepared for then that love him,"* (I Corinthians 2:9).

It's important to consider, that throughout the pages of the Bible, we recognize God's practice to define the number *forty* within the *refining process* of His purpose. It was often used to spiritually prepare the hearts of many notable servants; those who God appointed to carry out His mission as presented throughout the biblical drama of Christ's story. This number is significant as it is often applied in the form of testing, trial, preparation, and purification. Shared below are just a few examples: In *Noah's day* it rained for forty days and forty nights after he entered into the ark with his family and a boatload of paired-up critters. *Israel's first kings*, Saul, David, and Solomon each reigned for forty years.

Moses' life was profoundly divided into three segments of forty-years. He was raised and served in the courts of the Egyptian Pharoah for the first forty-years of his life, before being exiled to the wilderness for killing an Egyptian overseer who was beating a Hebrew slave. He spent the next four decades tending his flocks in the wilderness before being called by God Almighty to serve as the deliverer of the Hebrew slaves. This became his time of divine preparation before responding to God's call for the final forty-years of his earthly days. It was during this final phase of his life that he became Israel's initial liberator. Even though his efforts never allowed him access into the Promised Land as the Israelites wandered in the wilderness because of God's discipline for their lack of faith. But it was during those years of wandering that Moses scribed the first five books of the Bible, or as the Jews refer to that collection of ancient writing, the Torah. It's important to recognize that Moses was a *foreshadow of the Promised Messiah*. He served as a precursor to Israel's *Promised Deliverer*, called to lead God's Chosen, out of bondage and into a life of abundance.

Personally, one of the more intriguing applications of the number forty contained within the Old Testament is also connected to Moses, at least in my estimation. It involved the nation of Israel's grumbling, as well as her disobedience during their forty-year exile to the wilderness. I believe it was a culminating factor involving God's response to *Israel's cyclical rejection* of His word throughout her history. The Lord's discipline to these ten-cycles of disobedience, actually resulted in the four-hundred-years of silence between the last prophetic word from God to His chosen by any Old Testament prophet, and the arrival of the Messiah into the world.

The entire ordeal of Israel's recurring rejection of God is recorded in the Old Testament books of Exodus and Numbers. To briefly summarize: Through the initial journey of deliverance out of Egypt, the Israelite's arrived at the edge of the Promised Land. During this time, there are ten examples of the Hebrews complaining, ignoring Moses' directives, grumbling against God, and ultimately rejecting Joshua and Caleb's report regarding the true blessing of God's provision within the Promised Land. In Numbers we read God's response to the Israelite's continued rejection, grumbling, hard-heartedness, and disobedience. *The Lord said to Moses, "How long will these people treat me with contempt? How long will they refuse to believe in me, in spite of all the signs I have performed among them?* (Numbers 14:11 NIV).

Fast forward one-thousand years and you will come to the end of the Old Testament prophets. Israel was no longer a sovereign nation;

she would remain under foreign rule from that point on for more than two-thousand years. Even though the Jews were allowed to live in the region, including the Holy City of Jerusalem until 70 AD. Israel's continued disobedience involving her adulterous relationship with foreign gods, had placed the people under the heavy hand of various conquering nations through the centuries. God had turned His back on her. But *He never let her out of His sight*. He still had a *sanctified plan and purpose for His Chosen People.* It would be four-hundred-years between the proclamations of the prophet Malachi and the birth of Jesus Christ.

What I find extremely interesting, and what I believe is worthy of some deep reflection at this point; involves the correlating relevance involved within the significance of *Israel's forty-years* of discipline before being allowed to enter into the Promised Land. That was God's initial consequence under the pleading heart of Moses for God to take pity on His people. Although they didn't get off scot-free, as none of the original adults of the Exodus were allowed entrance into the land because of their lack of faith. But let's take a moment to reflect on the significance of the 400 years of silence between Malachi and the birth of Jesus. Remember the *ten recorded* instances mentioned in Exodus and Numbers that involved the people's rejection, doubt, and irreverence to God's provision throughout their journey. It had been more than a thousand years since those days. Israel had become a nation, ruled by Judges, and then later on, by her own Kings. But the people continued down a *path of cyclical rejection*, resulting in *divinely applied discipline*, followed by the people's *repentance*, as they *turned back to God*. Their repentance would once again open their lives to an abundance of *blessing from the Lord's patient provision*.

Finally, God had His fill of Israel's adulterous ways. So, what happened? He took a step back from the people, and left them to manage on their own. Does it make you wonder how coincidental it is that God chose to be silent for four-hundred-years as He made plans for His Son to be delivered in a lowly, stable in Bethlehem? *Forty years* of wandering, multiplied by *ten counts* of Israel's rejection on their way to the *Promised Land*, resulted in a sentence of solitary separation from God for four-hundred-years. That's a fairly substantial length of time for

Abraham's lot to silently contemplate their relationship with the Almighty. Remember, God often applied the number forty to specific periods of time for the preparation of His purpose within the lives of both individuals and nations.

Israel was afforded four-centuries to once again, spend time isolated in the wilderness of their own making, in order to prepare for the Messiah. By the end of that four-hundred-years of God's silence, the masses were desperately prepared to welcome the *Man of Wonders* into their lives. Sadly, a lot of them still weren't able to receive or believe in Jesus. Case in point; most of the religious leaders couldn't get past the legality of their twisted religion to accept the truth of God's grace. The priests of Jesus' day embraced a totally legalist view of God's Law, and were totally incapable of understanding or relating to the spiritual nature of grace, embodied within the promise of the Messiah.

A legalist says God will love you if you change. But grace declares; God loves you just the way you are, and He's not about to leave you in the sad state of your personal circumstance. It is for that very reason that He sent His only Son to serve as the sacrifice necessary to save your very soul. The reality of the profound mercy offered to you from the Lord involves the truth declaring that God's grace always trumps legalism. Christ came not to destroy the law, but that through Him the Law would be fulfilled. The religious leaders of Jesus' day would never accept that profound truth as a legalistic view of God had been hard-wired into their minds and hearts over the centuries due to their unwavering devotion to the Laws of Moses. In their mind, that was the only way to gain access to God the Father.

Personally, I think it was no coincidence that there was such a great time span between the last words of God's final Old Testament prophet, Malachi, and the first words from the Supreme Prophet, Jesus Christ; Who was, and is, and is to come. Of course, this leads us into the consideration regarding two of the most important examples of the number forty in the Bible. The first involves *Jesus'* spending forty days and nights, fasting and praying in the wilderness before beginning His official, earthly ministry. The *second* even greater reference to a forty-day period of preparation with *Jesus* occurred immediately following His resurrection. He completed His final time on earth with forty-days of ministry-time, sharing His final words of instruction with the Disciples and the masses in His resurrected form. One might assume that this forty-day period was a final time of preparation for the Lord to take His place at the right-hand of God. Forty-days after He rose from the grave, Jesus ascended into heaven in order to prepare a place for all who would follow after Him. These final days were truly the capstone of His initial, earthly ministry. But wrapped within this time frame, ultimately, was an intense period of preparation for these anointed Apostles to go forth into all the world to share the Good News of the Gospel of Jesus Christ.

There are numerous instances of God using the number forty as a means to prepare His chosen servants for a specific, appointed calling. You can research other examples on your own. With that being said, *welcome* to your personal forty-day journey to fully discover the miraculous nature of Jesus, the Christ. Thank you for joining me on this journey. During this time, you will discover biblical truths regarding the life, death, resurrection, and purpose for Jesus' ministry. Each section begins with relevant scriptures that relate to the Messiah, as found within the pages of both the Old and the New Testaments of the Holy Bible. These passages are followed by a devotional that is intended to instill moments of reflection for what Christ offers to the world even during these modern times. Every section then concludes with words of poetic inspiration (much like David's Book of Psalms), designed to intimately awaken your soul as a means to draw attention back toward your personal relationship with the Lord. At the end of every section, you are provided an opportunity to ponder each day's lesson, and then journal the impact of that particular devotion.

I must warn you; this isn't the typical, run-of-the-mill-devotional that you can simply allot five-minutes a day toward, before running off to complete your personal obligations. I recommend you set aside at least forty-minutes a day for the next forty-days to really discover Jesus. The devotions you are about to experience require deep consideration, in order to truly experience the radiance of Christ's glory. I strongly encourage you to savor these moments, as you immerse yourself in a study to discover the true nature and grace of the Lord Jesus Christ. This journey requires a commitment on your part, just as your choice to follow Him involves great devotion. If it's too much to ask, remember Jesus' words to Peter in the Garden of Gethsemane, *can you not tarry with me for just one hour?*

It is my prayer that the words contained within the following pages, assist you in discovering Jesus Christ in a new and more passionate light. I pray that you will experience Him as the true *Radiance of God's Glory*, providing the strength and courage to not only manage life's challenges and trials, but to discover a deeper hope and a fuller assurance of grace, through the promise of God's love. During one of the times when Jesus was being confronted by the Pharisees in an effort to find some fault in His teaching, He spoke this profound bit of prophetic insight: **"I am the light of the world. Anyone who follows Me will never walk in the darkness but will have the light of life,"** (John 8:12 HCSB).

As you are drawn to the *Light* during this journey of discovery, may you embrace a more intimate and meaningful relationship with your Lord and Master---the One known as *Jesus, the Christ!* May God's *radiant light of glory*, forever shine upon your path. It is my prayer that He fills your heart with the bountiful riches of His grace, mercy, provision, and love!

Shalom and God bless! - *Lanny Cook*

Barukh atah Adonai Eloheinu melekh zokher hab'rit v'ne'eman bivrito v'kayam b'ma'amaro. - Blessed are You, Lord our God, Ruler of the Universe, who remembers the covenant, and is faithful to God's covenant, and keeps God's promise.[1]

---

[1]   Every Day Blessings & Rituals, *My Jewish Learning*,
       www.myjewishlearning.com/article/everyday-blessings-rituals/

Day 1

Is Jesus the Only Way?

Scriptural Reflection

Behold, I stand at the door and knock. If anyone hears My voice and opens the door, I will come in to him and dine with him, and he with Me. To him who overcomes I will grant to sit with Me on My throne, as I also overcame and sat down with My Father on His throne.
Revelation 3:20-21 NKJV

And if Christ has not been raised, our preaching is useless and so is your faith. More than that, we are then found to be false witnesses about God, for we have testified about God that he raised Christ from the dead. But he did not raise him if in fact the dead are not raised. For if the dead are not raised, then Christ has not been raised either. And if Christ has not been raised, your faith is futile; you are still in your sins. Then those also who have fallen asleep in Christ are lost. If only for this life we have hope in Christ, we are of all people most to be pitied.
1 Corinthians 15:14-19 NIV

In the beginning was the Word, and the Word was with God, and the Word was God. He was with God in the beginning. Through him all things were made; without him nothing was made that has been made. In him was life, and that life was the light of all mankind. The light shines in the darkness, and the darkness has not overcome it. [9] The true light that gives light to everyone was coming into the world. He was in the world, and though the world was made through him, the world did not recognize him. He came to that which was his own, but his own did not receive him. Yet to all who did receive him, to those who believed in his name, he gave the right to become children of God—children born not of natural descent, nor of human decision or a husband's will, but born of God. The Word became flesh and made his dwelling among us. We have seen his glory, the glory of the one and only Son, who came from the Father, full of grace and truth.
John 1:1-5, 9-14 NIV

Therefore, God exalted him to the highest place and gave him the name that is above every name, that at the name of Jesus every knee should bow, in heaven and on earth and under the earth, and every tongue acknowledge that Jesus Christ is Lord, to the glory of God the Father.
Philippians 2:9-11 NIV

The topic of this introductory devotion is a stumbling block for a majority of people, including many folks who claim to be Christians. It's also a bit longer than all the rest of the devotions that you are about to encounter. Please, bear with me through this initial portion of the journey as we lay the *foundational premise* for the time we'll spend together over the next forty-days.

Within this age of political correctness there are many who believe there has to be multiple paths that lead to heaven. The concept of heaven according to the modern cultural view, involves any and all personal preferences that meet an individual's specific viewpoint. As a society we have digressed to the point where every person appoints themselves capable of *defining truth* according to the desires of their human heart. The modern culture has usurped Godly morality and defends the right for every individual to determine what is acceptable or wrong - good or evil; or what is moral or immoral in accordance with the convenience of their twisted personal desire. There is no longer an acceptable standard of reference because God has been removed from the equation. Which means there is no truth to the modern-day definition of truth!

Is Jesus the Only Way? That's the question that will be answered within the confines of this introductory devotion. It's one that will literally decide your eternal fate. In this hypersensitive, politically correct, cancel-culture world; it has become extremely common to hear people say there are a multitude of ways to find god and enter into your own personal desire of eternal paradise. It's common place to define god according to your own standards. Since as an individual in today's world, you can be whatever you want to be. Whether it's true or not, your personal preference for a deity of your choosing, allows you to determine who or what you want him, her, or it, to be. It's pretty normal anymore to stuff your humanly-contrived deity into a box of tolerance created through a fabric of perverted, lifestyle choices. Of course, none of which bear any resemblance to righteousness, divinity, morality, or even Godly power. This of course is a contrived, secular perspective. It is a form of idolatry that originates through a limited human pursuit of any or all things spiritual or supernatural. In essence, the modern culture is very similar to all

2

previous cultures from the ancient of days.

Throughout the history of humanity, cultures have searched for *spiritual purpose*. Nearly all religious quests promote some form of heavenly award for its participant at their passing from this world. However, if you believe what the Bible says, these other paths are nothing more than an individually contrived, self-serving view of piety that involve a wide menagerie of false gods and idols. This form of feel-good promise is extremely palatable but flagrantly flawed. It's a devious concoction with deadly consequences.

According to the Bible, there is only one way to enter into heaven. There is no other road that will get you there. The truth of the Gospel message, is that this has nothing to do with religion. Rather, it has everything to do with your personal relationship with Jesus. One of the biggest, societal criticisms about Jesus being *the only way*, involves the critique that this is too exclusive. If it's not all-inclusive, then it is intolerant. Every world religion is *exclusive in their own right*, and has been throughout the history of mankind. Take a moment to reflect on the following considerations: First, religion is man's attempt to either find God or define himself as a god. Throughout history, mankind has worshipped multitudes of different deities. The culture in Ephesus worshipped a mixture of Roman and Greek gods; Diana, Zeus, Mercury, Artemis, Jupiter, Mars, Hades, Aphrodite, Ares, and Hermes. The Egyptians were also polytheists worshipping hundreds of gods - the sun god Ra, the creator god Amun, the mother goddess Isis, and Osiris the ruler of the underworld. The Philistines worshipped Dagon. The Canaanites were Baal Worshipers. Hindus choose a personal deity to worship, known as an *ishta devata*. Muslims worship Allah. Agnostics worship science through the defining pursuit of objective, secular truth. Naturalists worship nature. Narcissists worship self.

The desire to *worship* is written within the very essence of humanity's DNA. The right to freely worship in America has created a spiritual confusion based on religious equality under the law. This infers tolerance across the board. But spiritually, this isn't true. *Religious equality* is separate from *religious truth*, the difference between the two requires definition from a biblical perspective. Not all religions possess the sovereignty of *divine Truth*. Most of them have been derived by secular hopes, dreams, aspirations, and even wild imaginations. Take the Pharaohs of Egypt and the Cesars of Rome. In this life, they elevated themselves to the status of deity. But yet, when they died, they remained dead. I've visited the tombs of the Pharaohs in the Valley of the Kings in Egypt. Trust me, they never became gods. They never acquired the form of any sort of deity. Their mummified remains clearly proclaim that dead is surely dead, inside the confines of their religious pursuit of personal deification.

Religious equality doesn't equate to *spiritual validity* in God's sight! *Tolerance* doesn't translate to *truth*. The search for truth doesn't give anyone a license to discriminate, but it does provide the spiritual insight to discern the straight and narrow path. It's not possible for all religions to be a valid means to enter into relationship with the One True God, and the Holy Bible makes that perfectly clear. Many people believe nearly all religions worship the same god but call him by a different name. There is nothing further from the truth!

Although Judaism and Christianity both worship the same God; the God of Abraham, Isaac, and Jacob, no other religions worship Him. The difference between Judaism and Christianity involves the perceived status of the Promised Messiah. Orthodox Jews are waiting for Him to arrive. Christians believe that Jesus (Messiah) made His first appearance over 2,000 years ago. He was rejected by the Sanhedrin before being crucified for the blasphemy of claiming to be God. On the third day He rose from the grave. *Forty-days* later He ascended into heaven and will return at the end of this age in what is referred to as His *Second Coming*!

Judaism gave us the Old Testament, which is the inspired Word of God. Christianity proclaims that both the Old and the New Testaments are the completed Word, with emphasis being placed on the truth that Jesus is the Word. The New Testament confirms through a myriad of first-hand accounts by credible witnesses, that *Jesus is the fulfillment of the Old Testament Laws* and Prophets. Thus, those in the Jewish faith, pray to the Father, or Yahweh, while Christian's pray to the Father in the name of Jesus, as He is the Mediator between mankind and God Almighty. Christians have access to God the Father through the Son, Jesus Christ. In John 14:6 we are told by Jesus, Himself,

"I am the way, the truth, and the life, No one comes to the Father except through Me." The Apostle Paul in a letter to his friend Timothy, confirms the truth that Jesus is the only means to come to the Father.

> For there is one God and one mediator between God and mankind, the man Christ Jesus, who gave himself as a ransom for all people, *(I Timothy 2:5-6 NIV).*

Only in the Bible is God revealed as the One eternal, personal Creator, who brought the entire universe into existence through His spoken Word. Most other religions worship "gods" representing the personification of natural forces of the universe. Christianity alone is centered on historical events and evidence associated with a Person—the promise, birth, death, resurrection, and prophesied return of Jesus Christ. Nearly all other religions are based on the imaginations and teachings of their deceptive founders.

An often-overlooked reality of the scriptures involves the basic premise in the literal division between the Old and the New Testaments. That *division is Christ.* It's similar to the one contained within the very distinction that divides our calendar; AD, Anno Domini, or the year of the Lord, and BC, Before Christ. Foundational to the purpose of this biblical division, is the revelation of promise regarding the Messiah, as presented in the Old Testament. The fulfillment, or completion of that revelation is presented in the New Testament proclaiming the arrival of the Messiah. All of which is contained within the life, death, and resurrection of Jesus Christ. Talk about historical confirmation. The Old Testament Prophets foretold of the miraculous events surrounding the promise of a redemptive Messiah. The New Testament confirms the details involving the fulfillment of those predictions within the record of Jesus and His mission. The prophetic promise within the Old Testament provides compelling confirmation to the reality of Jesus' own words.

> Do not think that I came to destroy the Law or the Prophets. I did not come to destroy but to fulfill,
> *(Matthew 5:17 NKJV).*

Jesus Christ is the only religious or spiritual figure who actually *conquered death*, as He was resurrected from the grave, and ascended into heaven with hundreds of first-hand witnesses. Christianity is founded on a *personal relationship* with the Creator offered through the life, death, and resurrection of Jesus Christ. Christianity is the only religion where a person is saved by grace rather than an individual's efforts, goodness, works, or own hand.

Skeptics will often try to discredit the divinity of Christ through the assumption that the Bible is the only record which attests to His life or purpose in this world. That's not true. The following historians all mentioned Jesus in their historical documents:

Suetonius – Roman Historian described the treatment of Christians under Claudius' rule: *They were committed to their belief Jesus was God and withstood the torment and punishment of the Roman Empire. Jesus had a curious and immediate impact on His followers, empowering them to die courageously for what they knew to be true.*

Lucian of Samosata– Greek Satirist wrote: *The Christians, you know, worship a man to this day—the distinguished personage who introduced their novel rites, and was crucified on that account.*

There were many other notable historians who mentioned Jesus within their historical records. Publius Cornelius Tacitus – a Roman Historian, Pliny the Younger – another Roman Historian. Josephus – Jewish Historian, Mara Bar-Serapion – a Syrian philosopher all record specific details regarding the life of Jesus Christ. Even within the tenants of Judaism – the Rabbinical Texts called the Talmud, refer to Jesus. But listen to what can be summarized through these various writings of ancient non-Christian sources: Josephus and Lucian indicate that Jesus was regarded as wise. Pliny, the Talmud (a central text of mainstream Judaism), and Lucian imply He was a powerful and revered teacher. Josephus and the Talmud indicate He performed miraculous feats. Tacitus, Josephus, the Talmud, and Lucian all mention that He was crucified. Tacitus and Josephus say this occurred under Pontius Pilate. And the Talmud declares it happened on the eve of Passover. There are references to Jesus' resurrection by both Tacitus and Josephus. Josephus records that Jesus' followers believed He was the Christ, or Messiah. Pliny and Lucian indicate that Christians worshipped Jesus as God!

History provides astounding evidence that Jesus lived over two-thousand years ago and even most critics won't argue that fact. Critics don't debate His teaching; they don't debate His existence. They are offended by His **exclusive claim** to be the *Son of God*, and His declaration that He is the *only way to God.* In fact, the reason Jesus was crucified had everything to do with His proclamation: *"when you see Me, you've seen the Father!"* Regardless of the overwhelming evidence from non-biblical sources, regarding the question as to "who Jesus is?" most skeptics are going to argue. So, this leads us back to the only viable source of verifiable evidence, which is contained within the pages of the Bible.

> **God has raised this Jesus to life, and we are all witnesses of it,** *(Acts 2:32 NIV).*

> **Salvation is found in no one else, for there is no other name under heaven given to mankind by which we must be saved,** *(Acts 4:12 NIV).*

> **Whoever believes in the Son of God accepts this testimony. Whoever does not believe God has made him out to be a liar, because they have not believed the testimony God has given about his Son. And this is the testimony: God has given us eternal life, and this life is in his Son. Whoever has the Son has life; whoever does not have the Son of God does not have life,** *(1 John 5:10-12 NIV).*

I will leave you with this question as you start out on this forty-day journey of discovering Jesus: *Do you believe that Jesus is the Only Way?* Before you answer that, reflect on this quote from C. S. Lewis.

> A man who was merely a man and said the sort of things Jesus said would not be a great moral teacher. He would be either a lunatic – on the level with the man who says he is a poached egg – or else he would be the Devil of Hell. You must make a choice. Either this man was, and is, the Son of God: or else a madman or something worse. You can shut Him up for a fool, you can spit at Him and kill Him as a demon; or you can fall at His feet and call Him Lord and God. But let us not come with any patronizing nonsense about him being a great human teacher. He has not left that open to us. He did not intend to. *(C.S. Lewis, Mere Christianity, pp. 55—56)*

Now it's time for you to draw your own conclusion. What do you say? Is Jesus the only Way to enter into relationship with God the Father, and for you to enter into His paradise when you pass from this world? It's up to you to decided for yourself. But be careful. Your eternal destination lies in the balance of this most consequential decision.

Jesus said, "Behold, I stand at the door and knock. If anyone hears My voice and opens the door, I will come in to him and dine with him, and he with Me. To him who overcomes I will grant to sit with Me on My throne, as I also overcame and sat down with My Father on His throne. (*Revelation 3:20-21NKJV*).

Have you heard Jesus knocking at the door of your life? Have you opened up your heart to let Him in? Take a moment to journal your thoughts about your relationship with Him in the space below.

_____

_____

_____

_____

_____

_____

_____

_____

_____

_____

_____

_____

_____

_____

_____

_____

Knocking on the Door

Do you hear Him knocking, before the sands of time?
Before the time when life began, God knew He'd need a plan,
  To one day come as one of us, to save the souls of man.
When the world was void and empty; when darkness filled the air,
  God planned a way for each of us to know how much He cared.

Do you hear Him knocking, as He softly calls your name?
Before the time our life began, He thought of you and me,
  Formed within our mother's womb, He knew who we would be,
Children of the living God, though born to sin and shame,
  The only path to heaven -is through the Savior's blessed name.

Do you hear Him knocking, as a baby faintly cries?
He's the Babe born in the manger, who opened up the door,
  In a humble common stable, He came from heaven's shore.
Lowly creatures there to witness, the Savior's virgin birth,
  God is now among us; True love has come to earth.

Do you hear Him knocking, as He humbly paved the way?
He paid the price for all our sins, He suffered, bled, and died,
  Through the agony of Golgotha, Our Lord was crucified.
The Babe born in the manger; He came to set us free;
  Redeemer, Savior, Sacrifice, He died for you and me!

Do you hear Him knocking, as He gently bids you come?
Step out onto the waters, In the midst of raging seas,
  Lift your eyes to His salvation, as you fall upon your knees;
With your humble adoration - He will save you from your sin;
  If you choose to hear Him knocking - If you choose to let him in.

Do you hear Him knocking? Do you know His name?"
He's the Babe born in a manger: Redemption from above;
  The Word who dwelt among us: The gift of God's full love.
He is Jesus Christ, the Savior, do you hear Him call your name?
  If you open up the door to Him, you will never be the same.

Do you hear Him knocking? Will you ask Him in?
When you realize God's mercy; He'll take away your fear,
  As you open up your heart, His gentle voice you'll hear;
May you take the time to seek Him: May you listen to His voice,
  He offers you, His gentle peace, let your heart & soul rejoice!

Lanny K. Cook

Day 2
Ancient of Days
Scriptural Reflection

"You are my witnesses," declares the Lord, "and my servant whom I have chosen, so that you may know and believe me and understand that I am he. Before me no god was formed, nor will there be one after me I, even I, am the Lord, and apart from me there is no savior. I have revealed and saved and proclaimed— I, and not some foreign god among you. You are my witnesses," declares the Lord, "that I am God. Yes, and from ancient days I am he. No one can deliver out of my hand. When I act, who can reverse it?" *Isaiah 43: 10-13 NIV*

I was watching in the night visions, and behold, One like the Son of Man, Coming with the clouds of heaven! He came to the Ancient of Days, and they brought Him near before Him. Then to Him was given dominion and glory and a kingdom, that all peoples, nations, and languages should serve Him. His dominion is an everlasting dominion, which shall not pass away, And His kingdom the one which shall not be destroyed. *Daniel 7: 13, 14 NKJV*

I cried out to God with my voice—To God with my voice; And He gave ear to me. In the day of my trouble. I sought the Lord; My hand was stretched out in the night without ceasing; My soul refused to be comforted. I remembered God, and was troubled; I complained, and my spirit was overwhelmed. Selah You hold my eyelids open; I am so troubled that I cannot speak. I have considered the days of old, The years of ancient times. I call to remembrance my song in the night; I meditate within my heart, and my spirit makes diligent search. Will the Lord cast off forever? And will He be favorable no more? Has His mercy ceased forever? Has His promise failed forevermore? Has God forgotten to be gracious? Has He in anger shut up His tender mercies? Selah

And I said, "This is my anguish; But I will remember the years of the right hand of the Most High." I will remember the works of the Lord; Surely, I will remember Your *wonders of old*. *Psalm 77: 1-11 NKJV*

To fully experience Jesus in a deep, personal way, it's essential to recognize Him through the biblical reference as the *Ancient of Days*. However, to do so, it's critical that we consider God's chosen nation of Israel which was called out from the days of old, in order to serve God's redemptive purpose for humanity. But before going there, it's important to answer one critical question: can we actually *rely on the Bible*, the *Word of God?* In other words, can we trust it? The reality of this question poses a dilemma for much of the scholarly world. Skeptics contend that much of the Bible is nothing more than storytelling or mythology gathered from old wives' tales of the nation of Israel. But those who come to the Scripture with an open mind will find that it truly is a divinely inspired piece of literature.

As we begin today's study involving the Ancient of Days, it requires a glimpse into the past involving the choosing of God's people, the Hebrews. They would serve as the conduit for sharing the Almighty's plan to bring humanity back into fellowship through the atoning blood of redemption. The Lord's purpose for salvation was put into play through a humble man named Abram. He was called to be the *patriarch of Israel's appointment* as God's chosen people. That appointment was specific, sanctified, and set forth from the foundations of the world. According to the Prophecy Study Bible:

> God chose the nation of Israel so that He would have a repository of divine truth for generations to come. Through Israel God has given the world the Word of God, the patriarchs, the prophets, Jesus Christ, and the apostles. There would be no Christianity without Jewish contribution. God's love for Israel produced Satan's hatred for Israel and the Jewish people. Anti-Semitism is driven by a demon spirit because of the righteous contributions the Jewish people made to civilization.[2]

Through Israel, God delivered the Laws of Moses, proclaiming the straight and *narrow path that leads to salvation*. Through His Law and the prophets, God shared with the world a path that would eventually lead to the foot of His throne. Israel was an integral part of that plan, yet there are many people today who think the Old Testament

---

[2]   *Prophecy Study Bible: New King James Version* (Nashville, TN: Thomas Nelson Publishing, 1997), p. 1590.

and Israel are no longer a viable component of God's purpose. They contend that ever since the gospel message was proclaimed to the world and the Church came into existence, God has no further plan or purpose for the Old Testament, the Jews, or Israel. These assumptions are nowhere near the truth. Jesus speaks directly to these misconceptions, as recorded in the Gospel of Matthew:

> Do not think that I have come to abolish the Law or the Prophets; I have not come to abolish them but to fulfill them. For truly I tell you, until heaven and earth disappear, not the smallest letter, not the least stroke of a pen, will by any means disappear from the Law until everything is accomplished. Therefore, anyone who sets aside one of the least of these commands and teaches others accordingly will be called least in the kingdom of heaven, but whoever practices and teaches these commands will be called great in the kingdom of heaven. For I tell you that unless your righteousness surpasses that of the Pharisees and the teachers of the law, you will certainly not enter the kingdom of heaven, *(Matthew 5:17–20 NIV)*.

The *Bible*, in its entirety, is *an amazing literary marvel*. It's not just a book of history, dates and times, or people and places. It's not just a compilation of philosophical ramblings or insignificant rhetoric. Rather, it is a meticulously refined manuscript that was carefully, thoughtfully, and divinely compiled for the sole purpose of providing humanity with God's redemptive revelation. It is *God's story*. Both the Old and New Testaments contain revolutionary insights and profound wisdom for enlightenment, not only for living in the current age but also, for understanding the plans and purposes of God Almighty. It is also the only book that offers the *key to eternity*, where true paradise is found through relationship with the Creator Himself.

The Holy Scriptures are by far the *most complex and intricate piece of literature* on the face of the earth. The individual threads of this monumental tapestry at times appear to have no relevance or meaning to us today, as they often come across as nothing more than tattered and torn ancient parchments. Yet within each individual thread, there is meaning, purpose, and an intricacy that cannot be explained through any other means than the divinity of its inspired authorship. Each individual thread, when revealed by God, allows us to

13

see it has neither a beginning nor an end. Its circular concentricity constantly winds its way back to the realization that God's love for His creation is eternal and that He has an everlasting plan for it.

Perry Stone Jr. notes, "The Old Testament is the New Testament concealed, and the New Testament is the Old Testament revealed. In fact, many of the future prophetic events predicted in the New Testament are actually concealed in the book of Genesis, the first book of the Bible. The name 'Genesis' in Hebrew is Bereshith, meaning 'First in order or beginning.'"[3] Simply stated, the *Bible leads, guides, directs, and proclaims that Jesus Christ is Lord.* Jesus is the Alpha and Omega, the Beginning, and the End. There is no other means for God's earthly creation to gain access to the Father than through the saving grace of the Lord Jesus Christ. Period!

The writings contained within the pages of this devotion proclaim this, as the revelation of Israel itself could never have been imagined or *conceived by mere mortal designers.* This is especially true when we consider that this piece of historical literature was written over a 1,500-year time span, by forty authors, in three different languages, and over three continents. It contains sixty-six books that proclaim historical facts, prophetic proclamations, profound insights to living, and, most importantly, the expression of God's love and plan for humanity. The continuity, and consistent focus within the collective writings specifically points the way to the Promised Messiah. This in itself provides solid evidence pointing to God being the Author, who inspired all forty of these scribes to pen His Words for humanity's redemption.

Theologians, Bible scholars, pastors, and biblical teachers who have studied the Word, examined the prophecy, and pondered the possibilities; agree that God is still actively *fulfilling His promise* to the covenants He made with the fathers of Israel. Paul Benware writes, "In light of Israel's disobedience *(Romans 10:21)*, has God cast them aside? The answer is an emphatic 'no.' Israel is stubborn, disobedient, and undeserving. However, the promises God made in the Abrahamic Covenant were eternal and unconditional. Israel's present spiritual

---

[3]   Perry Stone Jr., *Unlocking Secrets in the Second Coming Scrolls* (Cleveland, TN: Voice of Evangelism, 2004), p. 253.

blindness is limited in extent (it is 'partial,' *Romans 11:25*) and duration (it is 'until,' *Romans 11:25*). Someday, God will fulfill His promises to Israel and 'graft' Israel, as a nation, back into the Abrahamic Covenant experientially (*Romans 11:23–25*). They will finally be redeemed as a nation, partaking for the first time of the New Covenant."[4]

God's plan of salvation for humanity is intricately woven through the fabric, the fiber, and the very essence of *Jewish history* as provocatively proclaimed by its prophets of old. Jewish history is one of promise. It is centered on the need, hope, anticipation, yearning, and desperation for a Messiah. Jewish history not only paved the way for humanity's redemption, serving as the conduit for the Messiah's initial appearance, but also even today serves as the lightning rod that will perpetuate His return. For Jews, they are still anticipating the arrival of their Messiah. For Christians, Jesus Christ is the Messiah who will one day return to earth and establish God's kingdom for all eternity, bringing the realization of salvation to the Jewish people, the nation of Israel, and to all who call upon the name of the Lord.

The history of Israel has been quite colorful to say the least. The Hebrew people are unlike any other in the history of the world. Through God's chosen race, the world was filled with promise and hope. From the Jewish people the world witnessed the *preeminent nature, the power, and the benevolence* of the One true God. Through Abraham's lineage the world received the Torah, the Priests, the Laws, and the Prophets. Israel was called to not only bear witness to sovereignty and supremacy of the Lord, God Almighty, but they served as the chosen to usher in the long-awaited, promised Messiah. No other people have had the history, the purpose, the calling, the promise, or the future that has accompanied Israel for thousands of years. Truly, in this world of short-lived civilizations, Israel is the grandpappy of them all. The annals of time bear witness to the truth that Israel holds a place of honor in this world, from the ancient of days!

The Apostle Paul confirms the true origination of the inspired words contained within the Bible, as he writes: **All Scripture is given by inspiration of God, and is profitable for doctrine, for reproof, for**

---

4   Paul N. Benware, *Survey of the New Testament (Revised)* (Chicago, IL: Moody Press, 1990), p. 217.

correction, for instruction in righteousness, that the man of God may be complete, thoroughly equipped for every good work, *(2 Timothy 3:16, 17 NKJV)*. Paul writes specifically in regards to the Old Testament, but the same holds true for the divine inerrancy of the New Testaments, since it too is Scripture. Of course during Paul's time, and the days of the early Church, there was no New Testament. That came through the ministry, and letters of many of the original Disciples, and through Paul's efforts to share the message of Christ. Actually, Peter confirms the inerrancy of Paul's Epistles, which became a major portion of the books contained in the New Testament.

> Therefore, beloved, looking forward to these things, be diligent to be found by Him in peace, without spot and blameless; and consider that the longsuffering of our Lord is salvation—as also our beloved brother Paul, according to the wisdom given to him, has written to you, as also in all his epistles, speaking in them of these things, in which are some things hard to understand, which untaught and unstable people twist to their own destruction, as they do also the rest of the Scriptures, *(2 Peter 3:14, 16 NKJV)*.

Elsewhere Peter states the same truth using a reference to the Holy Spirit within the Triune nature of God: **No prophecy of Scripture came about by the prophet's own interpretation of things. For prophecy never had its origin in the human will, but prophets, thought human, spoke from God as they were carried along by the Holy Spirit,** *(2 Peter 1:20-21)*. So the truth to be gleaned from the previous references from both Paul and Peter, involve the profound confidence available, regarding the reliability involving all Scripture. It is God inspired and dependable for your eternal good works. It began and will aslo be finalized through Jesus Christ, who is the Word of God. All of which arrived through the earthly lineage of Abraham.

The history of Israel and the Jewish people is filled with passion, purpose, failure, accomplishment, celebration, tragedy, and destiny. No nation or people in the world can trace their roots back more than 4,000 years. The Jewish people's story is uniquely appointed. They are the only nation that began in the *ancient days* through an *eternal covenant* with God, and they are the only nation in the modern world that can still make that claim. Their journey from the humble beginnings of a man named Abram took them to places they could never have imagined, let alone planned. Their journey throughout a myriad of lands in the Mideast has been filled with promise, seasoned with failure, sprinkled with adversity, and garnished with glory as they served as the conduit for *presenting and proclaiming* God Almighty, to the world. There can be no doubt as we reflect on the historical records regarding Israel, that Israel's purpose, both past and present was miraculously appointed by the *Ancient of Days.*

As you take time to reflect on today's devotion, take a moment to realize that God used Israel as the people who ushered in the *Promise of the Ages*, Jesus Christ. That's quite a calling. That's a tremendous *legacy.* The proof that God isn't finished with Israel, is completely enveloped in her rebirth as a Sovereign Nation in 1948. The legacy of Israel's past, present, and future is intricately wrapped within the very promise of the Messiah, Jesus Christ. The reality of life is that not only do nations leave a legacy in this world, but so will you. Israel's legacy is totally defined within the continuing story of God's grace, mercy, and promise. All of which, only comes through Jesus.

So, for today's consideration, I leave you with this simple question to ponder throughout the remainder of your day. **Will your** *legacy* **share the radiance of Christ's glory for your loved ones to remember, when you pass from this world?** Take a moment to journal your thoughts in the space below.

_____

_____

_____

_____

_____

_____

_____

_____

_____

Days of Old

As in the days of Noah, this world continues on;
　　Generations come and go; life is quickly gone....
Selfish-stubborn-sinful lusts, consume the hearts of men,
　　Pursuing life for all its worth, engulfed by reckless sin.
Seeking pleasure all their days, engrossed in foolish gain-
　　Kindness, caring, thoughtfulness is held in sad disdain.
Independence, wealth, and fame were the idols of the day;
　　Humanity had wandered from the straight & narrow way.
Terror – riots- murder- hate, ran rampant through the land,
　　War and death led the charge as hatred took a stand.
Caught within a downward spiral, sin consumed humanity;
　　The darkness of the human heart, was all there was to see.
The world it seemed, was doomed to die- "hope" was hard to find
　　The harshness of a wicked world, left goodness far behind.

As in the days of Noah, this world continues on,
　　Tho' little seems to change; this life is quickly gone....
But God was always patient, He has never turned away,
　　From the children He created, at the dawning of "that day."
His love endures forever, and so He set in place a plan;
　　Redemption from a sinful path—to save the souls of man.
In a dusty, lowly stable, a child was born one night,
　　The Promise of the Ages, the Way, the Truth, the Light –
Jesus came to save the masses, to pay the price for sin;
　　He lived; He died; He lives today-He offers hope again.
Son of God – Prince of Peace, Messiah, Priest & King
　　A baby born, so long ago, salvation He would bring.

As in the days of Noah, this world continues on,
　　The days are not much different-life is quickly gone....
Yet, the baby born so long ago, offers you a choice,
　　Leave behind your broken past, and listen to His voice.
He offers true forgiveness, if you turn from sinful ways;
　　Accept His Gift of saving grace before your final days!
As you place your trust in Jesus, new hope will soon unfold
　　Life will change, it can't go back to wicked "days of old!"
As you celebrate salvation, may you praise his Holy Name;
　　Life is renewed in amazing grace -you'll never be the same.

Lanny K Cook

18

Day 3
Be Still and Know!
Scriptural Reflection

In the beginning was the Word, and the Word was with God, and the Word was God. He was with God in the beginning. Through him all things were made; without him nothing was made that has been made. *John 1:1-3 NIV*

God is our refuge and strength, an ever-present help in trouble. Therefore, we will not fear, though the earth give way and the mountains fall into the heart of the sea, though its waters roar and foam and the mountains quake with their surging. [10] He says, "Be still, and know that I am God; I will be exalted among the nations, I will be exalted in the earth." *Psalm 46:1-3, 10 NIV*

In the beginning God created the heavens and the earth. Now the earth was formless and empty, darkness was over the surface of the deep, and the Spirit of God was hovering over the waters. And God said, "Let there be light," and there was light. God saw that the light was good, and he separated the light from the darkness. God called the light "day," and the darkness he called "night." And there was evening, and there was morning—the first day. *Genesis 1:1-5 NIV*

The heavens declare the glory of God; the skies proclaim the work of his hands. Day after day they pour forth speech; night after night they reveal knowledge. They have no speech; they use no words; no sound is heard from them. Yet their voice goes out into all the earth, their words to the ends of the world. In the heavens God has pitched a tent for the sun. It is like a bridegroom coming out of his chamber, like a champion rejoicing to run his course. It rises at one end of the heavens and makes its circuit to the other; nothing is deprived of its warmth. *Psalm 19:1-7 NIV*

Stilling your heart from the hectic pace of modern life, requires a conscious effort. You *must choose* to take time to re-energize; to reflect on your priorities; and to nurture your emotions, as well as your soul. When was the last time you enjoyed the peace of a crackling fire, beneath the canopy of the heavenly twilight, at the end of a stressful, chaotic day? Gazing into the mesmerizing flames it's easy to get lost within your innermost thoughts. The dancing flames of blue, orange, yellow, and red can easily draw you into a deep state of tranquil reflection. Embers from the crackling logs float into the great expanse of the night air, silently absorbed into the brilliance of the flickering stars above. They dissipate within the breadth and depth of the Milky Way, quietly swallowed up throughout the majestic, celestial bodies which comprise the *heavenly expanse of God's miraculous creation*.

A cool, night breeze provides welcome relief from the heat and sweat of a long, hard day. Like the very breath of God, it whispers a message of hope through the branches and bows of the towering pines. The night sounds of the locust, the timber wolf, and the owl remind us that we are not alone in the darkness. The warmth of the fire's flickering light greets those who gather around to share a moment of fellowship and camaraderie with friends and family. The sound of voices and laughter fill the shadowy darkness with a sense of joy and contentment, as they too drift into the stillness of the star-filled, evening sky.

In moments such as these, it's natural to lean back and breathe in the *wonders of God's creation*. The magnitude of His mighty works become apparent. The mysteries of His very being and the eminence of His love for mankind becomes tangible in such moments. As you still your heart to His wonder and promise, you can literally feel the intimacy of His loving touch while sitting in the midst of His creation. It is true that the heavens declare His glory, and when you take the time to notice, you can't help but realize His *omnipotent* power, as well as His *omniscient* understanding and knowledge that was required to speak all of creation into existence. Truly, He is all-powerful *(omnipotent),* and all knowing, *(omniscient).* But you will never recognize that until you experience, and then ultimately acknowledge His omnipresence. That is, God's sovereign ability to be everywhere. His Spirit cannot be contained. Like the air that you breathe, God completely surrounds you, fills you, gives life, and completes you. This is true, whether you want to believe or not.

Remember His words from Psalm 46 which state, *be still and know that I am God!* Truly, He is the God of all creation. His existence cannot be denied! That is, when you pause to reflect on the glory and majesty of His marvelous creation! When you choose to take a moment and recognize Him for who He truly is, you just might discover that He truly is the Great I Am! He is the Genius that designed and spoke all of creation into existence. He is the God who not only created you, but has a specific plan and purpose for your life.

You were meticulously knit together in your mother's womb for such a time as this. You are living under the call of His appointment. It's a destiny founded on the very premise of connection: one that is dependent upon the physical relationship with others, including your family and friends. But more important you were also created for spiritual relationship with the Creator Himself. You will never fully realize the significance of your personal, sanctified calling until you respond: *Still your heart and recognize His majestic creation!*

Precious times of reflection, often occur during the quiet moments of life: at the beginning and end of every day; as each chapter in life comes to completion; and as the first sentence of the next chapter begins. At the beginning of each new life, as well as at the end of every precious one; we ponder this existence and its purpose. During those times we are most open to seeking the answers for life itself. Today, as you set out on this spiritual journey, your life is about to change forever, as you pursue a deeper understanding and relationship with the *promise of the Messiah*, Jesus the Christ. That is, if you choose to open your heart to the reality of *Who He truly is!*

Now, it is one thing to be still and know that the Lord is God when things are calm in your life, but what happens when you are overwhelmed by the *storms of this world?* How do you respond when tragedy strikes, times get tough, or all hope is lost? How can you sit still when job demands are consuming your thoughts, or the family drama is shredding your very last nerve? How easy is it to go to bed and get a restful night's sleep when your mind whirls with the chaos of financial pressure? You toss and turn all night long, worrying about how to pay the bills that keep piling up, or wonder how you'll ever afford the supplies your children need for school. How easy is it when bad news comes stomping up your doorstep? There are a multitude of storms that overwhelm you with bad news; the loss of a loved one, or the breakup of a relationship. There are health issues that arise, as well as relational misunderstandings that haunt you through the night and even into the days. The storms of life can come upon you without warning, and it becomes extremely difficult to manage those torrential squalls when they do their best to swamp your boat and sink all of your hopes, dreams, and aspirations.

We can refer to the Gospel of Mark to gain some insight into this very topic of concern that each of us have experienced, probably more than once in our recent past. It's the record of Jesus and His Disciples who took a fishing boat cruise across the Sea of Galilee in the evening in order to get to the opposite shore. I'm sure their retreat toward the other side of the Galilee had to do with getting away from the pressure and demands of ministering to the crowds.

> That day when evening came, he said to his disciples, "Let us go over to the other side." Leaving the crowd behind, they took him along, just as he was, in the boat. There were also other boats with him. A furious squall came up, and the waves broke over the boat, so that it was nearly swamped. Jesus was in the stern, sleeping on a cushion. The disciples woke him and said to him, "Teacher, don't you care if we drown?" He got up, rebuked the wind and said to the waves, "Quiet! Be still!" Then the wind died down and it was completely calm.
>
> He said to his disciples, "Why are you so afraid? Do you still have no faith?" They were terrified and asked each other, "Who is this? Even the wind and the waves obey him," *(Mark 4:35-41 NIV).*

Concerning the concept of *being still to know* that He is God, there's probably no more prolific of a story than this one as shared by Mark. The reality of being still is completely immersed within the premise of seeking to know Him. The truth is, you don't have the power to effectively still your heart when it's racing out of control without seeking His power. After all, Jesus is the key to not only *quiet* the torrential wind and rains of your storm, but He also has the power to command them to *be still!* In simple terms, through Jesus and His omnipotent power, he rebuked (controls), even the wind and the waves. Are you surprised? You shouldn't be. He spoke all creation into existence! Why wouldn't He be able to control all things created?

And yet, there's an even more profound reality found near the end of this passage, as Jesus defines the key that unleashes His power to control the storm. Jesus rebukes the wind and calms the waves through the *simplicity of faith.* Your faith in Him not only calms the storms of life, but it calms the very storm that you find yourself in at this very moment. I have a piece of artwork hanging in my bedroom to remind me of this amazing gift of assurance that brings the Lord's peace into my spirit, when things get tough. *Sometimes God calms the sailor; other times He calms the storm.*

> Then they cried out to the Lord in their trouble, and he brought them out of their distress. He stilled the storm to a whisper; the waves of the sea were hushed. They were glad when it grew calm, and he guided them to their desired haven, *(Psalm 107:28-30 NIV).*

As you spend time reflecting on today's devotion, ask yourself; *Do you have the faith to trust Jesus to calm the seas and rebuke the waves of your storms?* Then remember that *your faith in Him, leads to peace in your spirit.* To be still and know that He is God, requires you to seek Him, and to surrender your life into His capable hands. May His peace be upon you! So, for today's consideration, I leave you with this simple question to ponder throughout the remainder of your day. *Will you still your heart and diligently listen to His voice? What is He saying to you right now?* Record His words below.

_____

_____

_____

_____

_____

_____

_____

Gaze Out into the Distance

Gaze out into the distance, as the waves lap around your feet,
    The future is uncertain, yet in His promise you are complete.
New life and hope He offers – you're a child of the King,
    No need to fret or worry, you are called to praise and sing!

Gaze out into the distance, as the waves come crashing in,
    Now, Jesus is the answer, He's the atonement for your sin!
His life He freely offered, you must choose to seek His face,
    He is the souls' redemption, by God's mercy and His grace!

Gaze out into the distance, and seek the promised land,
    Follow God's direction; take hold of His strong hand!
He will walk you through this journey; guide each earthly stride,
    If you listen to His calling, He will stay right by your side!

Gaze out into the distance, at the rough and stormy sea,
    You're a child of the Promise; you are born of destiny!
Scan the far horizon, as you search for dreams and more,
    Let Jesus tread beside you, along His peaceful shore!

Gaze out into the distance; lift your eyes to heaven above,
    Accept His grace and mercy, now feel His righteous love!
Set your eyes upon the Master, as you walk from day to day,
    He'll watch you every moment – stay close along the way!

Gaze out into the distance, as you seek your destiny,
    His loving grace, and mercy, will set the sinner free.
Be still to know the Promise, lift your eyes to Him in prayer,
    He offers life, He gives you peace, you are always in His care!

Lanny K. Cook

Day 4
God's Vessel of Perfection
Scriptural Reflection

May His name endure forever; may it continue as long as the sun. All nations will be blessed through Him, and they will call Him blessed. Praise be to the Lord God, the God of Israel, who alone does marvelous deeds. Praise be to His glorious name forever; may the whole earth be filled with His glory. Amen and Amen. *Psalms 72:17-19 NIV*

"'I am the Alpha and Omega,' says the Lord God, 'Who is, and Who was, and Who is to come, the Almighty.'" *Revelation 1:8 NIV*

"'To whom will you compare Me? Or who is My equal?' says the Holy One. Lift your eyes to the heavens: Who created all these? He who brings out the starry host one by one, and calls them by name. Because of His great power and mighty strength, not one of them is missing..., but those who hope in the Lord, will renew their strength. They will soar on wings like eagles; they will run and not grow weary, they will walk and not be faint." *Isaiah 40:25-26, 31 NIV*

The law of the LORD is perfect, refreshing the soul. The statutes of the LORD are trustworthy, making wise the simple. The precepts of the LORD are right, giving joy to the heart. The commands of the LORD are radiant, giving light to the eyes. The fear of the LORD is pure, enduring forever. The decrees of the LORD are firm, and all of them are righteous. They are more precious than gold, than much pure gold; they are sweeter than honey, than honey from the honeycomb. *Psalm 19:7-10 NIV*

The world recently experienced a time that was unlike anything any modern generation had ever encountered. The fear and uncertainty associated with the unparalleled world event known as the Covid Pandemic, placed the world in a state of panic, unprecedented paranoia, and baffling uncertainty. *Americans turned to an idol* of hoarding, as they were stock-piling nearly everything they could find on the store shelves in fear of an apocalyptic end to the world as we had known it. Of course, it was easy to understand why so many people were so easily panicked by the media's depiction of this disastrous pandemic event, of biblical proportions.

All normalcy was cast aside as social distancing became the law of the land. Humanity was *sequestered to social isolation*. Businesses and the livelihoods of the masses became victims of the panic as they were shut down. Financial ruin covered the landscape and all non-essential workers became wards of the state. Their only option for income came from government handouts. Medical care was relegated to emergency care exclusively. Online appointments became the modus operandi of nearly all doctor visits, as routine procedures, preventive care, and nearly all elective surgeries were terminated.

Senior care facilities were locked down, as were all hospitals, leaving many patients to wallow in the misery of their afflictions, and in many cases, these patients were left to die in isolation, without any loved ones sitting by their side, holding their hand as they departed this world. It seemed that people had lost the ability to apply any form of common sense or practical thinking to the situation. Nearly every day the world awoke to another headline instilling even more doom and panic into the hearts of all humanity.

As the reality of this situation confronted the world, it was easy to lose hope. The hearts and minds of individuals were consumed with unanswered questions: What am I going to do? How am I going to get through this? What happens if I get sick or die from this dreaded virus? How can I pay all of these bills? What do I do with all this mess? How do I respond? How will I survive? The circumstances of those days were overwhelming.

It seemed like just when you thought it couldn't get any worse, it did. Everything had been turned upside down and this neat little world lost all semblance of sanity. *Where could you turn to find hope?* How could the world return to a sense of normalcy? In a culture that offered more panic than hope, there was only one place to turn. The *Bible – God's Word*. Throughout the challenges of those days, I was reminded of the story of Job. Maybe Job wasn't facing a world-wide pandemic, but he was in a season of his life that everything was working against him. He lost his family, all of his possessions, his livelihood, he was sick, cast into isolation, and destitute. At the worst of his suffering, even his wife tried to convince him to curse God and die. Tragedy after tragedy, loss after loss, Job persevered. But I'm pretty sure that every time another tragedy struck, or something else fell apart, he would be consumed with questions, wondering where was God? What else could go wrong? Why is God punishing me? What did I do to deserve this? Why doesn't God love me? Or, why does God allow these terrible things to happen?

Similar cries come out of our own lips when we experience desperate times. Even though they arrive as a response to our severe desperation, they soon transform into an exasperated prayer for God's intervention. Dear God, *Now What?* Job never blamed God for his problems. As recorded in the Book of Job it took thirty-nine chapters for Job's deliverance to arrive. In dog years, I'm sure that seemed like an extremely long time. But Job's life was eventually restored completely. It took time and it took a vast amount of perseverance and faith before Job saw the light at the end of his tunnel of suffering. In many ways, we have all experienced times, such as in the days of Job. Faith delivered Job; it will you too when you call upon the name of Jesus!

This world is filled with challenges, trials, and even suffering. When those times arrive, there is *only one way* to triumphantly manage your way to the other side. What is that you ask? By stilling your heart and seeking God's guidance, peace, and assurance. Personally, I found there are two moments in a day, that accommodate the stilling of my heart. In the quiet of the evening after the activities of the day are complete, and in the early morning hours as the light of a new day dawns over the horizon. If the truth were told, those are my favorite times of any given day. I love to get up at the crack of dawn to get my day started. But not in a frantic way or at a hectic pace.

When was the last time you started your morning sipping on a cup of coffee, while sitting on a porch, watching God's creation awaken in a fresh, new way? Hearing the birds chirp within the fullness of the trees while, watching the butterflies playfully darting above the dew-covered garden, fills the heart with awe and wonder. The freshness of the morning air declares the tranquil serenity contained within the very essence of creation. Natural aromas of a new day arouse the senses as they surround us with their early morning passion. The sweet smell of pine; the fragrant bouquet of daffodils, gladiolas, and geraniums; the freshness of soft green grass, covered with a vibrance of fresh, morning dew; *invigorate the heart and soul.* While rays of light from the rising sun bid welcome to the promise of a new day, you discover a radiance and warmth that refreshes you.

Within the anticipation of the rising light, the morning glories open in splendor to blossom in the light of radiant beauty. Like a silent trumpet they proclaim the very promise of hope and life to the world. The tranquility of the morning calm conveys God's *perfect* message of love to anyone willing to pause and reflect - to *be still and to know that He is God.* Within the silence of the heart; the calming of the mind, and the stilling of your soul, God's voice can be heard. He is whispering your name; bidding your spirit to take notice of the beauty and the promise of His magnificent creation. The serenity of the early morning hours, when you take your eyes off of the circumstance and lift them toward the mountains from whence your help comes; you will be offered a glimpse into the perfection of God's love, mercy, and grace that only comes within His Peace.

> Very truly I tell you Pharisees, anyone who does not enter the sheep pen by the gate, but climbs in by some other way, is a thief and a robber. The one who enters by the gate is the shepherd of the sheep. The gatekeeper opens the gate for him, and the sheep listen to his voice. He calls his own sheep by name and leads them out. When he has brought out all his own, he goes on ahead of them, and his sheep follow him because they know his voice. But they will never follow a stranger; in fact, they will run away from him because they do not recognize a stranger's voice." *(John 10:1-5 NIV).*

Where do you go to experience the magnificence of God's splendor or feel the perfection of His presence in a profound way? Take a moment to journal your response in the space below.

_____

_____

_____

_____

_____

_____

_____

_____

_____

_____

_____

_____

_____

_____

_____

_____

_____

_____

_____

_____

_____

_____

_____

_____

_____

_____

_____

God's Vessel of Perfection

Who has believed our message? And to whom has the arm of the LORD been revealed? For He grew up before Him like a tender shoot, and like a root out of parched ground; He has no stately form or majesty that we should look upon Him, nor appearance that we should be attracted to Him. Isaiah 53:1-2 NASB

God's *Vessel of Perfection* – the righteous, Holy One,
      For God so loved this darkened world, He sent His only Son.
Born within a manger, amongst the dusty, stable hay;
      He is the Truth; He is the Light – He is the only Way!
Yes, God so loved His children, He chose to craft a plan,
      New life and hope and healing... He offers wayward man!
The *Vessel of Redemption*, wrapped in mercy, love and grace –
      This precious gift of sacrifice – for all the human race.

He was despised and forsaken of men, a man of sorrows and acquainted with grief; and like one from whom men hide their face He was despised, and we did not esteem Him. Surely our griefs He Himself bore, and our sorrows He carried; yet we ourselves esteemed Him stricken, smitten of God, and afflicted. Isaiah 53:3-4 NASB

God's *Vessel of Forgiveness* – sent to conquer sin and death;
      Came upon a midnight clear, thru His hallowed, precious breath.
Our Father's heart opened, to the broken and the lost;
      The Savior born to make a way, no matter what the cost.
This world would soon reject Him– despised with callous hate;
      They would not accept this holy Child, the Key to heaven's gate.
The *Vessel of Atonement* would bare our grief and pain–
      This humble Man of Sorrow, would suffer for our gain!

32

He was pierced through for our transgressions, He was crushed for our iniquities; the chastening for our well-being fell upon Him, and by His scourging we are healed. All of us like sheep have gone astray, each of us has turned to his own way; But the Lord has caused the iniquity of us all to fall on Him. Isaiah 53:5-6 NASB

The *Vessel of Salvation* – is the sacrificial Lamb of God,
　　　Pierced for our transgressions, for a world so deeply flawed.
Bruised for our iniquities, sharing peace we never knew,
　　　And by His stripes, healing comes - to give us life anew!
The world had turned away from Him, to wander on their way,
　　　Upon the cross our iniquity, was placed on Him that day!
God's *Vessel of Deliverance* – hung broken on a tree,
　　　He paid the price for sin and death – His gift will set you free!

The Lord is close to the brokenhearted; He rescues those whose spirits are crushed. Psalm 34:18 NLT

This *Vessel of Perfection* – the righteous, Holy One-
　　　Arose to life and conquered death as the Resurrected Son!
Born within a manger, amongst a stable strewn with hay;
　　　Redemption for this broken world, was born to us that day!
The Creator of the Universe, endured such brokenness,
　　　He offers life for those who choose; His atoning righteousness.
God's *Vessel of Eternal Love* – Jesus born to be the Way,
　　　He will lift you out of bondage, if you merely pause to pray!
　　　　　　　　　　　　　　　　　　　Lanny K. Cook

The Lord Himself will give you a sign:
Behold, the virgin will conceive
and give birth to a son,
and she will name Him Immanuel!
Isaiah 7:14 NASB

Day 5
The Word Became Flesh
Scriptural Reflection

Then the angel said to her, "Do not be afraid, Mary, for you have found favor with God. And behold, you will conceive in your womb and bring forth a Son, and shall call His name JESUS. He will be great, and will be called the Son of the Highest; and the Lord God will give Him the throne of His father David. And He will reign over the house of Jacob forever, and of His kingdom there will be no end." *Luke 1:30-33 NKJV*

The birth of Jesus Christ came about this way: After His mother Mary had been engaged to Joseph, it was discovered before they came together that she was pregnant by the Holy Spirit. So her husband Joseph, being a righteous man, and not wanting to disgrace her publicly, decided to divorce her secretly. But after he had considered these things, an angel of the Lord suddenly appeared to him in a dream. *Matthew 1:18-20a HCSB*

Be anxious for nothing, but in everything by prayer and supplication, with thanksgiving, let your requests be made known to God; and the peace of God, which surpasses all understanding, will guard your hearts and minds through Christ Jesus. *Philippians 4:7-7 NKJV*

Finally, brethren, whatever things are true, whatever things are noble, whatever things are just, whatever things are pure, whatever things are lovely, whatever things are of good report, if there is any virtue and if there is anything praiseworthy—meditate on these things. The things which you learned and received and heard and saw in me, these do, and the God of peace will be with you. *Philippians 4:8-10 NKJV*

One of the most compelling **stories of *faith*** comes from the story of Mary as recorded in the Gospel of Luke when the angel arrived to bring her the news of what was about to happen in her life. I can almost guarantee that Mary in this moment had one of those "You've got to be kidding me?" responses. This surely didn't sound like good news for her. This didn't seem to bare any semblance to the thought that she had found favor with God. This threw a big wrench in the works of where she thought her life was going. She was engaged to be married and she had never been with a man in the biblical sense.

Mary must have been in a near state of shock, as she realized that Joseph would know that this child was not his. In that day, a common punishment for this sin would be death by stoning. At the very least, Joseph could send her off to fend for herself and live out her life in shame. But then, after the severity of her situation began to set in, I'm sure she was quickly overwhelmed with questions: ***Now What? What can I do? How can I tell my parents? Where will I go? How will I tell Joseph? What will he do to me?*** I'm sure her mind was whirling with fear and dread, while her heart raced in panic-stricken terror. But do you know how Mary responded? She reacted in two profound ways.

First, she chose to take God ***at His Word.***

> Trust in the Lord with all your heart, and lean not on your own understanding; In all your ways acknowledge Him, And He shall direct your paths, *(Proverbs 3:5-6 NKJV).*

Second, she chose to ***prayerfully reflect***, or ponder the true depth and meaning of God's Word.

> But Mary kept all these things and pondered them in her heart, *(Luke 2:19 NKJV).*

> Your word I have hidden in my heart, That I might not sin against You, *(Psalm 119:11 NKJV).*

There is a significance in the term ***Word*** that needs to be realized within the context of this devotion. Again, it's found within the true definition regarding the use of the term ***Word*** within the Bible.

> In the beginning was the Word, and the Word was with God, and the Word was God. He was with God in the beginning. Through him all things were made; without him nothing was made that has been made. In him was life, and

that life was the light of all mankind. The light shines in the darkness, and the darkness has not overcome it... ¹⁴ The Word became flesh and made his dwelling among us. We have seen his glory, the glory of the one and only Son, who came from the Father, full of grace and truth, *(John 1: 1-5, 14 NIV).*

Mary took God at His Word. She placed her faith in the Word of God. She accepted God's will for her life and her calling; to be the mother of the child, Jesus. It wasn't going to be an easy journey and she knew it. But she placed her trust in God. She bore the Son who became her guiding light and Redeemer. Mary wasn't the only one in this story that experienced some serious, *life-altering* moments. Joseph had several of his own mind-boggling challenges to wrestle through.

> This is how the birth of Jesus the Messiah came about: His mother Mary was pledged to be married to Joseph, but before they came together, she was found to be pregnant through the Holy Spirit. Because Joseph her husband was faithful to the law, and yet did not want to expose her to public disgrace, he had in mind to divorce her quietly. But after he had considered this, an angel of the Lord appeared to him in a dream and said, "Joseph, son of David, do not be afraid to take Mary home as your wife, because what is conceived in her is from the Holy Spirit. She will give birth to a son, and you are to give him the name Jesus, because he will save his people from their sins."

> All this took place to fulfill what the Lord had said through the prophet: "The virgin will conceive and give birth to a son, and they will call him Immanuel" (which means "God with us"). When Joseph woke up, he did what the angel of the Lord had commanded him and took Mary home as his wife. But he did not consummate their marriage until she gave birth to a son. And he gave him the name Jesus, *(Matthew 1: 18-25 NIV).*

One of the most haunting, as well as probably the most traumatizing experience is realized through the act of *unfaithfulness* by a partner within the confines of a committed relationship. If you have never experienced the betrayal of a relational partner, count yourself extremely lucky. But within that bit of God's grace of protection, you should realize how deep the anguish goes, or how difficult it is to manage. Literally, it will turn your whole world upside down and, in many cases, it will require years to recover from the tormenting anguish of rejection. So, with that in mind, consider the extreme emotion that Joseph had to deal with when he discovered that his betrothed was pregnant. He knew for certain that he wasn't the father.

The shock of learning of Mary's condition, must have triggered a whirlwind of emotion; from disbelief, to anger, to despair, to hopelessness, to bitterness, to hatred, to overwhelming grief, and even to debilitating horror, for Joseph. Unless you've ever endured such a situation, you have no way of relating to what he actually endured. Even the death of a loved one can't compare to this type of grief. At least in death, well, in many cases, you're left to hold on to the memories of special moments. When someone is betrayed, not only is the relationship most often destroyed, but every good memory you ever had with that particular individual, turns against you.

In spite of all the emotions Joseph obviously experienced with the devastating news of Mary's pregnancy, all of his plans changed when He heard the Angel share *a message from God* Almighty. Joseph was a man with a good heart. That fact is confirmed as he pondered to secretly send Mary off, rather than turn her over to the Sanhedrin to be stoned. After all, that was the punishment for adultery according to the Mosaic Law. Joseph couldn't bring himself to do such a thing to a woman he obviously loved. So, when the Angel appeared, and spoke to him, *Joseph, son of David, do not be afraid to take Mary home as your wife, because what is conceived in her is from the Holy Spirit,* he was certain that he had to be obedient to God's word. After all, who wouldn't respond in obedience to the directive of an Angel, besides you, me, and the grand collective of the manly gender to ever live.

Mary and Joseph not only heard the words of the Angel, but they took heed to the divine message that each of them received. They surrendered to God's will for their lives, after they prayerfully considered His call. Because of their obedience, the *Word did become flesh and dwelt among them.* The world has never been the same. So, I leave you with this question? *When you hear that still small voice speaking to your heart, or when you feel the Holy Spirit urging you to step out in faith and obedience, what will you do?* Would you turn and run like Jonah did before getting swallowed by a great fish and spit up on the shores of Ninevah? Would you prayerfully seek the Lord's guidance and conviction to walk in obedience, according to His Word? Or, would you do your best to ignore Him? You do have a choice, when the Lord calls. *How will you respond?*

Take a moment to journal your thoughts in the space below.

_____

_____

_____

_____

_____

_____

_____

_____

_____

_____

_____

_____

_____

_____

_____

_____

_____

_____

_____

_____

_____

_____

_____

_____

The Word became flesh among us, and we beheld His glory, the glory as of the only begotten of the father, full of grace and truth.
John 1:14

The *Word became flesh* among us, on a cold and starry night.
      A Savior born in silence, within a stable's shadowed light.
Prophets proclaimed His glory, predestined before the birth,
      King of kings and Lord of lords; to reign over all the earth!

Yet no one paid attention, just a few who seemed to care,
      While the silence of this wonder filled the evening air;
Prophets foretold the story, of the One who was the Light,
      The baby born of a virgin, within the silence of the night!

Still, no one saw Him enter; no one heard Him cry,
      Born in a lowly manger, with the cattle standing by.
Prophets declared His purpose; the Heavens displayed His worth,
      Just a few would pay homage, to the Savior's holy, birth.

The *Word became flesh* among us, to begin salvation's plan,
      A Savior come for redemption; for the sinful way of man.
Prophets defied the skeptics to proclaim God's perfect Word;
      Yet few would seem to notice, a miraculous birth occurred.

Today there are those who listen to the Word and seek the Light:
      For most, were just too busy - to admit their sinful plight.
Prophets forewarned of the hardness of life in this fallen state,
      To reject the gift from the Father; is to seal a dreadful fate.

The Light of the world is upon us - The Word has been full-filled,
      The Glory of the Father, by His Son has been revealed.
Prophets proclaimed the Messiah, He was born, He lived, He died;
      He rose again triumphant; in *Radiant Glory* He does abide.

Will you take the time to seek Him? To save you from your plight.
      Will you accept God's gift of mercy within His radiant light?
God's Word now bids you welcome; will you answer mercy's call?
      His voice cries out to everyone; through a lowly, manger stall!

Lanny K. Cook

Day 6
In the Stillness of the Midnight
Scriptural Reflection

In the year that King Uzziah died, I saw the Lord seated on a throne, high and exalted, and the train of His robe filled the temple. Above Him were seraphs, each with six wings: With two wings they covered their faces, with two they covered their feet, and with two they were flying. And they were calling to one another: 'Holy, holy, holy is the Lord Almighty; the whole earth is full of His glory!' At the sound of their voices the doorposts and the thresholds shook and the temple was filled with smoke. *Isaiah 6:1-4 NIV*

Who has believed our message and to whom has the arm of the Lord been revealed? *Isaiah 53:1 NIV*

The thief comes only to steal and destroy; I have come that they may have life, and have it to the full. I am the Good Shepherd. The Good Shepherd lays down His life for the sheep..., I am the Good Shepherd; I know My sheep and My sheep know me---just as the Father knows Me and I know the Father---and I lay down My life for the sheep. The reason the Father loves me is that I Lay down my life--only to take it up again. No one takes it from Me, but I lay it down on My own accord. I have authority to lay it down and authority to take it up again. This command I received from My Father! *John 10:10-18 NIV*

The bridegroom was a long time in coming, and they all became drowsy and fell asleep. At midnight the cry rang out: 'Here's the bridegroom! Come out to meet him!' *Matthew 25:5, 6 NIV*

It is like a man going to a far country, who left his house and gave authority to his servants, and to each his work, and commanded the doorkeeper to watch. Watch therefore, for you do not know when the master of the house is coming—in the evening, at midnight, at the crowing of the rooster, or in the morning— lest, coming suddenly, he find you sleeping. *Mark 13:34-36 NKJV*

Life on earth had begun and Adam and Eve enjoyed perfect paradise. All of their needs; physical, emotional, and spiritual were provided by God. Within this perfect world, known as Eden, they enjoyed true communion and fellowship with God as their lives progressed. They had dominion over all of paradise; over all of the animals, the birds of the air, and the fish of the sea. They had no worries, no toils, or burdens to bare, as life provided sustenance and perfect tranquility. Literally, Eden was heaven on earth!

Within *His ultimate creation* which He called man, or humanity, God created a *free will.* The ability to choose what he wanted to do, and the directions or the paths that he wanted to follow. God's desire for man was to choose to daily commune and fellowship with Him. But within this free will, man chose to follow a different path. God had given them free access to all of Eden, and to all it offered. Everything except the fruit from the tree of the knowledge of good and evil was theirs to enjoy. This was the only stipulation God placed upon Adam and Eve, in order for them to remain in the garden to abide in perfect communion with Him. This one restraint became the stumbling block for all mankind.

You see, Satan also had a plan. One to pull God's ultimate creation into communion with the *evil powers that rule the darkness.* After God created light, the prince of this world did his best to block out the rays of God's goodness-of His love and His truth. So, man's *fate was sealed* as he chose to pursue the desires of the flesh. The desires which are not only hidden in the darkness of sin, but also consumed within the fires of its torment. Sin had entered God's perfect creation, as Satan, known as the prince of darkness, began his reign over all the earth's inhabitants. God created life in a sinless world, yet man chose death by falling prey to the temptations of his worldly desires.

So, it is today, people are usually not open to accept what God has to offer. It is not until we reach a point in life, when *all hope is lost* and we have *lost total control of our situation* that we reflect on our circumstance. When all hope is gone, and no answer can be found, it is then that we realize our only hope comes from the Father above. It is then that we realize we need to find a way to once again commune with Him - to find rest in His love, and fellowship in His presence. When circumstances of life become so overwhelming and we finally realize that no human means or understanding can free us from our strife, or from the sins that have consumed our life and our being, it is then that we begin to search for the answer.

Just as the old devil devised a plan to separate man from fellowship with God, the Lord returned the favor by presenting the Way of salvation from sin so we can once again gain access to the Father. Of course, the plan was based on man's free will, and he would have to personally choose to accept God's gift of salvation. So, God sent His son into the world; Emmanuel, the Prince of Peace, the Lamb of God, was sent to *serve as the sacrifice* for the sins of humanity. It was Adam's free will which brought sin into this world, and it is God's desire for each of us to choose to accept the gift of His Son in order for us to once again, enjoy the fellowship and communion of His presence.

> And behold, an angel of the Lord stood before them, and the glory of the Lord shone around them, and they were greatly afraid. Then the angel said to them, "Do not be afraid, for behold, I bring you good tidings of great joy which will be to all people, *(Luke 2:9,10 NIV).*

All the situations that you face in this life requires you to *make a choice* to decide the direction of your path. All of this is part of God's design, intricately woven throughout the DNA of mankind. He always provides an option; when one door closes, He allows another to open. You can decide to dwell in the House of the Lord, or you can partake of the worldly fruit from the tree of the knowledge of good and evil. Each and every one of us must make that decision for ourselves.

Therefore, my friend, choose wisely. *Will you follow the ways of the world, or will you accept the gift God freely and graciously offers you?* Each and every person in this world is destined to make a choice regarding their eternal destination. You can believe that there is more to this world than meets the eye, or you can live your life in denial of a loving God who sent His Son to this earth as the sacrifice for mankind's sin. You may choose to live in pursuit of self-serving pleasure, or you can surrender yourself into the loving, caring arms of the Redeemer.

Life is nothing more than a long, tedious journey of choices.

Each of us will not only live with our decisions, but we will ultimately die with the actions and directions we set for ourselves. Throughout this devotional I try to not interfere with the power and authority of the scriptures, as in many cases, I will simply share specific passages and let the Spirit of the Lord provide you with the discernment to understand their meaning. So, I will begin this strategy by simply sharing the words of the Apostle Paul in his first letter to the Church in Corinth. I will not add any commentary to it, or try to define it from my personal perspective of human understanding. I will leave that up to the Spirit of God to inspire for your own, particular circumstance.

> The message of the cross is foolish to those who are headed for destruction! But we who are being saved know it is the very power of God. As the Scriptures say, "I will destroy the wisdom of the wise and discard the intelligence of the intelligent."

> So where does this leave the philosophers, the scholars, and the world's brilliant debaters? God has made the wisdom of this world look foolish. Since God in his wisdom saw to it that the world would never know him through human wisdom, he has used our foolish preaching to save those who believe. It is foolish to the Jews, who ask for signs from heaven. And it is foolish to the Greeks, who seek human wisdom. So, when we preach that Christ was crucified, the Jews are offended and the Gentiles say it's all nonsense.

> But to those called by God to salvation, both Jews and Gentiles, Christ is the power of God and the wisdom of God. This foolish plan of God is wiser than the wisest of human plans, and God's weakness is stronger than the greatest of human strength. Remember, dear brothers and sisters, that few of you were wise in the world's eyes or powerful or wealthy when God called you. Instead, God chose things the world considers foolish in order to shame those who think they are wise. And he chose things that are powerless to shame those who are powerful. God chose things despised by the world, things counted as nothing at all, and used them to bring to nothing what the world considers important. As a result, no one can ever boast in the presence of God.

> God has united you with Christ Jesus. For our benefit God made him to be wisdom itself. Christ made us right with

God; he made us pure and holy, and he freed us from sin. Therefore, as the Scriptures say, "If you want to boast, boast only about the Lord," *(1 Corinthians 1:18-31 NLT).*

Coming into a personal relationship with Jesus doesn't happen through your own, human understanding, intellectual capacity, or even biblical understanding. It happens through a *divine revelation* offered through the gift of God's wisdom and Spirit. As you continue through this devotional study on your journey to discover Jesus, make sure to pray before you enter into your study time. Pray for the Lord's discernment as you read through the material. And also, be sure to pray that the Lord will quicken His message to your heart and mind.

Throughout this journey stay mindful that Jesus is the *preeminent Son of the Triune God.* He is the *promised Messiah* who is *the visible image* of the *invisible God.* I pray that you keep that in mind as you contemplate today's devotion. Through the *Word* of hope and inspiration, may you be touched with the un-merited gift of grace, offered to you through the life, death, and resurrection of God's only begotten Son! His grace is freely offered and it is yours to receive. It is also yours to reject. Ultimately, the choice is completely yours! It is a decision based on the merits of *faith.* Shared in 1 John 5:12-13: **Whoever has the Son has life. Whoever does not have the Son of God does not have life. I write these things to you who believe in the name of the Son of God, that you may know you have eternal life.**

As you ponder the words within today's study, take the time to *still you heart, seek the Lord, and listen for His voice.* I'm not even going to leave you with a question to ponder for the rest of the day. I will simply urge you to focus on Him, as you reflect on His words that He shares with you throughout the day. Meditate on them through the midnight hours. Many of the most memorable messages that you will hear from the Lord, arrive in the stillness of the midnight. Make sure you don't roll over and fall back to sleep and snooze through those moments when the Lord bids you to wake up out of a sound slumber. Tomorrow when you rise to the dawning of a fresh day, remember that His love and mercy are new every morning! You have been given the gift of another day. Now, today's assignment can wait until you've slept on today's devotion. *When you wake up tomorrow morning, take a few moments and record what came to you throughout your day or night.* Maybe it wasn't a word, or a thought that came from your time reflecting on your relationship with Jesus; rather, you may have received a feeling, a sensation, an impression, or a leading. Use the lines below to record what came out of your time of deep reflection.

_____

_____

_____

_____

_____

_____

_____

_____

_____

_____

_____

_____

_____

_____

_____

_____

_____

_____

_____

_____

_____

_____

In the Stillness of the Midnight

In the stillness of the midnight, Jesus prayed beneath a tree,
>   For God to take the cup from Him; that was filled with agony.
"Not My will, but Thine be done" Jesus cried to God above,
>   As He became the sacrificial Lamb, thru His never-ending love.
He gladly paid the price for sin, when He was nailed to the tree,
>   He was born to be the sacrifice; then He died on Calvary.

In the stillness of the midnight, as Jesus lay within the tomb,
>   The Spirit came upon Him within that stone-cold room.
The power of God released new life, into His broken form,
>   A breath of everlasting life enveloped Him that morn.
He was born to be the sacrifice as He died for you and me.
>   Yet, He lives today within your heart for all eternity!

In the stillness of the midnight, after a long and weary day,
>   Do you seek the Lord in solace, as you close your eyes to pray?
Do you feel His very presence, as you face your many trials?
>   Is Jesus there beside you as you trek across the miles?
Have you ever opened up the door, to ask the Savior in?
>   Does He dwell within your heart; has He washed away your sin?

Be still and know that He has come, to save you from your sin,
>   Be still and know that He is God, as He shed His blood for men.
Be still and know that Jesus died in agony on that tree,
>   But rose again to conquer death, and lives in Victory!
May the glory of the Risen Lord, shine bright throughout each day;
>   May He fill your life with endless love as you walk along His way!

Lanny K Cook

Day 7
Through a Child
Scriptural Reflection

Yet to all who received Him, to those who believed in His name, He gave the right to become Children of God - Children born not of natural descent, nor of human decision or a husband's will, but born of God. The Word became flesh and made His dwelling among us. We have seen His glory, the glory of the One and Only, who came from the Father, full of grace and truth. *John 1: 12-14 NIV*

But after he had considered these things, an angel of the Lord suddenly appeared to him in a dream, saying, "Joseph, son of David, don't be afraid to take Mary as your wife, because what has been conceived in her is by the Holy Spirit. She will give birth to a son, and you are to name Him Jesus, because He will save His people from their sins." When Joseph got up from sleeping, he did as the Lord's angel had commanded him. He married her but did not know her intimately until she gave birth to a son. And he named Him Jesus.
Matthew 1:20-25 HCSB

After they were gone, an angel of the Lord suddenly appeared to Joseph in a dream, saying, "Get up! Take the child and His mother, flee to Egypt, and stay there until I tell you. For Herod is about to search for the child to destroy Him." *Matthew 2:13 HCSB*

After Herod died, an angel of the Lord suddenly appeared in a dream to Joseph in Egypt, saying, "Get up! Take the child and His mother and go to the land of Israel, because those who sought the child's life are dead." So he got up, took the child and His mother, and entered the Land of Israel. *Matthew 2:19-21 NKJV*

When his parents saw him, they were astonished. His mother said to him, "Son, why have you treated us like this? Your father and I have been anxiously searching for you." "Why were you searching for me?" he asked. "Didn't you know I had to be in my Father's house?" But they did not understand what he was saying to them. *Luke 2:48-50 NIV*

50

Other than the initial stories about Jesus' birth, the Bible doesn't share much information about Joseph, Mary's husband, who was the earthly step-father of Jesus. But the Gospels record four events that are significant for us to look at in regards to Joseph and his role in Jesus' early life. Three of these references involved dreams where an angel of the Lord appeared to Joseph to give him *guidance, direction, and assurance.* Each of these encounters served to reassure Joseph as to God's plan and purpose for his life, specifically as it related to Jesus. The final scriptural reference shares significant insight regarding Jesus' purpose as a child in the Temple at the age of twelve-years old. At this time, Jesus defined His divine legitimacy as the true Son of the Heavenly Father. But during those early years of Jesus' childhood, Joseph was called to be the earthly father who served as the paternal guardian of the Promised Messiah. Through it all, Joseph consciously chose to open his heart to God's will. He surrendered himself into obedience for the Lord God's plan and purpose.

After Joseph's first encounter with the Angel of the Lord, who assured him to take Mary as his wife, he had a *second life-altering message* from God. It's safe to say that this moment probably came at a time when he thought things were finally moving forward pretty well!

> After they were gone, an angel of the Lord suddenly appeared to Joseph in a dream, saying, "Get up! Take the child and His mother, flee to Egypt, and stay there until I tell you. For Herod is about to search for the child to destroy Him." So he got up, took the child and His mother during the night, and escaped to Egypt. He stayed there until Herod's death, so that what was spoken by the Lord through the prophet might be fulfilled: Out of Egypt I called My Son, (*Matthew 2:13-15 HCSB*).

Joseph's *third life-altering* moment is recorded in this scripture:

> After Herod died, an angel of the Lord suddenly appeared in a dream to Joseph in Egypt, saying, "Get up! Take the child and His mother and go to the land of Israel, because those who sought the child's life are dead." So he got up, took the child and His mother, and entered the land of Israel. But when he heard that Archelaus was ruling over Judea in place of his father Herod, he was afraid to go there. And being warned in a dream, he withdrew to the region of Galilee.

Then he went and settled in a town called Nazareth to fulfill what was spoken through the prophets, that He will be called a Nazarene, *(Matthew 2:19-23 NKJV).*

As you consider the calling that Joseph had on his life, there is one main consideration that is essential to also apply to your situation within the reference which we just discussed. Open your heart to God's voice and be willing to walk through this life with obedient confidence as you fully trust Him. In simple terms, *you must surrender* to God's purpose and plan for your life. That's what Joseph did during those early days leading up to the birth of our Savior, and throughout the remainder of his earthly days. Joseph chose to answer his call with determined focus and relentless trust in God's purpose and promise. Both Joseph and Mary *took God at His Word* and held tight to His Promise. Of course, the Promise was completely immersed within the purpose of Jesus Christ, the Lamb of God. Which would be revealed within the revelation of God's mercy and grace as the atonement for sin.

The final mention of Joseph comes within the pages of the Gospel of Luke. At first, this record involving the circumstance of Jesus at twelve years old is a bit perplexing. Mary, Joseph, and their entire family were heading home from the Passover festivities in Jerusalem when they realized Jesus wasn't with them. Frantically, they returned to Jerusalem, searching for the missing Jesus.

> Every year Jesus' parents went to Jerusalem for the Festival of the Passover. When he was twelve years old, they went up to the festival, according to the custom. After the festival was over, while his parents were returning home, the boy Jesus stayed behind in Jerusalem, but they were unaware of it. Thinking he was in their company, they traveled on for a day. Then they began looking for him among their relatives and friends. When they did not find him, they went back to Jerusalem to look for him. After three days they found him in the temple courts, sitting among the teachers, listening to them and asking them questions. Everyone who heard him was amazed at his understanding and his answers. When his parents saw him, they were astonished. His mother said to him, "Son, why have you treated us like this? Your father and I have been anxiously searching for you."
>
> "Why were you searching for me?" he asked. "Didn't you know I had to be in my Father's house?" But they did not

52

understand what he was saying to them. Then he went down to Nazareth with them and was obedient to them. But his mother treasured all these things in her heart. And Jesus grew in wisdom and stature, and in favor with God and man, *(Luke 2:41-52 NIV).*

Within the context of this passage, it's important to note two significant aspects of this reference as they relate to Joseph. Look first, at verse 52 where Luke shares that *Jesus grew in wisdom and stature, and in favor with God and man.* Joseph was divinely appointed to serve as the fatherly influence to model righteousness and integrity to the child, Jesus. He was also assigned to guide, protect, and provide for God's Son as He grew in stature and into full maturity.

The most misunderstood section of this scripture involves Jesus' response, *didn't you know I had to be in my Father's house?* The passage even states that Mary and Joseph didn't understand what Jesus was saying to them. Of course, this is understandable since within their human understanding, they could not yet comprehend the intricate details of Jesus' purpose or promise at the tender age of twelve. However, we can see that at that moment, Jesus was proclaiming something extremely profound.

First, he was declaring that from a legal perspective, Joseph had taken on the role and the responsibility as His earthly father. In modern language it's comparable to say that Joseph was the custodial parent of Jesus. But within the profound dynamic of Jesus' statement that He *had to be in my Father's house,* it becomes obvious that Jesus was declaring the legitimacy of His preeminent relationship with God the Father. If we take it just one step farther, we can see that Joseph served as the context of the Old Testament Law, while God the Father represents the Grace contained within the New Testament promise.

With this final reference from Luke, nothing else is known regarding Joseph's life. Scholars agree that by the time Jesus began His earthly ministry, Joseph had died and Mary was a widow. Personally, even though there is no historical evidence to confirm this assumption, I believe that within the divinely appointed, circumstance of God's purpose, Joseph probably died not too long before Jesus began His earthly ministry. I assume that Joseph's fatherly role served as the representative of Jewish Law for Jesus' formative years, but Joseph had to die before the promise of grace could unfold within the ministry of the Messiah.

Regardless, Joseph provided the *paternal influence* for Jesus' formative years. It was through his influence that the Child Jesus was molded, guided, protected, and nurtured into the Man of God's purpose. Through Mary and Joseph's Child, the Law of Moses was fulfilled, and God's grace brought life more abundant into the world.

> Do not think that I have come to abolish the Law or the Prophets; I have not come to abolish them but to fulfill them. For truly I tell you, until heaven and earth disappear, not the smallest letter, not the least stroke of a pen, will by any means disappear from the Law until everything is accomplished, *(Matthew 5:17-18 NIV)*.
>
> I have come that they may have life, and that they may have it more abundantly, *(John 10:10b NKJV)*.

As you consider Joseph's ability to surrender to God's calling: How have you responded to the Lord's voice? Have you opened your heart to God's purpose? Are you able to live in obedient confidence, fully trusting Jesus? *Are you surrendered to God's calling and plan for your life?* Record your thoughts in the space below.

_____

_____

_____

_____

_____

_____

_____

_____

_____

_____

_____

_____

_____

_____

_____

Through a Child

Through a Child, we hear the promise, in a Child we find true love,
    For this Child will be the blessing, a gift from God above.
He came to earth, so long ago; He was born in Bethlehem,
    Immanuel - "God with us," – He is the great "I Am."
Through a Child we seek forgiveness. by a Child we gain God's grace,
    This Child will be God's mercy, as we seek to touch His face.
He's the Babe born in a manger, the Bright, Morning Star;
    The Word dwelt among us, proclaimed both near and far.
Through a Child we find God's guidance, in a Child we see the plan,
    For this Child provides the pathway, to save the souls of man.
Prince of Peace, the Bread of Life, He is the Truth - the Way,
    The Gate that leads to heaven, and the never-ending day!
Through a Child we are accepted, from a Child we find God's Peace,
    For this Child brings contentment, that will never, ever cease.
He's the Alpha and Omega, the Beginning, and the End,
    Master, Teacher, Comforter; Prophet, Priest, and Friend.
Through a Child we find new purpose. through a Child we find relief,
    For this Child provides a miracle, as He frees us from our grief.
He feeds the hungry masses, He heals the sick and lame,
    He bears our hurts and burdens; He takes away the pain.
Through a Child we gain salvation, in a Child we have new life,
    For this Child will break the bondage: of sin and all its strife.
The sacrifice for all mankind, He died to set us free,
    He conquered death and lives again, He reigns eternally!
Through a Child we share God's promise, in a Child we see the Light,
    For this Child was born long ago, on a silent star-filled night.
He's the Holy One of Israel, the Gift from Heaven's Throne,
    The Living Word – Promised One – He is the Cornerstone.
Through a Child we are united, by a Child we find our place,
    For this Child is our Redeemer – He is God's amazing grace.
 May the message of the Christ Child; touch your heart today;
    As He whispers a reminder, "I'm the Life, the Truth, and Way!"

Lanny K. Cook

Day 8
What Can I Offer?
Scriptural Reflection

May he also rule from sea to sea, and from the Euphrates River to the ends of the earth. May the nomads of the desert bow before him, and his enemies lick the dust. May the kings of Tarshish and of the islands bring gifts; May the kings of Sheba and Seba offer tributes. And may all kings bow down before him, all nations serve him. *Psalm 72:8-11 NASB*

Arise, shine; for your light has come,
And the glory of the Lord has risen upon you.
For behold, darkness will cover the earth
And deep darkness the peoples;
But the Lord will rise upon you
And His glory will appear upon you.
Nations will come to your light,
And kings to the brightness of your rising.
"Raise your eyes all around and see;
They all gather together, they come to you.
Your sons will come from afar,
And your daughters will be carried on the hip.
Then you will see and be radiant,
And your heart will thrill and rejoice;
Because the abundance of the sea will be turned to you,
The wealth of the nations will come to you.

Isaiah 60:1-5 NASB

Now after Jesus was born in Bethlehem of Judea in the days of Herod the king, behold, wise men from the East came to Jerusalem, saying, "Where is He who has been born King of the Jews? For we have seen His Star in the East and have come to worship Him." When they saw the star, they rejoiced with exceedingly great joy. [11] And when they had come into the house, they saw the young Child with Mary His mother, and fell down and worshiped Him. And when they had opened their treasures, they presented gifts to Him: gold, frankincense, and myrrh. *Matthew 2:1, 2, 11 NKJV*

The *Magi of the East* had journeyed for several years as they followed the star in search of the promised Messiah. These wise men knew from their studies of the heavenly expanse that this brilliant light represented something beyond magnificent. Unlike modern day astrologers, they understood the meaning of God's plan as they studied the heavens above. They recognized that this was an *historic event* which they were divinely compelled to pursue and witness. They knew that they were called to journey from the comforts of their palaces to seek after the light.

The hearts of the Wisemen ached to discover the wonder that the brilliant radiance of this star's message offered to the human soul. They were devoted star gazers, gifted in the interpretation of the galaxies, and they were also well versed in the prophecy contained within the *Hebrew scriptures*. These were highly knowledgeable astrologers. But there is also no doubt that their hearts and minds were actively seeking and listening to the voice of God. It's no coincidence that they just happened to see a star and decided to chase off after it.

The Magi fully understood the significance of this heavenly wonder. They were well aware that this was an unparalleled, celestial occurrence; proclaiming the arrival of a miraculous appointment. It was one which would ultimately divide the calendar of human history. Truly, they knew full well that this was the greatest event to ever be recorded within their own lives, as well as within the annals of world history. At least up to that point in time. Of course, this explains why they ventured out to travel for years searching for the light at the end of this stellar rainbow. We know that their journey was a rather lengthy one, since the scriptures tell us that Herod in his rage over being mocked by the Magi...

> Then Herod, when he saw that he was deceived by the wise men, was exceedingly angry; and he sent forth and put to death all the male children who were in Bethlehem and in all its districts, from two years old and under, according to the time which he had determined from the wise men. Then was fulfilled what was spoken by Jeremiah the prophet, saying: "A voice was heard in Ramah, Lamentation, weeping, and great mourning, Rachel weeping for her children, refusing to be comforted, because they are no more, *(Matthew 2:16-18 NKJV).*

The Magi were the first men to *follow the light of Christ* by faith. They couldn't even begin to realize the glory or the joy that awaited them at the end of their spiritual quest. But they fully realized that it represented the birth of a very special child---truly, more than just an ordinary prince. The heavens had declared the splendor of God's plan, announcing the birth of the King of kings and the Lord of lords. But just like the rest of the world, the Magi could never completely comprehend the incredible significance regarding the impact this Child would have on mankind. Yet, they journeyed for years in search of a prophecy; in search of a promise! The commitment they exhibited was astonishing!

How many of us would leave the comfort of our homes and way of life, or leave our country to follow a star in pursuit of a vision? Would you? The Kings from the East had no idea when they would finally discover the promised King. There was no way to tell how long their journey would take, before being able to return to their homeland, their families, and friends. But yet, they were so *sure of God's promise* that they carried with them precious gifts of gold, frankincense, and myrrh. Expensive gifts; elaborate presents which signified the prominence of this Child. These gifts comprised so much more than just a gift with a simple monetary value. They also declared a profound cultural, spiritual, and prophetic component.

Tradition has it that the three Magi who traveled from Tarshish, Sheba, and Seba were named *Caspar, Melchior, and Balthasar.* Now, Melchior's gift of gold to the Christ-child *symbolized royalty,* and was a tribute to Jesus' divine nature, along with the recognition that He was the King of kings, and Lord of lords. Jesus was the Christ, which means the Anointed One. Truly He is the Son of God. Caspar's gift of myrrh also holds profound significance. It is a *spice for embalming* the dead, and it's associated with suffering, bitterness, and affliction. It represented Jesus' human nature, defining Him as the Son of Man. This gift prophetically proclaimed Jesus' role as the Sacrificial Lamb of God. Finally, the gift of frankincense given to the Christ-child by Balthasar was symbolic of *Jesus' holiness and righteousness,* as it was a resin used in perfumes and incense. It was the sweet aroma of worship that proclaimed Christ as the High Priest, as well as the Name above all names. The tributes of the three-Wisemen were freely and willingly given in adoration to the holy miracle of Christ's arrival in the world! The gifts they bore were given in humility and honor to the only King who is worthy to be worshipped and adored!

As you reflect on the significance of the gifts from the Magi to the baby Jesus, take a moment to consider what you have to offer the only begotten Son of God. *What do you possess that has any significance or value to Christ?* What do you have that is deserving of His sacrifice? It's true that you can give your time, energies, and even a tithe to today's church. But it is also true, that none of these things will save you from your sin, or allow you to enter into the presence and glory of God.

The only tangible gift that God has required since the day of Christ's resurrection, involves the *surrender* of a life into His hands and into His care. The only thing that Jesus asks in return for the price He paid to forgive your sins and free you from the shackles of that sin, is you! He wants you to accept His gift of redemption so that your name can be written down in the Lamb's Book of Life. His greatest desire is for you to come back into relationship with the Father! *"I am the way, the truth and the life, no man cometh unto the Father, but by Me!"* The birth, death, and resurrection of Jesus allows the world an opportunity to find their way back into a personal relationship with God the Father! That only happens when you accept Jesus, the visible image of the invisible God, into your heart.

Adam's sin separated you from a relationship with God. The birth of Jesus provided a way for humanity to be redeemed from the bondage of sin. God's grace for the world became flesh nearly two-thousand years ago, and the Magi sought after this gift in order to honor Him as the newborn King of the Ages. Jesus longs for you to seek Him and then simply present your life into His care. Jesus loves you just the way you are. There is nothing you can ever do, and there is nothing that you could have ever done to keep God's love from reaching you. All you have to do is open the door of your heart and let Him in.

> But God, who is rich in mercy, because of His great love with which He loved us, even when we were dead in trespasses, made us alive together with Christ (by grace you

have been saved), and raised us up together, and made us sit together in the heavenly places in Christ Jesus, that in the ages to come He might show the exceeding riches of His grace in His kindness toward us in Christ Jesus. For by grace you have been saved through faith, and that not of yourselves; it is the gift of God, not of works, lest anyone should boast. For we are His workmanship, created in Christ Jesus for good works, which God prepared beforehand that we should walk in them, *(Ephesians 2: 4-10 NKJV).*

The question you need to answer today after reflecting on this topic, is simple. *What do you have to offer Jesus? What are you willing to give to your King?* Take a moment to record your response on the space below.

_____

_____

_____

_____

_____

_____

_____

_____

_____

_____

_____

_____

_____

_____

_____

_____

_____

_____

_____

_____

_____

What Can I Offer, what shall I bring?

What can I share with the newborn King?

I have nothing of value, nothing of worth,
> How can I honor, the Holy One's birth?
The Kings of the world, from lands far away;
> Traveled to seek Him - their tribute to pay!
From Tarshish and Sheba they followed the Light
> To seek out the promise, and to witness the sight!
Melchior came and offered pure gold,
> He followed the star the prophets foretold!
'Twas gold for a King, the Light of the world;
> Precious and pure, God's love was unfurled!
Caspar then offered his gift to the Child,
> Anointed in Myrrh, with aromas so mild,
Sweet smelling virtues, yet so bitter to taste,
> Suffering and sorrow, Christ was destined to face!
Balthasar followed in adoration and praise,
> Frankincense given; burned through the days;
The incense of worship, the fragrance of prayer,
> The sacrifice offered, God's atonement to bare!
Jesus would live and then die on the cross,
> The price to be paid for a world that was lost!
Yet, what can we offer, to worship the Christ?
> This child that was born, the Divine Sacrifice!
We have nothing of value, nothing of worth,
> Nothing to offer, the dear Savior's birth!
So, give of yourself - your soul - and your life,
> He has forgiven all sin – you're free from all strife!
The option is yours, may you follow His ways,
> To worship and praise Him, all of your days!
May you follow the path to the mountain of myrrh,
> May you walk through the hills of frankincense pure,
May the Light of His love, shine brilliant as gold,
> May you seek out Redemption, as the wise men of old!

Lanny K. Cook

62

Day 9
The Child Jesus
Scriptural Reflection

Who has believed our message? To whom has the Lord revealed his powerful arm? My servant grew up in the Lord's presence like a tender green shoot, like a root in dry ground. There was nothing beautiful or majestic about his appearance, nothing to attract us to him. He was despised and rejected— a man of sorrows, acquainted with deepest grief. We turned our backs on him and looked the other way. He was despised, and we did not care. *Isaiah 53:1-3 NLT*

My son, do not forget My teaching, but keep My commandments in your heart, for they will prolong your life many years and bring you prosperity. Let love and faithfulness never leave you; bind them around your neck, write them on the tablet of your heart. Then you will win favor and a good name in the sight of God and man. Trust in the Lord with all your heart and lean not on your own understanding; in all your ways acknowledge Him, and He will make your paths straight....... Blessed is the man who finds wisdom, the man who gains understanding, for she is more profitable than silver and yields better returns than gold. She is more precious than rubies; nothing you desire can compare with her. Long life is in her right hand; in her left hand are riches and honor. Her ways are pleasant ways, and all her paths bring peace. *Proverbs 3:1-6, 13-17 NIV*

When Israel was a child, I loved him, and out of Egypt I called My Son. *Hosea 11:1 NIV*

And the child grew, waxed strong in spirit, filled with wisdom: and the grace of God was upon Him. *Luke 2:40 KJV*

There is *no greater love* exhibited on earth then when a mother gently draws a newborn baby close against her breast. With adoring eyes, she inspects every inch of her newborn miracle. Tenderly she strokes her fingers along his cherub-like cheeks while softly grooming the silk-like hairs on the top of his head. She lovingly sways back and forth in rhythmic serenity, as she gently cradles him in her caressing arms. With bated-breath she sweetly sings a prophetic lullaby. Her loving voice is a reassurance to this precious child, that his mother is simply a breath away.

The sweet songs of love emanate from the depths of her soul as she partakes of the treasure who she lovingly caresses. This is a moment that only a mother can ponder; one that only a mother can understand and appreciate. The sweetness of her lullaby quietly floats across the room as it disappears into the night. It sends a message to all within reach of her melodic serenade, of a love that will never die. Hers is a devoted love. One that will never depart; no matter how great the distance that separates a mother from her child.

Intertwined within the strains of a mother's soft lullaby, is a message conveying the hopes, dreams, and prayers that she offers to God as a covering over the life of her precious child. Lyrics filled with prayers for happiness, joy, laughter, and love; saturate her child. She envisions a bright future for this tiny miracle - a life filled with prosperity, good fortune, and possibly fame. Her chorus radiates with prayers for protection and guidance as this child ventures out into life. Petitions from her heart echo across the room; requesting God to dispatch a legion of angels to watch over her bundle of joy as he grows into a man. Her song pleads for God's grace, to fill his heart with peace, goodwill, and just enough tribulation in life to keep him humble, reverent, and secure in his faith. The sweetness of a lullaby which flows from a mother's heart and through her lips is much more than just a melody. It's a *whisper of joy*, a moment of *prayer*, a profession of *faith*; a blessing of *love*; as well as a declaration of trust, begging for *divine intervention* over the life and soul of her bundle of joy.

Mary and Joseph, were literally hand-picked to raise Jesus, to train Him up in the *Way of the Lord God*. Both played a significant role in the emotional, physical, and spiritual nurturing that was required according to His prophetic purpose. After all, Jesus was not just an ordinary child, He was the Son of God: *Who was, Who is*, and *Who is to come.* Even at the age of twelve it was apparent that this child Jesus, was the son of God. The scriptures contain few records of the life of Christ from the time of His birth until the time that His ministry began. Nearly thirty years of His life is hidden from the records of antiquity. We know that as a newborn baby, His family fled to Egypt in obedience to God's warning. It was a flight required to avoid the persecution and wrath of Herod the king, who had sent forth a decree requiring all of the male children less than two years old in that region to be slaughtered. Herod's rage over the news from the Magi that the King of kings was born in the region, led him to massacre hundreds of innocent young lives as he tried to preserve his kingdom and reign over the land. We also know, that after several years of living in Egypt, Mary and Joseph brought the young boy Jesus back to live in Nazareth. During this time, Jesus apprenticed in his father's carpenter shop, working side by side with Joseph, learning the skills of the trade.

The brief mention of Jesus' appearance in the Temple at the age of twelve provides insight into the fact, that even as a child, Jesus astonished the most educated teachers of His time with both His understanding of the Jewish laws and also, His responses to their questions. Even at this young age it's evident that He understood His destiny and purpose for this world. When He replied to His parent's admonishments of where He had been and why He had treated them in such a way, He simply said, *"Don't you realize that I must be tending to my Father's business?"* He knew what His existence in this world required. For thirty-years God prepared Him, as He grew in stature and grace for the ministry and purpose to which He was born.

One can only speculate the experiences Jesus had as He grew up in Nazareth. Did He have friends that He often played with? Did they spend hours in the fields playing together, wrestling, running, trying to catch lizards and toads. Or, did they lie on their backs for hours watching the clouds float overhead, imagining all forms of animals, creatures, and mystical creations? More than likely Jesus was adored by the adults of the community. A Child who always did the right thing; always polite, never rude, and who was the perfect Son. But I'm sure that there were many adults, maybe even Mary and Joseph, who at times could not understand why He acted or responded in the manner that He did. After all, He was the Son of God! Constantly, He displayed wisdom and knowledge far greater than even the brightest teachers of the day.

There was definitely something different about Jesus. He just wasn't mischievous and deceitful like some of the other children. He never lied about anything, and constantly exhibited honesty and obedience. He always had to do what was right and refused to participate in any of the typical rebellious actions or defiance toward parents and authority figures like some of the other children. In fact, Jesus was probably perceived as a rather odd boy by many of the inhabitants of Nazareth. Undoubtedly, there were times He would go off by Himself in the countryside to meditate and pray. Definitely odd behavior for a boy of that age.

More than likely, Jesus had a few close friends with whom He played and shared. Even at a young age, *He must have had a presence and a joy which attracted people toward Him*. There had to be an aura that radiated through His smile and sparkled out of His eyes. I'm sure there were many who may not have understood Jesus, but wanted to be near Him. They were drawn to share the essence of light which radiated from His being. Truly, this Child, was special!

To stand in the temple at any age before the greatest minds of Israel, would unravel the nerves of even the most courageous of men. But here stood this twelve-year-old Boy, astonishing everyone with His knowledge, as well as His answers to their questions. Obviously, this wisdom was not derived from earthly means, but through His divine appointment.

> Trust in the Lord with all your heart and lean not on your own understanding; in all your ways submit to him, and he will make your paths straight, *(Proverbs 3:5-6 NIV)*.

Jesus spent thirty years, preparing for His three-year earthly ministry. A ministry which culminated with His death on the cross, and the resurrection from the grave. All that time He was devoted to the preparation of a ministry that would forever change the world. The time required to mold, shape, and temper the soul and character of Jesus was necessary, so that He could successfully complete His mission on earth. The *destiny of mankind* lay in the balance of the preparation for His ministry.

It's easy to become impatient and depressed with the daily situations that you face. You become discouraged by the challenges that life throws your way. You turn to the world and earthly means as a way to find the answers to life. Answers that appease the desires of your heart. Often times, it's not until all hope is gone and no other option exists that you *turn to find God* in search of sanctuary. As a last-ditch effort, you decide to seek Him in His Holy Temple. Mary and Joseph searched for the young Jesus in all the wrong places. It never even crossed their minds to look for Him in the Temple. None of us are really much different. Most of the time, we wander around, looking for the answers to life's biggest questions in all the wrong places.

Deep insight and wisdom are never obtained through your own efforts. *Wisdom comes from the Divine*, and it will never arrive until you *silence your heart*, in an effort to *listen* to the Lord's voice. You must seek God's wisdom and understanding as you face the challenges of life. You must learn to seek Him first, rather than searching through your own understanding! The only way to do that is to pray. That's the first thing Joseph and Mary should have done as they frantically searched for Jesus. I have a pretty good hunch that the Lord would have lead them to the Temple, much sooner.

Honestly, I can't even begin to imagine the daunting task to raise God's only begotten Son. Talk about an intimidating assignment. Even though the biblical records don't share too much information about Joseph, I can't help but believe that he was *a great prayer warrior.* Actually, I'm confident that *Mary was as well.* They'd have to be in order to have been chosen for such a divine undertaking. I'm thinking that they both spent countless hours seeking the Lord's guidance and praying for wisdom and grace to raise the Christ Child into the Man of God that He was born to become. Jesus' parents not only *served as a prayer covering* over Him during those early years, but they saturated their Son with *God's glory* through the *power of prayer.*

And when you pray, do not be like the hypocrites, for they love to pray standing in the synagogues and on the street corners to be seen by others. Truly I tell you, they have received their reward in full. But when you pray, go into your room, close the door and pray to your Father, who is unseen. Then your Father, who sees what is done in secret, will reward you. And when you pray, do not keep on babbling like pagans, for they think they will be heard because of their many words. Do not be like them, for your Father knows what you need before you ask him, *(Matthew 6:5-8 NIV)*.

As we close today's devotion, I want to ask two simple questions. The first: *Who is in your life that covers you with prayer?* The second: *Who do you need to lift up in prayer before the Lord?* Ponder those thoughts as you enjoy a prayer that may slightly resemble one that Joseph could have recited, as the earthly father of the Son of God. *Write the names of those individuals in the space below.* While you're at it, go ahead and list any specific needs of your own. Then after you've done that, take a moment and say a prayer, for the people and the things that you have listed. And, remember the words that the Apostle Paul shared in his first letter to the church in Thessalonica. **Rejoice always, pray continually, give thanks in all circumstances; for this is God's will for you in Christ Jesus,** *(I Thessalonians 5:16-18 NIV)*.

_____

_____

_____

_____

_____

_____

_____

_____

_____

_____

_____

_____

_____

A Father's Prayer

Mary gently rocks the Christ Child to sleep while softly singing a sweet lullaby. Joseph watches with peaceful contentment as the melody gently floats across the quiet stable. In the stillness of this precious moment, he closes his eyes and whispers this solemn prayer to God the Father...

Thank you, Lord, for Your beautiful child,
> Which You have given us, to nurture and love for a while.
Keep this Child in Your loving care,
> Help Him to grow and His crosses to bear.
Help us to guide Him to the path of Your light,
> Please fill His life with Your mercy and might!
Allow Him to trust You with a faith that is strong,
> While filling His heart with Your heavenly song.
Let His eyes sparkle, and glitter, and shine ......
> With mercy and laughter, and wisdom sublime.
Harden His heart to the worldly ways,
> And lift up His soul through glorious praise.
May His Radiance shine bright, as a great burning blaze;
> Now, help Him to seek You through all of His days!
Send down Your angels to watch over Him,
> Let Your presence be felt when the shadows creep in.
Most of all Lord, I ask in this prayer,
> Take care of Your Child, when we cannot be there . . .
For life is uncertain, there are no guarantees,
> There are mountains, and valleys, and treacherous seas;
So, help Him to find You, to know You are real,
> To seek You with passion, and serve You with zeal.
Please fill His life with Your bountiful love,
> And send down Your blessings from heaven above!
Joseph closed his prayer with a quiet amen,
> Then he opened his eyes to the present again!

Lanny K. Cook

And Jesus grew in wisdom and stature, and in favor with God and man, *(Luke 2:52 NIV).*

Day 10
A Voice, Crying in the Wilderness!
Scriptural Reflection

Behold, I will send my messenger, and he shall prepare the way before me: and the Lord, whom ye seek, shall suddenly come to his temple, even the messenger of the covenant, whom ye delight in: behold, he shall come, saith the Lord of hosts. *Malachi 3:1 KJV*

A voice of one calling: 'In the desert prepare the way for the Lord; make straight in the wilderness a highway for our God. Every valley shall be raised up, every mountain and hill made low; the rough ground shall become level, the rugged places a plain. And the glory of the Lord will be revealed, and all mankind together will see it. For the mouth of the Lord has spoken.' *Isaiah 40:3-5 NIV*

A voice of one calling in the desert, 'Prepare the way for the Lord, make straight paths for Him. Every valley shall be filled in, every mountain and hill made low. The crooked roads shall become straight, the rough roads smooth. And all mankind will see God's salvation.' *Luke 3:4-6 NIV*

Jesus did grow in wisdom and stature, as well as in favor with God and man after the experience in the Temple at the age of twelve. Not another word is mentioned about Him in the biblical record until the time comes for His ministry to begin. It's like there's an uncomfortable pause in the biblical script. All that we know for certain is that the *Child of God* became the fully grown, *Son of God*, as the Gospel records confirm Jesus' Messianic anointing by His baptism at the hands of John the Baptizer.

John was a cousin to Jesus, and was a descendent of the priestly tribe of Levi. Even though he is considered to be a Prophet of God, the truth is that according to the lineage from which he descended, he would have been considered a priest. He is famous for serving as the voice, *crying in the wilderness* to prepare the way for the Lord, Jesus. He had his own band of disciples, and his teachings had developed a rather large contingent of devoted followers.

Many people considered him to be a prophet in the form of Elijah. John dressed in a garment of camel's hair with a leather girdle or belt wrapped around his waist. He was a man of the wilderness, nourished by eating locust and honey, and sustained through the calling of God Almighty. He was called as the *Forerunner* to Jesus. His teaching involved a cry for people to repent of their sinful ways as a means of preparation for the coming of the true Messiah; the Deliverer of Israel.

> The beginning of the gospel of Jesus Christ, the Son of God. As it is written in the Prophets:
>
> "Behold, I send My messenger before Your face,
> Who will prepare Your way before You."
> "The voice of one crying in the wilderness:
> 'Prepare the way of the Lord;
> Make His paths straight.'"
>
> John came baptizing in the wilderness and preaching a baptism of repentance for the remission of sins. Then all the land of Judea, and those from Jerusalem, went out to him and were all baptized by him in the Jordan River, confessing their sins.
>
> Now John was clothed with camel's hair and with a leather belt around his waist, and he ate locusts and wild honey. And he preached, saying, "There comes One after me

who is mightier than I, whose sandal strap I am not worthy
to stoop down and loose. I indeed baptized you with water,
but He will baptize you with the Holy Spirit." It came to
pass in those days that Jesus came from Nazareth of Galilee,
and was baptized by John in the Jordan. And immediately,
coming up from the water, He saw the heavens parting and
the Spirit descending upon Him like a dove. Then a voice
came from heaven, "You are My beloved Son, in whom I am
well pleased," *(Mark 1:1-11 NKJV).*

John, a Prophet from the wilderness; was preparing the way for
redemption to arrive. He was called to proclaim the arrival of the Good
News. Finally, the broken and lost would soon be delivered out of their
own, personal, desert of barren desperation. Israel was ripe for such at
time as this. People, were destitute, broken, lost, hurting, oppressed;
desperately hoping, praying, and openly crying out to God, for the
promised Messiah to come! The message that John was preaching to the
masses; Behold it's time to receive the **Lamb of God, who would take
away the sins of the world.** The reality of those days along the Jordan
River was about to become reality, as the Messiah's time had finally
arrived on the banks of this life-giving water. The Living Water, was
about to enter His anointing.

As John baptized the long-awaited Messiah, and when Jesus
emerged from His submersion from the waters of the river, He received
His official *consecration* through the purpose of God the Father. As
Jesus rose to His feet, the heaven's opened and the Spirit descended
upon Him like a dove. His purpose was sealed as God's voice
proclaimed, "You are my beloved Son, in whom I am well pleased." The
gates had been opened to release mankind from the barren wilderness
of relational bondage that had imprisoned them through the
disobedience of Adam. It was the consequence of Adam's sin that cast
all of us out of the garden of personal relationship with God. Jesus, the
visible image of the *invisible God* had opened the door once again to
relational access with the Almighty. But yet, the official seal required to
forever decree that door to remain open was yet to be proclaimed. That
edict would not be decreed until the end of Jesus' three-year ministry.

Those were extremely desperate times for the Hebrew people
when the Messiah heard their cry, and poured Himself out, as the

redemption for sin. Today, it's hard to imagine the harshness of the wilderness from which they cried out to God. However, even within the confines and the constraints of this world, mankind is still immersed in the desperate wasteland of personal struggle. The circumstance of the human plight may have changed, but the harsh intensity of an individual's wilderness experience will never decrease.

There's not much difference between our lives and the lives of those who heard the message of John the Baptizer. Our hearts and basic desires are pretty much the same as those who walked the earth during the ministry of John. The harsh landscape that we struggle through hasn't changed much, either. The hectic pace of today's lifestyle has only served to intensify the heat of the modern desert that is intent on consuming life. Why? Because we ignore the need to feed our spiritual nature and neglect any form of deep relationship with God the Father. In that regard, nothing has changed over the past two-thousand years.

> **In those days, John, the Baptist came preaching in the Desert of Judea, and saying, 'Repent, for the kingdom of heaven is near.' This is he who was spoken of through the prophet Isaiah: A voice of one calling in the desert, 'Prepare the way of the Lord,'** *(Matthew 3:1,2 NIV).*

The cry of the people is no different today than it was when John first proclaimed the arrival of the Messiah. It's still time to *repent and turn back towards God!* Now is the time to *prepare your heart for the way of the Lord.* There's no better time than the present to lift your eyes to the Savior and cry out for His redeeming grace. It's no longer John's voice echoing across the desert. But rather, Jesus Himself calls out to you and to me in a still small voice; a voice that radiates throughout the innermost recesses of your life. He's calling you into repentance: To accept His free gift of grace, provided through the shedding of His own blood. Are you ready to turn your back on the past and lift your eyes to Him. He is softly whispering your name. He's calling for you to come into relationship with Him. Or, maybe you have stepped off the narrow way and need to just turn back to Him.

Regardless, if you want to hear His voice, you must *be still and fervently listen.* You need to seek Him daily through times of quiet reflection and devotion to His Word. Notice I didn't just say devotion "in" His Word; but rather "to" His Word. That makes a huge difference. Actually, it makes all the difference. It is during the times of *solace and prayer* as you struggle through the barren moments; that you are inclined to listen to His voice, and to seek His instruction. That is when you are most open to correct your course in life. Only Jesus can deliver you from the circumstance of your own, personal desolation.

Do you hear Jesus' voice, calling out your name? Will you respond to the voice of the Shepherd, calling out to the lost sheep of His flock? As the lover of your soul, He is whispering your name, calling out to your soul; bidding you to come home. *Will you answer His call,* or will you continue down the worldly path seeking your own direction? How have you responded to His still, small voice, as He tries to guide your steps? Following His voice is the only means to survive as you wander through the wilderness of your earthly days. Will you continue to wander in the wasteland of desolation, or will you follow His voice out of the parched desert and into paradise? The choice is yours!

> Whether you turn to the right or turn to the left, your ears will hear a voice behind you saying, 'This is the way, walk in it,' *(Isaiah 30:21 NIV).*

Over two-thousand years ago, John the Baptist publicly prepared the way for the Messiah, proclaiming to the world the One who would be God's redemptive grace. Grace would once again afford mankind, the luxury of finding communion and fellowship in God's presence, as the Spirit of the living God was about to be unleashed across the land. John's ministry proclaimed that it was "time to repent and be baptized!" Today, that message is still relevant. God's purpose had come to earth and it continues on to this very day.

> Finally, they said, "Who are you? Give us an answer to take back to those who sent us. What do you say about yourself?" John replied in the words of Isaiah the prophet, "I am the voice of one calling in the wilderness, 'Make straight the way for the Lord.'" Now the Pharisees who had been sent questioned him, "Why then do you baptize if you are not the Messiah, nor Elijah, nor the Prophet?" "I baptize with water," John replied, "but among you stands one you do not know. He is the one who comes after me, the straps of whose sandals I am not worthy to untie."
> This all happened at Bethany on the other side of the

Jordan, where John was baptizing.

 The next day John saw Jesus coming toward him and said, "Look, the Lamb of God, who takes away the sin of the world! This is the one I meant when I said, 'A man who comes after me has surpassed me because he was before me.' I myself did not know him, but the reason I came baptizing with water was that he might be revealed to Israel." Then John gave this testimony: "I saw the Spirit come down from heaven as a dove and remain on him. And I myself did not know him, but the one who sent me to baptize with water told me, 'The man on whom you see the Spirit come down and remain is the one who will baptize with the Holy Spirit.' I have seen and I testify that this is God's Chosen One," *(John 1:22-34 NIV).*

We are living during a time that will more than likely allow us to serve as eye witnesses to the second coming of the Lord Jesus Christ. It is an exciting time! The hour is drawing nigh, when He returns to take His children home to spend eternity in sweet fellowship and communion in His presence. The timetable of the ages persuades us to heed the call and obey His voice as we prepare ourselves for *the way of the Lord!* Truly, it is time to fully anticipate the return of Jesus Christ. It is time to *repent, for the Kingdom of heaven is near!* You cannot continue to live in the shadow of darkness. The Light of Christ will dispel all darkness, if you simply repent, and ask Him into your heart. *Will you step into the light of God's Chosen One and let Him in? Are you ready to walk on the path of Light that leads to life everlasting?* It's entirely up to you. Take a moment to share your response in the space below.

_____

_____

_____

_____

_____

_____

_____

Shadows in the Night

I see the rays of the golden sun at the close of another day –
      While the warming light that emanates, swiftly slips away.
The once blue sky, lined with clouds, is swallowed in the night,
      Anxious awe fills the heart, while shadows replace the light.
Twilight ebbs to softened light, as stars begin to shine,
      The moon ascends above the trees, for shadows to define;
A silhouette of brokenness, where branches seem to stretch—
      Obscurities of a sullen world, dull the brilliance of a crèche.

I hear the sounds that emanate from the stillness found within,
      The serenity of the locust strain, can still the hearts of men.
The blissful song of the nightingale, will share a message clear;
      To a somber soul, filled with sin, who stills their heart to hear.
The cricket's cheerful symphony, serenades within the shadow,
      A beckoned cry within each chord, breathes across the meadow.
The message sent throughout the night, is seldom, crystal clear,
      To seek respite for a weary heart – deep reflection brings a tear.

Within the coolness of the breeze, absorbed within the night,
      Solace from the searing heat, and this journey's weary plight.
A time for rest - to meditate - to reflect upon the day,
      Hope, the only sustenance as I strive to find the way!
The journey of a thousand miles is filled with many branches,
      I walk this trail in solitude; but alone, I take my chances.
So, I scan the far horizon, as I trudge along through time—
      Searching for a little peace - for grace - for life sublime.

Immersed within a shadow - life is darkened, dreary, cold,
      Hiding from a shameful past; life's hope and dreams grow cold.
Then a voice cries out of the wilderness; repent, to find the Way,
      Still engulfed within the shadows, I must lift my eyes to pray;
'Til the morning dawn that warms the soul, with His radiance of Light.
      He offers me, redemptive love, through His mercy, grace and might.
His Light dispels the shadows, from the darkness of my sin,
      To turn away from a sullen past, I must simply ask Him in!

Lanny K. Cook

Day 11
Disciples of the Lord and Master
Scriptural Reflection

And Jesus, walking by the Sea of Galilee, saw two brothers, Simon called Peter, and Andrew his brother, casting a net into the sea; for they were fishermen. Then He said to them, "Follow Me, and I will make you fishers of men." They immediately left their nets and followed Him. *Matthew 4:18-20 NKJV*

Then Jesus said to His disciples, "If anyone desires to come after Me, let him deny himself, and take up his cross, and follow Me. For whoever desires to save his life will lose it, but whoever loses his life for My sake will find it. For what profit is it to a man if he gains the whole world, and loses his own soul? Or what will a man give in exchange for his soul? For the Son of Man will come in the glory of His Father with His angels, and then He will reward each according to his works. *Matthew 16: 24-27 NKJV*

"'Awake, O sword, against My Shepherd, against the man who is close to me!' declares the Lord Almighty. 'Strike the Shepherd, and the sheep will be scattered, and I will turn My hand against the little ones. In the whole land,' declares the Lord, 'two-thirds will be left in it. This third I will bring into the fire; I will refine them like silver and test them like gold. They will call on my name and I will answer them; I will say, 'They are my people,' and they will say, 'The Lord is our God.'"
Zechariah 13:7-9 NIV

Then He said to His disciples, "The harvest truly is plentiful, but the laborers are few. Therefore, pray the Lord of the harvest to send out laborers into His harvest." *Matthew 9:37-38 NKJV*

The Gospels are filled with accounts of *Christ's teaching* to the multitudes and even within the Temple. Many of the most baffling teachings where shared with His Disciples as He provided them with deep insight regarding the promise of His Kingdom and God's ultimate purpose for both Israel, as well as the Church. However, many of the lessons He shared within His three-year ministry focused on *preparing the twelve chosen;* for the challenge of both understanding and sharing the Good News of the Gospel after the miraculous glory of His resurrection and His ascension to the Father. From these twelve, devoted followers, came the greatest Church the world has ever seen.

All of the original twelve were just ordinary men who came from all walks of life. There was nothing special about any of them until *Christ transformed their lives from ordinary to extraordinary.* Initially, these men didn't seek out on their own to follow the Lord. Each and every one of them had personal ambitions and obligations. Individually, they embraced their own pursuit of fulfilling their own hopes, and realizing their own dreams. Engrained deep within their daily activities were all sorts of responsibilities, challenges, and demands. One could assume that most, were established in their livelihood and probably rather comfortable within their own right; content with their life and the bounties of their labors.

Content that is, until they heard the voice of Jesus calling, *Come and follow Me, and I will make you fishers of men.* The Lord's still, small voice touched their hearts; it intrigued their minds, and beckoned them to follow a new calling! A new way of life! His voiced drew them out of their own pursuits, and cast them onto the path of God's promise. They were transformed; completely and totally changed. Their lives would never be the same from the moment they answered the call of the Lord Jesus Christ! They were chosen by God to serve His purpose - to share the Good News with all of the world, and to serve as the founders of the greatest Church the world has ever known.

But *who were these common men* who were divinely chosen by Jesus to be trained up and to carry on His ministry after His death and resurrection? A majority of them were fishermen by trade, one was a tax collector, and one was even a zealot who fervently opposed the Roman rule over Israel. They were *ordinary men*, who were each *called* into the fold of Jesus' flock; His appointed followers. Andrew was a follower of the prophet John. He was an eye witness to Jesus being baptized and the heavens opening up for the dove to descend upon the Messiah. Once He saw Jesus' interaction with John, he instantly became a follower of Jesus. Andrew was the one who provided an introduction of his brother, Simon Peter, otherwise known as Cephas, to Jesus. Then there were the sons of Zebedee, James the Greater, and John the Beloved. Jesus referred to them as the sons of thunder because of their impetuous nature. One by one the men were called: Philip, Bartholomew, Thomas, Matthew, James the son of Alphaeus, Jude who was also referred to as Thaddeus, Simon the Zealot, and finally Judas the betrayer of Christ.

This bedraggled gang of hand-chosen *spiritual interns* were all simple, ordinary men but received an extraordinary calling. There was nothing particularly special or impressive about any of them. It's easy to apply an old adage to describe this rag-tag team of followers, when you look at the lack of societal status these typically average men appeared to possess. *God doesn't call the equipped, He equips the called.* Maybe that's something you need to seriously consider within your own circumstance of following Jesus. There wasn't anything stellar or even promising within the nature of any of these men. But they were all handpicked by the Son of God, to become *fishers of men.* That actually provides a significant amount of hope for all of us then, don't you agree?

These twelve men served as *eye witnesses* to the greatest miracles and wonders ever encountered throughout all of humanity. They witnessed the *spiritual transformation of mankind* as their Master's hand reached out to touch a lost and hurting world. The sick found healing, the blind gained sight, the lame were allowed to walk again, the deaf could hear, the dumb would speak, and the dead brought back to life. Can you imagine the excitement and exhilaration these twelve found as they witnessed daily miracles and wonders as Jesus continued His ministry throughout the land? It is even harder to imagine the anguish, the fear, and the feeling of complete loss and confusion as their hopes and expectations were destroyed at Jesus' crucifixion on the cross. However, "then came the morning" when nothing could compare to the excitement, the wonder they must have felt at their first glimpse of the risen Christ.

After Jesus' ascension and through the baptism of the Holy Spirit at an event known as *Pentecost*, the Disciples' convictions became so strong and so bold, that they professed their faith even unto their own deaths. Most were martyred for what they believed as their critics plotted and schemed to destroy their testimonies, trying to discourage the ever-expanding body of Jesus' believers.

Christ warned His chosen ones that their journey would not be easy. He cautioned them that the world would be set against them and would try to destroy not only their mission, but also their lives. But Jesus promised Peter that *the gates of hell would not prevail against* the truth of the Good News. Yet, the greater the persecution against Christ's chosen witnesses, the greater the number of converts who decided to follow Him with a deep, profound faithfulness! For the efforts of these original followers, they were promised the *keys to the Lord's Kingdom;* that's a significant thought to contemplate. As followers of Jesus, we too are given a profound promise. We are *joint-heirs* with Jesus Christ within the expanse of His eternal Kingdom and will stand by His side as He rules in power and glory forevermore. That too is quite the promise for all who believe.

These men of faith delivered a message to the world regarding the miracle called salvation. One which is only offered through God's grace. It is God's unmerited gift that you can freely accept or reject! This is the good news -- the Gospel of Jesus Christ offered to all the world, during this unique period of time, known as the *Age of Grace*.

> He that loveth his father or mother more than Me is not worthy of Me; and he that loveth a son or daughter more than Me is not worthy of Me. And he that taketh not his cross, and followeth after Me is not worthy of Me. He that findeth his life shall lose it: and he that loseth his life for My sake shall find it, *(Matthew 10: 37-40 KJV).*

The Disciples served as first-hand witnesses to the miraculous wonder of the Jesus.' ministry Their lives became a living testimony to the world as they formed the foundation for the Church of the risen Savior. It wasn't that any of them left a personal legacy behind in their own right, but rather they left behind the legacy of the Light of the

World. When people encountered any of these men, they didn't see the person, they saw the *radiance of His glory*, brilliantly shining out of their lives. It was to God that they gave all glory, and honor. These original followers became the first *cloud of witnesses*, watching with their own eyes, the transforming power of Jesus as He performed miraculous wonders that forever changed people, along with their eternal destiny. But most important they became the conduit of grace as they responded to the Lord's calling to continue the mission of sharing the Salvation message to a lost, and broken world.

The true Disciples answered the Master's call, (I'm not including Judas Iscariot in this reference), and all of them except John, died a martyr's death. They carried their *devotion for the Master to their graves*. All of their deaths were extremely gruesome. James the Greater, was the first disciple to be martyred after Jesus ascended to heaven. He was beheaded at the command of Herod Agrippa. Peter, Andrew, Philip, and Simon the Zealot were all crucified. Thomas was killed by a spear; Matthew was slain by a sword. Thaddeus was shot with arrows. James the son of Alphaeus was thrown from the pinnacle of the Temple and then beaten to death as the fall didn't kill him. Bartholomew was flayed, or skinned alive. John, the beloved was the only disciple to not die as a martyr, although he was thrown into boiling oil while facing persecution in Rome, but somehow, miraculously survived the horrendous ordeal. He actually lived a rather long life, and died naturally in the city of Ephesus.

What's important to remember regarding the Disciples of Jesus, involves the frailty within their individual, human nature. They weren't perfect. They couldn't be. They had their character flaws and made plenty of mistakes. But *Jesus called them*. He loved them, used them, and embraced them in spite of who they really were. Think about it for a moment as we close today's devotion. Peter was bold, brash, forceful, and denied Jesus three times when push came to shove. Thomas was a doubter. The sons of thunder were prideful and impetuous. Remember how they argued about who would be the one appointed to sit next to Jesus in His Kingdom? Matthew, the tax collector was despised by all of society. Judas was a greedy sneak and the traitor to Jesus.

When Jesus was betrayed in the garden, all of His followers

scattered like sheep as the shepherd was struck down. All of them went into hiding as they struggled with their personal doubts and unbelief. When their faith was put to the test, every one of them failed as they all fled into the shadows, fearing for their own safety. You and I are no different than any of these original followers of Jesus. We share the same human weakness. We can relate to their failures, mistakes, and nature of self-preservation. All of us have *moments of doubt.* I'm pretty sure that somewhere you even *denied knowing* Him. Maybe not by just saying it out loud, but by not speaking up while remaining silent regarding the faith you claim to have in Him. All of us have also *betrayed* Him at some point in life. Maybe that betrayal came by worshipping something or someone more than you did Him at the time. Betrayal is also found within the times that you ignore His call, or act out against the direction He's telling you to go. Yet, even still, just like those examples of the Disciples' human frailty didn't stop Jesus from continuing to use them for the purpose of *His Kingdom come;* they won't stop Him from using you, either. Of course, that still leaves Judas Iscariot as the exception to that consideration.

Just as it was nearly two-thousand years ago during the time of our Lord and Master; so, it is today. He is still calling out to every heart and to every soul: *Come, follow me, and I will make you fishers of men! Have you answered His call? Have you made the choice to follow Him? Are you willing to go to your grave, confessing Him as your Lord and Savior?* Briefly share your reflections on these questions.

_____

_____

_____

_____

_____

_____

_____

_____

_____

_____

Disciples of our Lord and Master!

Jesus, Lord, and Master, left His heavenly throne,
>To come to earth long ago, man's sins He would atone;
Once His sacrifice was finished upon this sin-filled earth,
>He needed men to carry on, to teach the world "rebirth."
He would call the faithful, from many walks of life,
>Some were rough and rugged, while others knew no strife;
He would fill them with the spirit, make their life anew,
>Take away their load of sin, give them redemption, too.
He "knew" each one He needed, from deep within His heart,
>Predestination came alive right from the very start.
These chosen men, the famous twelve, found favor with the Lord,
>A blessed, consecrated group, joined in one accord.
It is written in the scriptures, "He calleth unto them,
>Who so ever will, may come" and they cometh unto Him.
Unto the many that cometh, "He appointed only twelve,
>He sent them forth to preach, "a sinful world to delve,"
Christ gave authority to these twelve --- of miracles divine,
>The power of God overcame them; awe and reverence sublime.
From thence they served the Master, the Messiah, the Promised One,
>The Redeemer of all the ages, God's only begotten Son.
For they have laid the ground work for the Church, His chosen bride,
>When He gave His last commandment, standing by their side:
Go ye now into all the world, and preach of what I've taught,
>For by My blood upon the cross, the sinner's soul I've bought,
Spread the saving Gospel to every creature here:
>Believe in me, accept this day --- to My riven side draw near;
Put your faith and trust in me, the Sacrificial Lamb,
>For I am He, the Promised One, I am the Great I Am.
Go to all the nations, baptize those who trust in Me,
>In the name of the Father, Son, Spirit. I have set the sinner free.
Unto the remaining eleven, this command of His was given . . .
>Then came His final words spoken; He was taken into heaven,
As nail pierced hands reached out to them in tender, loving care,
>"Lo, even unto the end of the age, I'll be always with you there."
Go, He said into all the world --- not just here or there,
>Make disciples of all people, Believers everywhere.
Therefore, His great commission, before He ascended thus
>Was not only to those faithful few, it still calls out to us.
As He called those twelve Disciples, He now calls you and me,
>I will make you fishers of men --- My follower you will be!

Clarice D. Cook

Day 12
Simple Faith
Scriptural Reflection

So then faith comes by hearing, and hearing by the word of God.
Romans 10: 17 NKJV

"For He will deliver the needy who cry out, the afflicted who have no one to help. He will take pity on the weak and the needy and save the needy from death. He will rescue them from oppression and violence, for precious is their blood in His sight. . .; May His name endure forever; may it continue as long as the sun. All nations will be blessed through Him, and they will call Him blessed. Praise be to the Lord God, the God of Israel, who alone does marvelous deeds. Praise be to His glorious name forever; may the whole earth be filled with His glory. Amen and Amen." *Psalm 72:12-14, 17-20 NIV*

"Then the eyes of the blind will be opened and the ears of the deaf unstopped. Then will the lame leap like a deer, and the mute tongue shout for joy. Water will gush forth in the wilderness and streams in the desert." *Isaiah 35:5, 6 NIV*

He was not far from the house when the centurion sent friends to say to him: "Lord, don't trouble yourself, for I do not deserve to have you come under my roof. That is why I did not even consider myself worthy to come to you. But say the word, and my servant will be healed. For I myself am a man under authority, with soldiers under me. I tell this one, 'Go,' and he goes; and that one, 'Come,' and he comes. I say to my servant, 'Do this,' and he does it." When Jesus heard this, he was amazed at him, and turning to the crowd following him, he said, "I tell you, I have not found such great faith even in Israel." Then the men who had been sent returned to the house and found the servant well! *Luke 7:6-10 NIV*

The Scriptures are filled with accounts which depict *man's faith in God.* Noah, Abraham, Sarah, Isaac, Jacob, Joshua, Moses, King David, Daniel, Joseph, Elizabeth, Mary, and Paul were but a few of the individuals who placed their trust in a power greater than their own. The common thread between all of these individuals was their *faith in God.* A faith in an Almighty Creator who promised to see them through this journey of life. But what is this thing called faith? Is it not knowing what lies ahead---not knowing what tomorrow will bring, and then simply trusting that God will take care of you? Is it believing that there is an Almighty Creator who spoke the heavens and the earth into being? Could it be knowing that there is a greater power who controls our destinies and our futures? Perhaps it is knowing that no matter what circumstances we face in life, there is always a ray of hope and through it all, God will prevail? The author of Hebrews tells us that "Faith" is. .

> The substance of things hoped for, the evidence of things not seen! Through faith we understand that the worlds were framed by the word of God, so that things which are seen were not made of things which do appear, *(Hebrews 11:1-3 NKJV).*

It appears then, that faith is believing in the "Word of God." By His word the worlds were framed. By His word the servant was healed. Jesus Christ is the Word...

> ... and the Word was made flesh, and dwelt among us, (and we beheld His glory, the glory as of the only begotten of the Father), full of grace and truth! *(John 1:14 KJV).*

God's Word, provides a promise of forgiveness and of life! Jesus Christ is that promise. He is the Messiah! The Savior of the world! *Only through Him can you find life!* Through Him you will find hope! Only by believing through faith in God can you accept the fullness contained within the precious Promise of God's Word!

> Do not think that I came to destroy the Law or the Prophets. I did not come to destroy but to fulfill. For assuredly, I say to you, till heaven and earth pass away, one jot or one tittle will by no means pass from the law till all is fulfilled, *(Matthew 5:17, 18 NKJV).*

Throughout the Bible we read accounts of people like you and me; ordinary people who *accepted God at His Word.* They sought after and followed the One known as Jesus. They reached out in "faith" to the miracles that He wanted to perform in their lives. They took their "faith" and put it into action. By "faith" we too can accept the blessings and grace God desires to bestow on each and every one of us, His children. Through "faith," we seek God in prayer. Through prayer, we seek God in "faith." By exercising our faith through prayer, God bestows upon us His grace and His mercy. Therefore, *seek ye first the kingdom of God, and His righteousness; and all these things shall be given unto you,* (Matthew 6:33KJV)!

His Word tells us that faith the size of a mustard seed can move mountains. We cannot begin to imagine or comprehend the power of faith when we place our lives into His control. Only by *faith* - simple, child-like faith; can you reach out and touch the hand of God. Through this intangible phenomenon called "faith," you and I will become heirs to His Kingdom! Through Jesus Christ, you can enter into relationship with your Creator. Only through Him will you find true life.

> I am the door. If anyone enters by Me, he will be saved, and will go in and out and find pasture. The thief does not come except to steal, and to kill, and to destroy. I have come that they may have life, and that they may have it more abundantly, *(John 10: 9-10 NKJV).*

Jesus is the door that allows you to discover true life. Not just an ordinary life, but life more abundant. Abundant life is yours for the asking. Will you reach out in child-like faith to allow God's power to work in your life? Life in Him provides healing, forgiveness, and the promise of eternal relationship with the One who created you. The only requirement to secure this promise of abundance is to reach out and invite Him into your life.

There are two specific examples of people reaching out to Jesus that are worthy of consideration at this point in our study. The first one involved the woman with the issue of blood who in total desperation after years of sufferings, approached Jesus in order to just simply touch the hem of His garment. Her faith was so strong that she believed all she had to do was touch Him and she would receive healing. Rather than try to describe the scene to you, I will simply share the scripture.

> So Jesus went with him. A large crowd followed and pressed around him. And a woman was there who had been subject to bleeding for twelve years. She had suffered a great

deal under the care of many doctors and had spent all she
had, yet instead of getting better she grew worse. When she
heard about Jesus, she came up behind him in the crowd and
touched his cloak, because she thought, "If I just touch his
clothes, I will be healed." Immediately her bleeding
stopped and she felt in her body that she was freed from her
suffering. At once Jesus realized that power had gone out
from him. He turned around in the crowd and asked, "Who
touched my clothes?" "You see the people crowding against
you," his disciples answered, "and yet you can ask, 'Who
touched me?'" But Jesus kept looking around to see who had
done it. Then the woman, knowing what had happened to
her, came and fell at his feet and, trembling with fear, told
him the whole truth. He said to her, "Daughter, your faith
has healed you. Go in peace and be freed from your
suffering," *(Mark 5:24-34 NIV).*

This woman had heard of the miraculous wonders being
performed by Jesus as He went around the countryside teaching, and
healing the masses. She *believed* with such a great faith in His healing
power, she knew all she had to do was get close enough to reach out and
touch Him for her healing to occur. You might be wondering why she
didn't just cry out to Jesus and have Him come to her like everybody else
in the massive crowd. It wasn't because she was too shy, or embarrassed
about her condition to call out to Him. She had to inconspicuously get
close enough to touch Jesus because of her condition. According to
Levitical Law, she was considered unclean because of her bleeding. She
wasn't allowed to get close to any one, for any reason, or for any
purpose. She was untouchable, and anyone who came in contact with
her would also be considered unclean. She had to get close enough to
Jesus to be able to reach out to touch Him without being seen. She was
a social outcast; literally exiled from the land of the living.

The second example of someone with profound faith involved a
father whose son was in desperate need of healing. The boy was
possessed, and out of the deep love and concern for his son, the father
came to Jesus. Once again, I think the Gospel of Mark does an excellent
job of sharing this story, so I'll let you read the passage for yourself.

When they came to the other disciples, they saw a large
crowd around them and the teachers of the law arguing
with them. As soon as all the people saw Jesus, they were

overwhelmed with wonder and ran to greet him. "What are you arguing with them about?" he asked. A man in the crowd answered, "Teacher, I brought you my son, who is possessed by a spirit that has robbed him of speech. Whenever it seizes him, it throws him to the ground. He foams at the mouth, gnashes his teeth and becomes rigid. I asked your disciples to drive out the spirit, but they could not." "You unbelieving generation," Jesus replied, "how long shall I stay with you? How long shall I put up with you? Bring the boy to me." So they brought him. When the spirit saw Jesus, it immediately threw the boy into a convulsion. He fell to the ground and rolled around, foaming at the mouth. Jesus asked the boy's father, "How long has he been like this?" "From childhood," he answered. "It has often thrown him into fire or water to kill him. But if you can do anything, take pity on us and help us." "'If you can'?" said Jesus. "Everything is possible for one who believes." Immediately the boy's father exclaimed, "I do believe; help me overcome my unbelief," *(John 9:14-24 NIV)*!

I share this example in order to encourage you to come to the Lord with concerns involving someone other than yourself. Too often, we approach Jesus because we have a need, or a challenge, or an affliction that we want Him to address. This is fine, especially when we consider that the woman with the issue of blood did just that. But too often, we lose focus of those around us, along with the challenges of life that they are trying to manage. Petitioning God on the behalf of others is a true sign of both your *spiritual maturity*, as well as the love you have for others. As a follower of Jesus, you are called to pray for the needs of others, but you can't forget to also pray for their spiritual needs. One of the biggest spiritual needs that is easy to overlook is the one involving faith. You need to realize that everyone, including yourself, needs to pray for a strengthened faith. As the father who brought his son to Jesus requested, *help me overcome my unbelief.*

Faith requires action on your part. You can't wait around waiting for faith to drop into your life. It doesn't just appear through the wave of some magic wand, or by some cosmic wonder. You have to seek after it before opening your heart to receive it into your life. Faith will only develop in your heart as you seek the answers to the questions, the challenges, and the circumstance of life. Faith is defined by your personal *search for God's promise of significance*. It is only available as you reach out to Him; to cry out and allow His power of promise to transform your life, as well as the lives who you continually lift up in prayer. It is at that moment when the power of Jesus' promise for life more abundant is released!

I'd like to close with a true story of persistent prayer that resulted in the salvation of my mother's uncle. My maternal grandmother grew up in a home that whole-heartedly followed Jesus. Her parents, sisters, and a younger brother had a strong faith in Jesus Christ. Everyone, believed in God's only Son, accept her oldest brother. My grandmother and all of her sisters prayed for their oldest brother to finally accept Jesus into his life throughout their entire lives.

Now, I have to tell you that most of them lived a really, long life. My grandmother made it to 102 years old, and her sister Ella lived to be almost a century old herself. For whatever reason, that oldest brother just couldn't believe anything that was contained within the Bible. He was convinced through the spiritual hardening of his heart that Jesus was nothing more than an old-wives-tale. But that never kept Grandma or aunt Ella for praying for him every chance they could. They had faith. *They trusted the Lord.* They were going to hold Him to His Word, that prayer changes things, including the hardness of the human heart. So, they prayed for their brother, throughout their entire lives. They prayed for the best part of a century. They didn't just pray, they would try to plant a seed of salvation every now and again too when they had a chance. But it seemed the power of prayer couldn't open the heart or mind of their beloved brother. The longer it went, the harder they prayed.

Finally, at ninety-nine-years old, their big brother had a conversation with a grandson. During that little talk, the grandpa was asked if he knew where he was going to spend eternity, since they knew his time one earth was quickly drawing to an end. My great uncle replied that he had no idea where he was going. So, his grandson showed him the way to the Lord that very day. Nearly ninety-years of continuous prayer by numerous sisters, finally paid off. Their prayers brought home the mother lode of *radiant glory*. Their brother finally accepted Jesus into his heart and his destiny was sealed. One month later, he passed on to his eternal reward.

Prayer and faith are strong components with the blade of the *double-edged sword of salvation*. In fact, the two are extremely relatable to the question as to what came first, the chicken or the egg? Are you required to have faith first in order to receive access to the Lord through prayer, or do you need to pray first before you can enter into His presence by faith? Actually, I believe you can't have one without the other. The only way to enter into the presence of the Lord is by having the faith to pray. Which in turn brings everything full circle as you enter into His presence through prayer; it is by faith that you receive His blessing, assurance, and peace. *Simple faith* is all you need to pray. To pray, all you need is faith the size of a mustard seed; that is an itty-bitty, teeny-weeny bit of faith. The simplicity of faith merely requires you to *open your heart and ask Jesus to come in*. Confess with your mouth and believe in your heart that He is Lord; that's all you need for faith to come alive. Simple faith starts with the simplest prayer.

Who do you know that needs to come to faith in Jesus? Are you willing to set your faith in action through prayer? Write down their name in the space below and then put your faith in action to begin praying for Jesus to meet them, wherever they are!

_____
_____
_____
_____
_____
_____
_____
_____
_____
_____
_____
_____

Simple Faith!

She merely touched the border, of His garment hanging low,
> Yet, in that single second, the Man of Miracles seemed to know
That something strange had happened here, this very day and hour ---
> Being pushed along the crowded street, He felt the loss of power,
While walking through the city, being jostled here and there,
> With hooded shawl gathered close, to enclose Him in sweet prayer;
She only touched the tasseled hem, of this holy, woven shawl;
> A garment worn for private prayer, when to His Father He'd call.

'Tis written in the Bible: "seek privately to pray,"
> The prayer shawl was the answer on any given day.
Now, with that reaching, grasping touch; somewhat hesitant, unsure ---
> Flowed forth the healing power, of the Master -- sinless, pure.
"Who touched me," was the question Jesus asked the thronging crowd;
> His Disciples were astonished that He felt "one" touch His shroud.
They sayest then unto Him, for in awe they surely be,
> "With this multitude about you, why ask, 'Who toucheth me?'"

Jesus looked around to find her --- the one who had done this thing ---
> The woman knelt before Him. . . in great fear and trembling.
She told Him the story of her life with all honesty and truth,
> How the physicians failed to heal her since her early days of youth.
Then she'd heard of the healing powers of this Man from Galilee;
> She knew in her heart He could heal her--- set her ailing body free;
She felt the need to only touch, the clothes Christ wore that day
> To heal the bloody fountain, her ridden body did portray.

In truth, she shared her story; laid bare the depths of her soul;
> Compassion shown upon Him, He whispered, "Dear child, I know!"
"This illness suffered many long years, indeed, has taken its toll ---
> Today, go in peace My Daughter, your faith has made you whole."
This Child of God, in remarkable faith, was healed of sickness and grief;
> Greater still -- freed from sin, through her powerful, simple belief!

You, too, My Child, can do the same, reach out in faith today;
> Touch this "Man of Miracles," He is the only way.
Give Him your heart, change your life, heal your hidden soul,
> Hear Him softly whisper to you, "Your faith has made you whole!"

> Clarice D. Cook

Day 13

Who Do You Say that I Am?

Scriptural Reflection

He has saved us and called us to a holy life—not because of anything we have done but because of his own purpose and grace. This grace was given us in Christ Jesus before the beginning of time, but it has now been revealed through the appearing of our Savior, Christ Jesus, who has destroyed death and has brought life and immortality to light through the gospel. *2 Timothy 1:9-11 NIV*

When Jesus came into the region of Caesarea Philippi, He asked His disciples, saying, "Who do men say that I, the Son of Man, am?" So they said, "Some say John the Baptist, some Elijah, and others Jeremiah or one of the prophets." He said to them, "But who do you say that I am?" Simon Peter answered and said, "You are the Christ, the Son of the living God." Jesus answered and said to him, "Blessed are you, Simon Bar-Jonah, for flesh and blood has not revealed this to you, but My Father who is in heaven. *Matthew 16:13- NKJV*

Fellow Israelites, listen to this: Jesus of Nazareth was a man accredited by God to you by miracles, wonders and signs, which God did among you through him, as you yourselves know. This man was handed over to you by God's deliberate plan and foreknowledge; and you, with the help of wicked men, put him to death by nailing him to the cross. But God raised him from the dead, freeing him from the agony of death, because it was impossible for death to keep its hold on him. *Acts 2:22-24 NIV*

In man's finite wisdom we tend to try to make things conform to meet our personal needs instead of trying to see things from a spiritual perspective. This was the case nearly 2,000 years ago as Jesus walked upon the fertile soil of this earth. Within His ministry He performed miraculous wonders which displayed His *awesome power and Divine authority.* Jesus turned water into wine, healed the sick and lame, restored sight to the blind, provided hope to the hopeless, fed the multitudes, taught, and prophesied with the authority of God. He even raised the dead from the grave. Yet, the people still didn't truly believe or accept Him for His atoning purpose. They hungered for His teachings, thirsted for His blessings, and sought Him out in an effort to see what miraculous wonders He would perform next. They sought after Him to catch a glimpse to the One they dreamed would be the Deliverer of Israel. They saw Him as an earthly King, who would destroy the tyranny of Rome.

Even though Jesus performed *miraculous wonders* that could only come through the *power of God,* the majority of people never understood. They couldn't comprehend the mission and full purpose that Jesus was destined to perform. Even the twelve chosen, Christ's closest companions, could not understand what the Lord tried to share with them. Peter stood up to Jesus, rebuking the idea of Christ dying and being raised on the third day. He allowed his earthly vision to cloud the purpose of Christ's mission on earth. Jesus responded to him, *you are a stumbling block to me; you do not have in mind the things of God, but the things of men,* (Matthew 16:23).

Peter, in his limited wisdom, could not even begin to see God's all-knowing, omniscient plan. All he could see were the desires and fears of his heart as he struggled to make Jesus conform to his human understanding. How many of us maintain the *thoughts of man,* instead of seeking the *thoughts of God?* How many times have you struggled to make Christ conform to your personal views with all of your humanly limited constraints? How many times have you neatly packed Him away into a confining box that defines Him according to your personal wants and self-indulgent desires? *So often we fight to seek our own desires instead of surrendering our lives to the Lord.* Too often we strive to make Christ into something that is transformed into our own twisted purpose, trying to have it our own way in this ego-centric world! We turn Him into something that suits our own purposes! We fight for control of life's circumstances as we struggle to take away from the hands of God the very essence of our lives, of our futures, and our well-being. How many can truly say that they accept Jesus Christ for who He truly is as presented within the confines of biblical evidence? Can you?

A major stumbling block regarding Jesus' identity even within Christian circles involves his *Person within the Trinity* The *Father, Son,* and *Holy Ghost*. Since this concept is difficult for any of us to truly grasp, many people believe that each of these attributes of God are separate entities. Another challenge involves the reality that the term Trinity isn't found anywhere in the Bible, and so many people get hung up on that fact. The reality of the Triune God can only be revealed through the study of scripture in its entirety. Let's take a look at what the Apostle Paul has to say regarding the defining relationship that involves the concept of the Holy Trinity.

> For he has rescued us from the dominion of darkness and brought us into the kingdom of the Son he loves, in whom we have redemption, the forgiveness of sins. The Son is the image of the invisible God, the firstborn over all creation. For in him all things were created: things in heaven and on earth, visible and invisible, whether thrones or powers or rulers or authorities; all things have been created through him and for him. He is before all things, and in him all things hold together, *(Colossians 1:13-17 NIV).*

This scripture clearly defines the reality that Jesus is the *visible image of the invisible God.* This will be further discussed in one of the last devotions of this study. But to simply finish triangulating the third person of the Trinity, I will just briefly share this summation for your consideration. God the Father is comparable to the *invisible power source* of the Trinity, while Jesus is the *image of the invisible Father.* Within the final aspect of the Trinity, the Holy Spirit becomes the *conduit for God's power to flow.* What's important to note here is that within the consideration of the question, *who do you say that I am?* -the scriptural reality is that Jesus, God, and the Holy Spirit are one. Jesus said, as recorded in John 14: 9; *when you have seen me, you've seen the Father.* The mystery of the Trinity, along with the divine nature of Jesus, is embodied within the makeup of the Eternal God Almighty.

Getting back to the previous scripture from Colossians, we discover that God rescued us from the dominion of darkness, and brought us into the Kingdom of the Son whom He loves. It is only through the Son that we obtain redemption and the forgiveness of sin. How do you receive that? By turning your life over to Him, when you believe in Him, and ask Him into your life.

Have you totally surrendered yourself to Jesus, the Christ for the dreams, plans, and purpose for which you were created? Or are you continually striving to define your own path, only letting Him walk beside you when it's convenient? Of course, it's easy to willingly surrender when it's not too much of a distraction, or if it doesn't require too much of a commitment of energy or money. During those times, it's no problem to let Him creep into your life. As long as it doesn't really interfere, take you down a path you don't want to go, or put a crimp on the lifestyle you seek for your secular happiness and pleasure.

If Jesus Christ is truly the Master and Savior of your soul, then you have a responsibility to surrender your life into His care. This includes your finances, focus, adoration, time, relationships, and energies. No matter what definition you devise to describe Him; how much access you allow Him in your life; or even how determined you are to stay away from Him, *He is always* by your side. He will *never leave you or forsake you.* So, there is simply one question you must answer. It requires you to reconcile His Truth within your heart. *Who do you say that Jesus is?* Briefly share your thoughts below.

_____

_____

_____

_____

_____

_____

Who Do You Say I Am?

Who do you say that I am? What name's been given me?
　　I am the Christ, the Anointed One, known as The Nazarene.
I am He Who Sent Me, I Am the Great I Am.
　　I am the Savior of the World, God's Sacrificial Lamb.
I am Alpha and Omega, the Beginning, and the End.
　　I am Master, Prophet, Holy One, Jehovah, Priest, and Friend.
I came as that Babe-in-the-manger, I left my heavenly throne;
　　The Word of Life put on a robe, as Jesus I am known;
The long-awaited Messiah, The Almighty, Lord of Hosts,
　　Refiner's Fire, The Fuller's Soap, Father, Son, and Holy Ghost.

My Lineage answers questions, of who I really am:
　　I am the Son of David, and the Key of Abraham,
I am the Root of Jesse, and The Promised One, Most High,
　　The only Begotten Son of God----the Prince of Peace am I.
Governor and King of kings, Ruler over all,
　　Redeemer of the Ages, to those who heed My call;
Eternal Light, The Righteous, Guardian of your Souls,
　　The One Whom God Exalted, the Victor O'er Your Foes.
I am The Name Above All Names, I am The Cornerstone----
　　I am the Light of All the World, your sins I will atone.

I bear your grief and burdens, I'm Healer of your pain,
　　The Man of Sorrows dries your tears, He gives you life again.
Known as the Faithful Witness, I am The Truth, the Way,
　　The Bread of Life, the Living Word, Creator of the Day.
Jesus Christ, Head of the Church, Good Shepherd of the Sheep,
　　Look to Me, The Son of Man, you little lambs I'll keep.
I am the Keeper of the keys; I hold the master key;
　　Lord of lords o'er life and death, I know your destiny.
As the Lily of the Valley, and the Bright & Morning Star,
　　My name rings out as Wonderful, tis heard both near and far.
Comforter or Counselor, the Fairest of the Fair,
　　The Carpenter of Nazareth, the Rose of Sharon rare.

The Teacher with authority, True wisdom shall increase;
      The favor found by God and man will never ever cease.
I, Jesus Christ, the Son of God, Who died upon that tree,
      Was buried but arose again, to set each sinner free;
The Water of Life is flowing, 'neath that old rugged cross,
      Drink and quench your thirsty soul, shake off the evil dross;
For a Little Child shall lead you, The Day Spring of your life---
      I'll take away all your sin, and free you from all strife;
This Beloved Son of God, In Whom He is Well Pleased,
      Gave My life that all could come.... I trust you're one of these.

I am The Vine. The branches you, in faith I'll help you grow,
      Just ask, it shall be given you, because I love you so!
Indeed, My names are countless, but, regardless of what name,
      You need to know that I am He, Whoever stays the same . . .
Today, Tomorrow, and Yesterday, the Spirit of Pure Love,
      Guiding Hand, The Watchful Eye, Who leads you from above.
As Holy One of Israel, I'll be the Great Bridegroom,
      When this Lord of All the Harvest, calls His children home.
For one day soon I will return, to draw each one to Me;
      Until that day I do remain, simply Emmanuel; "God with Thee".

Clarice D. Cook

Day 14
Sermon on the Mount
Scriptural Reflection

My people, hear my teaching; listen to the words of my mouth. I will open my mouth with a parable; I will utter hidden things, things from of old—things we have heard and known, things our ancestors have told us. We will not hide them from their descendants; we will tell the next generation the praiseworthy deeds of the Lord, his power, and the wonders he has done. He decreed statutes for Jacob and established the law in Israel, which he commanded our ancestors to teach their children, so the next generation would know them, even the children yet to be born, and they in turn would tell their children. Then they would put their trust in God and would not forget his deeds but would keep his commands. They would not be like their ancestors— a stubborn and rebellious generation, whose hearts were not loyal to God, whose spirits were not faithful to him.
Psalm 78:1-8 NIV

In the beginning was the Word, and the Word was with God, and the Word was God. He was with God in the beginning. Through him all things were made; without him nothing was made that has been made. In him was life, and that life was the light of all mankind. The light shines in the darkness, and the darkness has not overcome it. The true light that gives light to everyone was coming into the world. He was in the world, and though the world was made through him, the world did not recognize him. He came to that which was his own, but his own did not receive him. Yet to all who did receive him, to those who believed in his name, he gave the right to become children of God— children born not of natural descent, nor of human decision or a husband's will, but born of God. The Word became flesh and made his dwelling among us. We have seen his glory, the glory of the one and only Son, who came from the Father, full of grace and truth. *John 1:1-5, 9-14 NIV*

There is something almost mystical, even spiritual, about taking a trek into the mountains. Perched on top of an outcropping of granite where a meadow unfolds, the view takes on a pastoral significance. Momentarily, we are allowed to partake of *God's magnificent creation*, while the wind whips our hair and softly whispers through the branches of a towering pine tree. The fragrance of pine and wildflowers permeate the air, as the eagle majestically soars high within the vast expanse of blue sky. The chipmunks frantic chatter echoing overhead softly fades into the distant woods as they playfully scamper among the branches. The strumming of the woodpecker resonates across the meadow as the morning dew glistens from the rays of the rising sun. A deer grazing at the meadow's edge lifts her head to quickly scan the field while nearby, her fawn contently slumbers within a grassy bed. Found within the limits of this natural sanctuary is a solitude, a *quiet reverence* reserved in adoration for God's creation. Nothing brings us closer to Him than time spent in solemn reflection within the midst of His unspoiled splendor.

Whenever I read the scripture regarding Jesus' Sermon on the Mount, I'm taken back to my early teenage years at a small church camp in the Rocky Mountains. The camp staff and all of the youthful campers would gather at the edge of a meadow at days end, in front of a large campfire. It was here, beneath the glory of God's heavenly expanse where we would assemble to listen to Salvation's message from one of the pastors. As my childhood pastor shared a message one evening, I could imagine Jesus standing before us, just like the time He shared that infamous, *Sermon on the Mount*. I don't remember the exact message from Pastor Bob on that particular evening. But I vividly remember how moving it was as it brought me to the realization that Jesus, the Redeemer is the Truth, the Way, and the Life for anyone who accepts Him into their life.

On that very special night, I remember surrendering myself at the foot of the cross and placing my life into the hands of Jesus. He was the One who opened the door of grace that allows access to the Father. Jesus gave His all so that anyone who believes can enter through that door. It was a night that I will never forget. That's why today's devotion is so important. It reminds me of the night Jesus found me sitting in that mountain meadow. My life was changed forever.

Can you envision Jesus standing on top of an outcropping of rock at the edge of a meadow, with the anxious multitudes gathered all around Him? People came from far and near to catch a glimpse of this Man of Miracles: To hear the words of this mighty Teacher. They came from all walks of life – those who were curious and others who were desperate. The multitude was engrossed within the desires, hopes, and dreams of a culture defined by those days from long ago: Rich and poor, Greek and Jew, free and slave, the weak and affirmed, the hopeless and lost, the religious and the spiritually blind, the destitute and the outcast. Every individual gathered at that meadow's edge, eagerly awaited the chance *to see, hear, witness, or even receive the miraculous words and wonders* of this gifted Prophet.

Take a moment to close your eyes and imagine that you are sitting in the middle of that crowd. Can you see Jesus standing there in front of you? A breeze gently whips through His hair, while He stretches forth His Hand as He begins to formulate the opening remarks of His teaching. He has a message to proclaim from God the Father; words of hope and comfort. As He glances around to engage the faces within the crowd, He remains silent, and the anticipation builds. You know that His message will deeply touch the very heart and soul of everyone that surrounds you, including yourself. *For those who take Him at His word, their lives will be forever changed.*

With the crowd pressing in around the Teacher, He lifts His eyes toward heaven. A calm covers the scene with a tense anticipation. As you look around at the crowd, you can see every man, woman, and child stretching their necks, trying to catch a glimpse of this miraculous man known as Jesus. They turn an ear toward the Prophet as they impatiently wait to hear His words. Silence engulfs the landscape as everyone is focused upon this Man from Galilee. Many of those who are anxiously waiting to hear Jesus speak, including yourself, are keenly familiar with the words of the prophets; Isaiah in particular. Many of his prophetic words have been engrained into your mind . . . *Who has believed our report? And to whom has the arm of the Lord been revealed?* (Isaiah 53:1 NKJV).

Jesus finally begins to speak. His commanding voice resonates across the meadow and down the valley, with a power that rolls like thunder. Yet, there is a softness in His voice that tenderly relays compassion and understanding. A sense of peace, filled with hope greets you as the words project from His mouth. There are those like yourself in attendance, who *hunger and a thirst* for God's message of hope, love, and forgiveness. But there are others, who are listening out of curiosity or suspicion. Those who want to use His words against Him, or to discredit who He says He is!

> But they have not all obeyed the gospel. For Isaiah says, "Lord, who has believed our report?" So then faith comes by hearing, and hearing by the word of God, *(Romans 10:16, 17 NKJV).*

Regardless of the motives of those listening, Jesus speaks with an authority never before heard. *He commands a presence* never before witnessed throughout the history of mortal man. He speaks with a conviction that resonates with passion and assurance. His words penetrate to the depth of your heart, along with all of those who have opened their minds to hear and accept His message. He speaks and it's like He's talking directly to you, not as a stranger, but as a friend. It's as if He knows you personally, along with everyone else assembled around that mountain amphitheater. It's as if He can read each and every mind; know each thought; understand each fear; realize each hope; and speak directly to every dream. You are *captivated* by His words. *Intrigued* by His wisdom. *Stirred* by His presence. *Energized* by His authority. *Touched*, like never before by a simple teaching. As He shares His last thought, you realize that you have witnessed a miraculous wonder. You heard the very *Word of God* speak directly to you. You are convinced that He truly is the long-awaited Messiah.

> And Jesus went about all Galilee, teaching in their synagogues, preaching the gospel of the kingdom, and healing all kinds of sickness and all kinds of disease among the people. Then His fame went throughout all Syria; and they brought to Him all sick people who were afflicted with various diseases and torments, and those who were demon-possessed, epileptics, and paralytics; and He healed them. Great multitudes followed Him—from Galilee, and from Decapolis, Jerusalem, Judea, and beyond the

Jordan, *(Matthew 4:23-25 NKJV).*

As we conclude today's devotion, take a moment to think back to a time in your life when you witnessed something miraculous, or you heard something that was extremely inspirational. Can you remember an event when something sent chills down your spine, or your breath was taken away by a sight, a sound, or moment; causing you to breathe in a sense of God's glory? The *heavens truly display the glory of the Lord.* But so does your life and the world all around you. His glory is obviously evident when you take the time to notice; it's right there in front of you if you choose to still you heart and mind to focus on Him. It's not enough to *simply listen* to God's word, you have to *apply it* to your life. Only then will you truly experience the splendor of His majesty and His promise of a life more abundant.

> But don't just listen to God's word. You must do what it says. Otherwise, you are only fooling yourselves. For if you listen to the word and don't obey, it is like glancing at your face in a mirror. You see yourself, walk away, and forget what you look like. But if you look carefully into the perfect law that sets you free, and if you do what it says and don't forget what you heard, then God will bless you for doing it. If you claim to be religious but don't control your tongue, you are fooling yourself, and your religion is worthless. Pure and genuine religion in the sight of God the Father means caring for orphans and widows in their distress and refusing to let the world corrupt you, *(James 1:22-27 NLT).*

Have you taken the time to hear God's voice today? What is He saying to you at this very moment? Focus on what He is telling you, or impressing on your heart right now, and then apply it to your life. Take a moment to briefly describe what He is saying in the space below.

_____

_____

_____

_____

_____

_____

_____

Sermon on the Mount

When Christ lived among men on earth, and began His ministry here,
   He went throughout all Galilee, teaching to all-both far and near.
He preached the Kingdom Gospel, And the many sick He healed;
   Those who listened and believed in Him, into eternal life were sealed.

Throughout Syria, His fame spread, as He preached and taught the word;
   There followed Him great multitudes, who before had never heard.
As he looked upon those multitudes, up onto a mount He went;
   After a time of preparing, for the Disciples He then sent.

He gazed upon His follower's, with great love that filled His heart;
   He "opened His mouth" to speak --- He knew just how to start.
He began His sermon simply, with "blessed are the poor,"
   For unto them is heaven given, they'll rejoice forever-more!

He knows of sorrows one suffers, as He referred to "those that mourn,"
   Take their burden to Jesus, grief-stricken hearts won't be so torn.
He remembered the meek, the timid, realized their fear from birth;
   For He said, "the meek are blessed, they shall inherit the earth."

Blessed are they who hunger for righteousness their hearts were stirred;
   Their hunger and thirst will be taken; filled with God's glorious word!
The merciful shall find mercy, by favor in God's marvelous grace;
   The "pure in heart" are richly blessed; they shall see Him face to face.

Children of God are peacemakers. Their love and joy may abound;
   By God's grace and forgiveness, peace in their hearts will be found.
Believers in Christ will find favor in the eyes of God, they'll be blessed;
   Stand firm when men shall revile you, fail not this redeeming test;

For Christian, you'll meet persecution, by men who'll mock your ways;
   Beloved, rejoice and be happy; Your reward? Infinite, heavenly days!
When Jesus had ended His message, the people were quite amazed;
   He taught with authority, and not as the scribes of those days.

When He finished and came down the mount, crowds followed Him yet;
   Dear One, the way is still open, if you only believe and accept.
You, too, can follow this Savior, as the multitudes did long ago;
   Just put yourself in His keeping; the way of salvation you'll know!

Clarice D. Cook

Day 15
Miracle of Faith
Scriptural Reflection

For you are all sons of God through faith in Christ Jesus. For as many of you as were baptized into Christ have put on Christ. There is neither Jew nor Greek, there is neither slave nor free, there is neither male nor female; for you are all one in Christ Jesus. And if you are Christ's, then you are Abraham's seed, and heirs according to the promise.
Galatians 3:26-29 NIV

"Most assuredly, I say to you, he who hears My word and believes in Him who sent Me has everlasting life, and shall not come into judgment, but has passed from death into life. Most assuredly, I say to you, the hour is coming, and now is, when the dead will hear the voice of the Son of God; and those who hear will live. For as the Father has life in Himself, so He has granted the Son to have life in Himself, and has given Him authority to execute judgment also, because He is the Son of Man. Do not marvel at this; for the hour is coming in which all who are in the graves will hear His voice and come forth—those who have done good, to the resurrection of life, and those who have done evil, to the resurrection of condemnation.
John 5: 24-29 NIV

For as many as are led by the Spirit of God, these are sons of God. For you did not receive the spirit of bondage again to fear, but you received the Spirit of adoption by whom we cry out, "Abba, Father." The Spirit Himself bears witness with our spirit that we are children of God, and if children, then heirs—heirs of God and joint heirs with Christ, if indeed we suffer with Him, that we may also be glorified together. *Romans 8: 14-17 NIV*

Then, behold, the veil of the temple was torn in two from top to bottom; and the earth quaked, and the rocks were split, and the graves were opened; and many bodies of the saints who had fallen asleep were raised; and coming out of the graves after His resurrection, they went into the holy city and appeared to many. So when the centurion and those with him, who were guarding Jesus, saw the earthquake and the things that had happened, they feared greatly, saying, "Truly this was the Son of God!" *Matthew 27: 51-54 NKJV*

When you take the time to consider the *intricacies of the human body*, you will quickly realize that you are truly a miraculous being. Think about the vast number of differing cells that make up the multitude of biological systems in your body. Your body is comprised of nearly a dozen distinct systems that are necessary for you to stay alive. A few examples of these involve a nervous system, a skeletal system, a digestive system, a respiratory system, a muscular system, a cardiovascular system, and a reproductive system. Each of these systems are made up of various organs, cells, and tissue for a uniquely designed and specific purpose. Individually, they would never support life. But collectively, they work in harmonic unison to allow you to breathe, live, move, think, and prosper. *Truly, the human body is a miraculous wonder.* The genius behind our design is beyond human comprehension. The complexity of the human design is a miracle, and most of us never fully appreciate the true wonder of life.

The same can be said about the miraculous wonder of faith. There is an unrecognized appreciation involving the human ability to develop the promise of faith. In the New Testament book of Romans, we are told, *So then faith comes by hearing, and hearing by the word of God,* (Romans 10:17 NKJV). The Bible in simple terms is a book of faith. Within God's Word are a multitude of promises, prophecies, historical records, and even poetry; requiring you to actively listen. All of which point to, while defining the purpose and the story of Jesus. Integral to instilling into the human heart a sense of faith, is the process of sharing *truth*. Truth builds trust - it shapes relationship. Truth is essential for faith. It determines life and instills a deep sense of security. Through the process of building trust, the manifestation of faith compels us to celebrate. Coming back full-circle, the Bible is filled with many holy celebrations. There were seven feasts commemorated throughout the Jewish calendar and all of them were commanded by God! He called them to celebration!

The Jewish Feast of Passover, has added significance for celebrating. This is the time when Jews observe the remembrance of the angel of death visiting the land of Egypt during the time of Moses. This angel passed over any house that had lamb's blood brushed onto its doorposts, otherwise, the first born of every family died. This caused

Pharaoh to finally let the Israelites leave Egypt to start their journey to the Promised Land. Approximately 1,600 years later, during this same week, *Jesus made his triumphal entry into Jerusalem.* It was there that Jesus enjoyed the Passover meal He had longed to share with His twelve Disciples.

It was during this Passover week that Jesus was betrayed, crucified, and buried, becoming the Sacrificial Lamb for the sins of the world. He rose from the grave on the third day conquering sin and death while providing salvation for anyone who believes in Him. Talk about an *amazing climax to the century's old celebration!* The ultimate fulfillment for a week of jubilation. This is the greatest reason the world has cause to rejoice, as you take time time to reflect on; salvation, forgiveness, and the redemption of your soul!

When you realize, Jesus forever changed the dynamic of the Passover Feast you begin to understand the significance, the grace, the mercy, and the unconditional love of God the Father! Talk about a miracle of faith! Jesus declared. **I have come that they may have life, and that they may have it more abundantly,** *(John 10:10b NKJV).*

During Jesus' three-year ministry, He shared many parables about celebration: **The** *Prodigal Son*, The *Lost Sheep*, **The** *Lost Coin* and The *Wedding Feast* are all great examples. Even within His many miracles there is a profound element of "commemoration." In the *story of Lazarus*, do you think that there was a bit of an unbridled revelry involved, after Jesus raised His dear friend out of the grasp of his earthly death? Even though Lazarus was a bit smelly after being dead for four days, do you think they just went back to the humdrum of daily life without taking time to praise and worship Jesus through unrivaled revelry? I think not. This was a celebration to end all celebrations. Within my personal pondering, my first thought is that Lazarus was assigned a downwind end of the banquet table because of the noxious stink that accompanied him from the grave. But actually, it's probably more likely that the miracle of being raised from the dead by Jesus, provided such an extensive healing that even the smell of death was completely, washed cleaned from his body! Regardless, it was the miracle of faith that moved Jesus to raise Lazarus from the dead.

Now faith is confidence in what we hope for and assurance

about what we do not see. This is what the ancients were commended for. By faith we understand that the universe was formed at God's command, so that what is seen was not made out of what was visible. ⁶And without faith it is impossible to please God, because anyone who comes to him must believe that he exists and that he rewards those who earnestly seek him, *(Hebrews 11:1-3, 6 NIV)*.

Where did Jesus perform His first miracle recorded in the Gospels? At the *wedding in Cana!* They had celebrated with so much exuberance that they were running out of wine. So, Jesus' mother mentioned to Him that the wine was all consumed and that the hosts would face complete, social humiliation if something wasn't done about the supply shortage. How did Jesus respond? He turned water into wine so that the celebration would continue! As Mark Lowry, the famous Christian singer and comedian has been credited with saying: *Jesus turned the water into wine just to keep the party going!* As Christians, we have more to celebrate than anyone else in this world and God loves a righteous celebration! Jesus proved that very point as He performed His first recorded miracle at the wedding in Cana. Again, through the miracle of faith, Jesus was moved to respond.

However, the greatest miracle of faith that is provided through a relationship with Jesus is forgiveness. *Do you know what you're saying when you refuse to forgive?* You're saying *Jesus' death on the cross wasn't enough for the offenses incurred against you.* Think about that for a minute. In fact, if there is somebody that you haven't forgiven, spend the remainder of the day thinking about that one! *Unforgiveness* isn't a *miracle of faith;* it's an *abomination to faith.*

> For if you forgive other people when they sin against you, your heavenly Father will also forgive you. But if you do not forgive others their sins, your Father will not forgive your sins, *(Matthew 6:14-15 NIV)*.

The *miracle of faith* in Jesus Christ allows you to live, not with reckless abandon or with hopeless resolve, but rather with the *assurance, hope,* and *promise* of salvation that comes when you enter into relationship with Him! You have a new future because of God's grace and mercy. When you ask Jesus into your life, your *eternal destiny* is set and your *earthly identity is defined.* The true miracle of faith is founded on the very foundation of God's promise in Jesus Christ!

> For the Lord himself will descend from heaven with a cry of command, with the voice of an archangel, and with the sound of the trumpet of God. And the dead in Christ will rise first. Then we who are alive, who are left, will be caught up together with them in the clouds to meet the Lord in the air, and so we will always be with the Lord. Therefore encourage one another with these words, *(I Thessalonians 4:16-18 ESV).*

Today is the time to revel in the mercy and grace that is provided through God's miracle of faith! It is time to celebrate your faith in Him. Are you ready for your personal *season of singing* to begin. Even within the challenges of life in this world, when you take a moment to consider the benefits of salvation that comes through Jesus, the Son; you have a lot to celebrate! I personally believe that each of us have a unique melody that radiates within our hearts. This is what some people refer to as your *soul song.* Maybe you've never paid much attention to it, or maybe you know exactly what I'm talking about. *Take a moment to listen to the melody that sings out in your heart.* Make note of it, and reflect upon it often.

> I am a Rose of Sharon, a Lily of the Valleys. The voice of my beloved! Behold, he comes, leaping over the mountains, bounding over the hills. My beloved speaks and says to me; "Arise, my love, my beautiful one, and come away, for behold, the winter is past; the rain is over and gone. The flowers appear on the earth, the time of singing has come, and the voice of the turtledove is heard in our land," *(Song of Solomon 2:1, 8, 10-12 ESV).*

Who do you need to forgive in order for your heart song to return? Maybe it's yourself or maybe you need to seek forgiveness from someone else. Write those names below. Let your season of singing begin.

_____

_____

_____

_____

_____

The Season for Singing

The Son of God arrived of flesh, in a stable strewn with hay!
>The Savior of the world was born, on that very special day;
"Glory to God in the highest," sang the angels in one voice;
>"Peace on earth, goodwill to men" let the hearts of all rejoice!

Promise of the Ages, as God's prophets did proclaim,
>The Redeemer born to free us, from a life of sinful shame!
Now arise and sing His praises, the winter's gone and past,
>The storm's no longer raging, the Son shines bright at last!

New life blossoms in His splendor, through soulful melodies,
>Refresh your hearts, verse by verse as a mild, summer breeze.
A season filled with singing, revives the broken heart,
>Melodies of atoning love – God's grace to now impart.

Arise and sing His praises, for the winter now is done,
>As you grasp the hand of Jesus – the only begotten Son!
Arise and sing His praises, for a new life now begun,
>Lift your voice toward heaven, to praise the Newborn Son!

Will you sing about God's glory? Will you sing about His Love?
>Will you sing about His coming, as a gentle turtledove?
As you celebrate redemption, may your heart be filled with praise;
>As your soul is filled with Promise, from the Ancient of Days!

May you sing throughout each season, may you sing without refrain,
>And lift your voice toward heaven, to praise His Holy Name!

Lanny K. Cook

Day 16
Jesus ~ Lord, and Master
Scriptural Reflection

See the sovereign Lord comes with power, and His arm rules for Him. See, His reward is with Him, and His recompense accompanies Him. He tends the flock like a Shepherd; He gathers the lambs in His arms and carries them close to His heart; He gently leads those that have young. Who has measured the waters in the hollow of His hand, or with the breadth of His hand marked all the heavens? Who has held the dust of the earth in a basket, or weighed the mountains on the scales and the hills in a balance? *Isaiah 40:10-12 NIV*

Do not store up for yourselves treasures on earth, where moths and vermin destroy, and where thieves break in and steal. But store up for yourselves treasures in heaven, where moths and vermin do not destroy, and where thieves do not break in and steal. For where your treasure is, there your heart will be also. The eye is the lamp of the body. If your eyes are healthy, your whole body will be full of light. But if your eyes are unhealthy, your whole body will be full of darkness. If then the light within you is darkness, how great is that darkness! No one can serve two masters. Either you will hate the one and love the other, or you will be devoted to the one and despise the other. You cannot serve both God and money. Therefore, I tell you, do not worry about your life, what you will eat or drink; or about your body, what you will wear. Is not life more than food, and the body more than clothes? Look at the birds of the air; they do not sow or reap or store away in barns, and yet your heavenly Father feeds them. Are you not much more valuable than they? Can any one of you by worrying add a single hour to your life? And why do you worry about clothes? See how the flowers of the field grow. They do not labor or spin. Yet I tell you that not even Solomon in all his splendor was dressed like one of these. If that is how God clothes the grass of the field, which is here today and tomorrow is thrown into the fire, will he not much more clothe you—you of little faith? So do not worry, saying, 'What shall we eat?' or 'What shall we drink?' or 'What shall we wear?' For the pagans run after all these things, and your heavenly Father knows that you need them. But seek first his kingdom and his righteousness, and all these things will be given to you as well. Therefore, do not worry about tomorrow, for tomorrow will worry about itself. Each day has enough trouble of its own. *Matthew 6:19-34 NIV*

There have been multitudes of people throughout the ages who desired to follow Jesus in order to experience a personal relationship with Him. Yet, many of them could not give up their *worldly treasures, pleasures*, and *desires* in order to enjoy *a daily walk with the Master.* Deep within their hearts they longed to find communion, while enjoying a deep fellowship with this Man of Miracles. But for some, secular reason, their priorities got in their way. They just couldn't make the decision to place Jesus ahead of their earthly desires. Selfish-pursuits are a distraction that are difficult to overcome to make Him *Master* of your life. Too often it becomes more important to clutch onto possessions, status, or ambitions of worldly idolatry. Hands become too full of *secular pursuits* to reach out and take the hand of Jesus. Such individuals are too dependent to place control of their lives into Jesus' care and follow after Him in order to seek His direction and guidance! Ultimately, these people are too *self-reliant* to let go of personal agendas; to accept the abundant blessings Christ offers to those who commit their trust, lives, and cares into His hands!

How often in today's world, do you find yourself pursuing the worldly desires of your heart, instead of seeking a lasting relationship with the *Lord* of lords and *King* of kings? It seems that the greater the material possession that you secure, the greater your desire to obtain more! You become obsessed with *gaining status, honor*, and *wealth* from within the *personal identity you seek to define.* Often, the greater the blessings from God, the greater you neglect being a *good steward.* It's easy to take His blessings for granted; forgetting the simple principle that all things come from the Father above. This leads to worrying and stressing about what you have; what you need, how you will pay for the collection of self-indulgence, as well as the great concern as to what you'll have to do to not lose your bountiful assets.

At one time or another, we have all been guilty of *neglecting* our health, family, and friends; as we pursue the acquisition of personal prosperity, as well as notable mention on the billboard of social status in this worlds' theatrical platform. Besides the *neglect* that is so often associated with great bounty in this life, humility often is a casualty of the war of Lordship, as you nearly break an arm, patting yourself on the back for *independently* securing profound success. In your ego-centric mind, you become the *lord and master* of your self-defined little universe. Sounds familiar to the ancient Pharaohs of Egypt and Cesars of Rome who defined themselves as gods through their own declaration.

As I share all of this, I'm including myself in every one of the scenarios mentioned. Whenever I take the time to consider the cost of following Jesus, I'm reminded of the story of the rich young ruler, out of Matthew's Gospel. Take a moment to carefully consider the details of this sad story.

> Now behold, one came and said to Him, "Good Teacher, what good thing shall I do that I may have eternal life?" So He said to him, "Why do you call Me good? No one is good but One, that is, God. But if you want to enter into life, keep the commandments." He said to Him, "Which ones?" Jesus said, "'You shall not murder,' 'You shall not commit adultery,' 'You shall not steal,' 'You shall not bear false witness,' 'Honor your father and your mother,' and, 'You shall love your neighbor as yourself.'" The young man said to Him, "All these things I have kept from my youth. What do I still lack?" Jesus said to him, "If you want to be perfect, go, sell what you have and give to the poor, and you will have treasure in heaven; and come, follow Me." But when the young man heard that saying, he went away sorrowful, for he had great possessions. Then Jesus said to His disciples, "Assuredly, I say to you that it is hard for a rich man to enter the kingdom of heaven. And again I say to you, it is easier for a camel to go through the eye of a needle than for a rich man to enter the kingdom of God." When His disciples heard it, they were greatly astonished, saying, "Who then can be saved?" But Jesus looked at them and said to them, "With men this is impossible, but with God all things are possible," *(Matthew 19:16-26 NKJV)*

The first assumption many people make about this exchange between Jesus and the rich young ruler is that you can't be wealthy or prosperous and still follow Jesus. That's not what He is saying here at all. What Jesus is telling you is that the things of this world can't mean more to you than a *relationship* with Him. Riches, fame, and prosperity can all be good things, but not when they become your *focus*. They can't *become your god!* Throughout this worldly journey, the *road to salvation* is paved with a *dependence* on Him. If you are overtly independent in your heart and mind, you'll never discover the *Truth* or the *Way* that leads to Life. That is the lesson of the rich young ruler's encounter with Jesus.

How many of us refer to Jesus as *Lord* and *Master*, yet we relegate Him to the confines of a church on a Sunday morning or a simple prayer before a meal or bedtime? If He is the *Master* of your life, then you need to place Him at the *very center of your existence*. He has to be the focus of your thoughts, the passion of your life, and the desire of your heart. You need to be thankful for all He has given you. In return, you need to give him your very best. Give Him your all! For all that you have is through His goodness! In actuality, all that you possess really belongs to Him. You need to be a *faithful steward* of His bountiful grace and mercies. Your finances, children, spouse, family, and friends are all gifts from the *Master*. He has given you *stewardship* over all these blessings. He has entrusted you with their care, in order that you might prove to be a good steward of His graciousness. So, strive to give the first fruits of your labors back to Him, to give your time, talent, and energy to the One you call Master! That's what the Lord proclaimed when He said, **choose you this day whom you will serve, as for me and my house, we will serve the Lord,** *(Joshua 24:15).*

Do you give your best to the Master, or do you keep the best for yourself and give Him the *remnants* from your *earthly gluttony*? Is He the honored guest at your table of life, or do you merely offer Him the leftovers from your elaborate celebrations? As you reflect on this thought, can you honestly say that you offer your best to Him? Have you *fully surrendered* your heart, soul, and mind into His care? If Jesus is to be the *Master* of your life, then you must choose to give complete and total control of all that is yours, *to Him*. You must entrust in His loving care, the most precious possessions of your life, including yourself. You must choose to allow Him the authority to tend to your deepest needs and cares. *Trust* Him to provide, to guide, and to direct your steps as you pursue any hopes, dreams, or prayers!

But the question that obviously is milling around in your mind at this point of the devotion, involves the *how of this process*. The Apostle Paul shared profound insight into the *how to* of surrendering your life to the Master. It's actually quite simple in concept, but much more difficult in the actual application, within your everyday life. Again, I don't want to paraphrase Paul's profound insight, so I will simply share it straight from the Bible.

> Rejoice in the Lord always. I will say it again: Rejoice! Let your gentleness be evident to all. The Lord is near. Do not be anxious about anything, but in every situation, by prayer and petition, with thanksgiving, present your requests to God. And the peace of God, which transcends all understanding, will guard your hearts and your minds in Christ Jesus. Finally, brothers and sisters, whatever is true, whatever is noble, whatever is right, whatever is pure, whatever is lovely, whatever is admirable—if anything is excellent or praiseworthy—think about such things. Whatever you have learned or received or heard from me, or seen in me—put it into practice. And the God of peace will be with you. I rejoiced greatly in the Lord that at last you renewed your concern for me. Indeed, you were concerned, but you had no opportunity to show it. I am not saying this because I am in need, for I have learned to be content whatever the circumstances. I know what it is to be in need, and I know what it is to have plenty. I have learned the secret of being content in any and every situation, whether well fed or hungry, whether living in plenty or in want. I can do all this through him who gives me strength, (Philippians 4:4-13 NIV).

A simple question to ask yourself regarding the truth to whether Jesus is the *Lord* and *Master* of your life involves the concept of *contentment*. I understand how difficult that is to secure. But, have you learned to be content in whatever circumstance life throws your way? Like Paul, I'm sure you fully understand what it's like to be well fed or hungry; to be in need, wanting more, or to enjoy the pleasure of basking in plenty. But have you been able to find contentment in your situation? Of course, contentment as defined by Paul in this specific passage, *only* arrives through the *Peace of God*. Which *only* comes through the *Prince of Peace*, otherwise referred to as Jesus. So, the process of finding contentment comes when you realize the need to totally surrender to Him. That's when you will finally rest in the assurance of His grace as the Lord is simply a prayer away. When you turn to Him, you will discover the peace of contentment that transcends all understanding. It will protect your heart and mind in the *power of Jesus' Name.*

As you implement this practice into your daily walk, your contentment will continue to grow like a mustard seed. As you meditate on those things that are *true, pure,* and *noble,* God's *peace* will settle your spirit. But you can't stop there. You need to come to the point where your identity, as to who you are; is totally defined by Jesus. That comes when you take your faith to the next level, by *actively, consistently surrendering* your life to His Lordship. Then, He will truly be the Master of your life. That is how you will discover contentment in its purest form. Remember it comes through Jesus Christ. Only in Him will you find the strength to do all things. To discover true contentment, you must define *Jesus,* as the *Lord* and *Master* of your life. Are you up for that challenge?

In the space below, list the areas of your life where you *acknowledge Jesus as Lord and Master.* Next, list the things that you *need to surrender into His care.* But don't stop there, take a moment to prayerfully consider what you need to do next in *order to completely define or align your identity in Christ.*

_____

_____

_____

_____

_____

_____

_____

_____

_____

_____

_____

Jesus ~ Lord, and Master

Jesus - Lord, and *Master,* in His loving way,
      Gives us light and mercy; watches o'er us day by day.
Be not anxious for the things of life, what ye shall drink or eat,
      For your Father up in heaven, will provide your daily meat.

Behold the birds so beautiful, they neither sow nor reap,
      They gather not, nor store away; yet them the Lord does keep.
If the *Father* keeps and feeds the birds, whose songs fill the air,
      Dear one, think, of all the love He gives to all within His care!

Why take ye thought of raiment, the things that you should wear;
      Behold the lilies of the field, in all their beauty fair,
With all their stately splendor, they neither spin nor toil,
      Still a king in all his glory, has yet to be so royal.

If *God* so clothes the fields of grass, so green and lush today,
      To be cast into the ovens, just to wither and burn away;
Won't He then clothe His children, those ones He holds so dear;
      Oh, child of faith, so finite, through God you have no fear!

Seek first the *Lord as Master,* give Him your heart and soul;
      Once you've found His righteousness, blessings then will roll,
Take no thought about tomorrow, God will see you through;
      The morrow shall take care of self, while God takes care of you.

Clarice D. Cook

124

Day 17
The Bread of Life
Scriptural Reflection

To everything there is a season, A time for every purpose under heaven: A time to be born, And a time to die; A time to plant, And a time to pluck what is planted; A time to kill, And a time to heal; A time to break down, And a time to build up; A time to weep, And a time to laugh; A time to mourn, And a time to dance; A time to cast away stones, And a time to gather stones; A time to embrace, And a time to refrain from embracing; A time to gain, And a time to lose; A time to keep, And a time to throw away; A time to tear, And a time to sew; A time to keep silence, And a time to speak; A time to love, And a time to hate; A time of war, And a time of peace. What profit has the worker from that in which he labors? I have seen the God-given task with which the sons of men are to be occupied. He has made everything beautiful in its time. Also He has put eternity in their hearts, except that no one can find out the work that God does from beginning to end.
Ecclesiastes 3: 1- 11 NKJV

He was despised and rejected by mankind, a man of suffering, and familiar with pain. Like one from whom people hide their faces he was despised, and we held him in low esteem. Surely he took up our pain and bore our suffering, yet we considered him punished by God, stricken by him, and afflicted. But he was pierced for our transgressions, he was crushed for our iniquities; the punishment that brought us peace was on him, and by his wounds we are healed. We all, like sheep, have gone astray, each of us has turned to our own way; and the Lord has laid on him the iniquity of us all. He was oppressed and afflicted, yet he did not open his mouth; he was led like a lamb to the slaughter, and as a sheep before its shearers is silent, so he did not open his mouth. *Isaiah 53: 3-7 NIV*

Jesus said to them, "Very truly I tell you, it is not Moses who has given you the bread from heaven, but it is my Father who gives you the true bread from heaven. For the bread of God is the bread that comes down from heaven and gives life to the world." [35] Then Jesus declared, "I am the bread of life. Whoever comes to me will never go hungry, and whoever believes in me will never be thirsty.
John 6:32, 33, 35 NIV

Have you ever endured any form of *extreme pain*? Either *emotionally, physically*, or even *spiritually*? I think it's safe to say that everyone, at least during some time in their life, will experience some form of nearly unbearable brokenness or trauma. Such pain comes in all sorts of ways. Maybe it was through relational loss like a divorce or separation; it could be that you or a loved one have endured a serious illness, or even suffered through a tragic accident. Maybe you have experienced extreme grief over the death of a loved one, or even the loss of a cherished, family pet. Maybe you had to deal with some great financial loss, or even the reality of getting fired from a job or demoted from a favored position.

It's pretty rare for someone to not have a falling out with a friend, coworker, or even a church body that causes such a riff that you have to completely part ways. Within the sad reality of this modern culture, there is a common tendency to be *offended, judge others*, and even make *false accusations,* making it impossible to continue with a relationship. The art of reconciliation is most often a lost art in this current society. Choosing to forgive someone for either their perceived or actual offenses has become a sign of weakness. The reality of life in the 21st century is that all of us have endured seasons of brokenness, loss, desperation, offense, and hopelessness at some point in time. Those situations are extremely hard to deal with, and it's even harder to let them go, choosing to move forward with life in a positive way. If you haven't gone through any such traumatizing event, you need to count your blessings and thank the Lord above for His gracious protection.

Most of us can muddle our way through an occasional event that is nearly unbearable. Given time, we can usually get back to an even keel and the waves of life are no longer threatening to swamp our lifeboat. But when the *perfect storm* hits, it's a totally different story. During the times of continuous, overwhelming squalls, the best that any of us can do is lash ourselves to the mast and pray that our lifeboat doesn't sink to the bottom of a watery grave.

A few years back, I found myself at the very center of an intense, personal storm. I wasn't sure I'd ever be able to navigate out of the ferocity of this tumultuous squall. Its hurricane force winds, the torrential rain, and its nerve-shattering lightning strikes crashing all around, were nearly overwhelming. Truly, it was the most challenging few years of my entire life. In a matter of a short span, our family experienced the unexpected loss of one of my closest cousins, who died within a week of being diagnosed with lung cancer. Two of my favorite uncles passed away, along with two of the aunts that I had spent a lot of time with throughout my entire life. I experienced the loss of my father after a long battle with respiratory disease. I went through a devastating divorce, immediately following Dad's death. The divorce resulted in the loss of several of my in-laws with whom I had become extremely fond and cared for deeply. I also endured the betrayal of extremely close, long-time friends during the darkness of these days.

Ultimately, I lost my position as an associate pastor, and nearly all of the friendships developed within a decade of full-time ministry. To top it off, my little pooch in his advanced years had to be put down. Literally, I felt like I had been exiled into the very pit of hell's desert. Many of the most important things in life had been taken away in a flash and I was helpless to do anything about it. Fortunately, I still had strong support from my immediate family, and most important, I still had my *faith in Jesus Christ*. In fact, through the desperation associated with my brokenness, it was my faith in Him that carried me out of that desert, and through it all, my dependence on Him became even stronger.

As I reflect on the nearly overwhelming loss experienced throughout those agonizing events, I realize this was a *season of sifting*. It was as if I had been whipped to pieces on the *thrashing floor of life*, then tossed in the air, allowing the wind to separate the chaff from the valuable grain. It is the grain that provides nourishment and new life, while the chaff is nothing more than a casing to be tossed out. The chaff included many of the things in this world I held close to my heart. It needed to be stripped away; cast off before life could *blossom and flourish in abundance*. I've considered whether my personal chaff was a distraction of some sorts; causing me to lose focus of the truth as to what is really important. Maybe a few of those distractions had become a form of an idol, causing me to turn my eyes and attention away from the *One that offers abundant life*.

With my world turned completely upside down, as Christmas approached that year, I realized something - "the *One* I chose to follow decades earlier; He is the only One who understood exactly what I had endured and the excruciating pain I had suffered." In fact, He too had been beaten and broken on the *world's thrashing floor*. But he had endured great affliction willingly. He *chose to suffer and die* for the forgiveness of my sin – for the redemption of all who would believe on Him. For me, I would have done nearly anything to avoid the pain and anguish that I had endured during the darkest times of my life.

Throughout those days and in the days that followed, I took great comfort in the reality that Jesus is the *Bread of Life*. He was born in a small town called Bethlehem. In ancient Hebrew the literal meaning of Bethlehem is *house of bread*. Jesus, as the *Bread of Life,* on the first day of *Unleavened Bread* was the *Passover Lamb*, Who was *sacrificed* over 2,000 years ago. On the *thrashing floor* of this earth, Jesus was prepared for a higher purpose, a divine calling. The punishment that brought *peace to earth* was placed upon Him as spoken about in Isaiah's 53rd chapter.

During the darkest days of my life, I realized the significance of Jesus being known as the *Bread of Life.* I finally got a lucid perspective into the reality of what He suffered for the peace of humanity. Truly His willing sacrifice is analogous to the process of wheat being prepared to serve the masses of hungry, thirsting, broken sinners – people, just like me and you. As grain being *pulverized by a millstone*, He was crushed for our iniquity. By the egregious wounds of His suffering and by the shedding of His blood, healing comes to the brokenhearted. Literally, *Jesus, the Christ*, was pierced for our transgressions and as the *Manna from God* that came down out of heaven, He offers *Life* to the world! The *Bread of Life* spoke to me personally throughout those dark, tumultuous storms. He reminded me that I could not live by bread alone, but by every *Word* that proceeds forth from His mouth.

After pondering these things in my heart for quite some time, I finally sat down at the computer in an effort to put into words the epiphany that had been afforded me through those nearly overwhelming storms of life. In a very short time, this poem flowed out of my heart and onto the keyboard. So, as you reflect on this piece, I pray you realize the great price that was required for Jesus to fulfill His calling as the *Bread of Life!*

So they asked him, "What sign then will you give that we may see it and believe you? What will you do? Our ancestors ate the manna in the wilderness; as it is written: 'He gave them bread from heaven to eat.'" Jesus said to them, "Very truly I tell you, it is not Moses who has given you the bread from heaven, but it is my Father who gives you the true bread from heaven. For the bread of God is the bread that comes down from heaven and gives life to the world." "Sir," they said, "always give us this bread." Then Jesus declared, "I am the bread of life. Whoever comes to me will never go hungry, and whoever believes in me will never be thirsty, *(John 6:30-35 NIV)*.

As you look back, considering the experiences where the chaff may have been removed on the thrashing floor of circumstance; can you see how you were distracted by things of this world? Can you see God's faithful hand carrying you through those terrible moments? *How did those difficult times impact you for the better?* In the space below, formalize your thoughts regarding today's topic. When you're finished, open up your heart in prayer. Seek the Spirit's insight as to how those wilderness experiences prepared you for God's greater purpose. *Can you see how He turned all things into good for His big-picture plan for your life?* Describe that time below.

_____

_____

_____

_____

_____

_____

_____

_____

_____

_____

_____

Bread of Life

But as for you, Bethlehem Ephrathah, too little to be among the clans of Judah, from you One will go forth for Me to be ruler in Israel. His goings forth are from long ago, from the days of eternity. Micah 5:2

Bethlehem the House of Bread, the least of any clan,
Brought forth the One to save the souls of sinful, fallen man.
Living Bread provides the Way foretold from long ago,
Redemption born in a tiny crèche because God loves you so.

Man shall not live by bread alone; but by every Word that proceeds from the mouth of the LORD. Deuteronomy 8:3

Manna sent in the wilderness, to feed their emptiness,
Unleavened Bread- God's love and truth, cloaked in holiness,
You cannot live on bread alone - You need God's holy Word,
Jesus is the Bread of Life, the Living, Righteous Lord.

The Bread of God is that which comes down out of heaven, and gives Life to the world." John 6:33

He feeds the hungry masses, He heals the sick and lame,
He bears our hurts and sorrows; He takes away the pain.
Bread of life, the Prince of Peace, He is the Truth - the Way,
The Door that leads to heaven, and the never-ending day!

Then came the first day of Unleavened Bread on which the Passover Lamb had to be sacrificed. Luke 22:7

"Do this in remembrance of me," were the words He shared with them,
A thankful prayer, in the brokenness, for what awaited Him!
As wheat beyond the harvest, He knew what lay in store-
Bruised & beaten - crucified - upon the thrashing floor.

Jesus said, "I am the Bread of Life; he who comes to Me will not hunger..." John 6:35

The Bread of Life from long ago - offers you a choice;
Accept His gift of grace and love, then heed your Savior's voice.
He offers true forgiveness, if you turn from sinful ways;
Embrace His gift of saving grace; find Hope for all your days!

Lanny K. Cook

He was pierced for our transgressions, He was crushed for our iniquities; the punishment that brought us peace was on Him, and by His wounds we are healed. Isaiah 53:5

Day 18

In Remembrance of Me . . .

Scriptural Reflection

Then Melchizedek, king of Salem, brought out bread and wine. He was priest of God most high, and He blessed Abram, saying 'Blessed be Abram by God Most High, Creator of heaven and earth. And blessed be God Most High, who delivered your enemies into your hand.'
Genesis 14:18-20 NIV

On that same night I will pass through Egypt and strike down every firstborn of both people and animals, and I will bring judgment on all the gods of Egypt. I am the Lord. The blood will be a sign for you on the houses where you are, and when I see the blood, I will pass over you. No destructive plague will touch you when I strike Egypt. This is a day you are to commemorate; for the generations to come you shall celebrate it as a festival to the Lord—a lasting ordinance.
Exodus 12:12-14 NIV

So anyone who eats this bread or drinks this cup of the Lord unworthily is guilty of sinning against the body and blood of the Lord. That is why you should examine yourself before eating the bread and drinking the cup. For if you eat the bread or drink the cup without honoring the body of Christ, you are eating and drinking God's judgment upon yourself. *I Corinthians 11: 27-29 NLT*

I speak to sensible people; judge for yourselves what I say. Is not the cup of thanksgiving for which we give thanks a participation in the blood of Christ? And is not the bread that we break a participation in the body of Christ? Because there is one loaf, we, who are many, are one body, for we all share the one loaf. *I Corinthians 10: 15-17 NIV*

For Jesus and His Disciples, it was time to celebrate Pesach, the *Feast of the Passover*, also known as the Feast of Unleavened Bread. This was a day of great celebration for the Jewish nation. A remembrance of their deliverance from slavery out of Egypt. It was a celebration of life. A time to remember how the Angel of Death had *passed over* the Jewish households in Egypt. The Israelites were commanded by God to cover the door post of their dwellings with the *blood of a lamb*. This would protect them from the plague of death, which instead, engulfed the nation of Egypt, temporarily bringing the mighty Pharaoh to his knees. It was then that he released the slaves of Israel to leave their chains of bondage and to seek out their promised land.

Ah, Passover --- truly, it was an extravagant *week of remembrance*. There was an overabundance of food, fellowship, laughter, singing, and praise for the blessings God had bestowed on His chosen people. It was a time devoted to family and friends. One can only imagine that the room prepared for Jesus and His chosen twelve was provided from a devoted friend. Possibly, it was a follower of Jesus, or maybe even someone who had received a life changing miracle from the Lord. There are those who speculate that it was the home of young Mark and his mother who provided the *upper room*. Regardless, the room was furnished and the feast prepared as Jesus and His Disciples ascended into that dimly lit upper room.

> When the hour came, Jesus and His disciples reclined at the table. And He said to them, 'I have eagerly desired to eat this Passover with you before I suffer. For I tell you, that I will not eat it again until it finds fulfillment in the kingdom of God'. . . And He took bread, gave thanks and broke it, and gave it to them, saying, 'This is my body given for you; do this in remembrance of Me.' In the same way, after the supper, He took the cup saying, 'This cup is the new covenant in My blood, which is poured out for you. But the hand of him who is going to betray Me is with Mine on the table. The son of Man will go as it has been decreed, but woe to that man who betrays Him,' *(Luke 22: 14-26 &19-23 NIV)*.

The Feast of Unleavened Bread or Passover, provides initial insight into the *salvation and deliverance of Israel* from Egypt. And yet, it is a mere *foreshadow* to the redemption that the Messiah, Jesus Christ would offer the world one-thousand-five-hundred years after the

Hebrew exodus from Egypt. Truly, it is a *festival of freedom* from slavery. It provides the ultimate *liberty from the bondage of death* formed through the shackles of sin. Passover provides a keen awareness to the miraculous promise of deliverance. Like all other Jewish Feasts, it is a foreshadowing of Jesus. Passover speaks of God's atoning work through the *Lamb of God*. It began as a remembrance of God's deliverance from the bondage of Egypt. For nearly four hundred years the Hebrews were enslaved under the rule of various Pharaohs. After centuries of inhumane suffering, God worked out the intricate details for a Deliverer to arrive. His name was Moses.

Moses came before the mighty Pharoah ten times, demanding that the ruler *let God's people go!* Every appearance before the royal court resulted in the same outcome. Pharoah refused to listen. After every appearance the Lord set a plague across the land. With each refusal to listen, the following plague would ramp up the suffering over the land. Finally, after Moses was rejected for the *tenth and final time*, God's patience had run out. He unleashed the *plague of plagues*. One that would strike down the firstborn of every household, both human and animal by the hand of the Angel of Death. The irony of this final notice involved the origin of this original decree. It was Pharaoh himself who ordered the killing of the firstborn Israelites eighty years earlier when Moses was a newborn infant. God turned the tables on Pharaoh and used the hardness of the ruler's heart against all of Egypt.

The ultimate plague would sweep over the land as the Angel of Death was scheduled to turn the Egyptian society into a wasteland of death and destruction. God commanded the Israelites to take the blood of a lamb—one without blemish and smear it over the doorposts of their homes. When the angel of the Lord saw the innocent blood on the doorpost, he would *pass over.* It was the *Angel of Death* that finally convinced Pharoah to let God's people go when the first-born prince of Egypt died on that very night. Every year for the past three-thousand-five-hundred years the Hebrew People have celebrated the Passover. Two-thousand years ago, Jesus and His chosen followed the same traditions. But Jesus took the symbolism, the remembrance of God's promise for deliverance upon Himself on that fateful night. On that night, Jesus changed the entire focus of the Passover. It would no longer be a celebration remembering God's deliverance of Israel from the bondage of slavery. It became the prophetic of remembrance of Jesus - God's *Sacrificial Lamb*. He became the *Great Deliverer*, Who freed the world from the bondage of death and sin.

Today, as followers of Jesus Christ, we have been covered by His atoning blood. He has *covered the doorposts of our hearts and souls with His life-giving blood*. We are *forgiven*. We have been washed clean of the stains of sin. Through Him we have been delivered from the penalty of death's hold. The intriguing part of Jesus' Last Supper as we've come to know it, involves the correlation of His *triumphal entry* into Jerusalem just four days before Passover. As He rode the foal of a donkey into the Holy City that morning, the welcoming crowds who excitedly greeted Him all shouted out, "Hosanna." The people were crying out to Jesus, the Lamb of God, "Save us!" Jewish tradition required that the Passover lambs be brought to the Temple for inspection, four days before they were to be sacrificed. Surely, Jesus was the true *fulfillment of all Levitical Laws*. The spotless Passover Lamb would serve as the ultimate sacrifice that just a few days later on a hill known as Golgotha.

From this point on the destiny of the world drastically changed. The Son of God was bound to serve as the sacrifice for mankind's sins. Jesus was about to take on the role as the Sacrificial Lamb of God. There was about to be a *new covering of Lamb's blood* over the door post of humanity. The Angel of Death would soon lose its stronghold over the future of the world. Isn't it ironic that at this point in Jesus' life, those closest to Him were about to be scattered as sheep. The twelve chosen, would now face the greatest challenge of their faith. One of them would betray his Master, another would deny His existence, and even another would doubt His resurrection.

None of us are any different than the original twelve chosen men. All of us have *denied* His existence, *betrayed* His love, and *doubted* His Word. Yet, Jesus accepts us as we are and just as He did with the Disciples, He invites us into His presence to join Him at the table of eternal communion: To share in the sacrament of the bread and the wine. It is Jesus' deep desire for you to share with Him in the intimate fellowship of God the Father, and to revel in the *sweet communion* that only comes when you enter into His presence!

> Jesus went out as usual to the Mount of Olives, and his disciples followed him. On reaching the place, he said to them, "Pray that you will not fall into temptation." He withdrew about a stone's throw beyond them, knelt down and prayed, "Father, if you are willing, take this cup from me; yet not my will, but yours be done." An angel from heaven appeared to him and strengthened him. And being in anguish, he prayed more earnestly, and his sweat was like drops of blood falling to the ground, *(Luke 22: 39-44 NIV).*

As you reflect on the events of the Last Supper within the confines of that dimly lit upper room, it is essential to remember the sacrifice that Christ made on your behalf. *This is my body and My blood, which is given for you... this do, in remembrance of Me!* Remember the price He paid for your redemption! Remember Him! As we close today's devotion, I think it's important to take a moment to still your heart and mind once again. I'm not going to ask you any questions today. But I want you to take a moment to focus on the Lord. *Carefully listen to see if God has a specific message for you now.* Within those thoughts, *write them down as a remembrance.* Sometime in the future, return to reflect on today's moment of communion with Christ.

_____

_____

_____

_____

_____

_____

_____

_____

_____

_____

_____

In Remembrance of Me

This do in remembrance of me,
    were the words Jesus spoke one day,
The Disciples readied the Passover,
    that night Judas our Lord did betray.
Remember Christ, our Savior,
    with the breaking of the bread,
This is my body; it's given for you
    with these words the believer is fed.
This body is our Bread of Life ---
    Eternal nourishment it gives;
Take - - -eat, as Christ commands,
    through Him the sinner lives.

In like manner, Jesus took the cup,
    in that furnished upper room;
Oh, the heaviness of our Savior's heart
    as He faced His impending doom.
The *New Testament* is in the cup,
    in *my blood which is shed for you*,
With these simple, spoken words,
    He shared His promise of life anew.
The *Old Testament* was the *law*,
    from Adam's fallen state;
The *covering of sin* by offerings
    then determined each sinner's fate.

Now, the cross provides salvation
    by the blood Christ shed that day;
When He became the sacrifice,
    our sins were washed away.
The *New* gives grace to sinners,
    through our Lord's eternal love;
By simple faith and trust in Him,
    we'll meet Him up above.
Believer, when you receive this bread,
    and from the cup partake,
Do this in remembrance of the One,
    Who died for mankind's sake!

Clarice D. Cook

Day 19
Gethsemane
Scriptural Reflections

Yet, it pleased the Lord to bruise Him, to make His soul an offering for sin, and the pleasure of the Lord shall prosper in His hand . . . He shall see the travail of His soul and shall be satisfied: by knowledge of Him shall many be justified. *Isaiah 53:10-11 NIV*

Even my close friend, whom I trusted, he who shared My bread, has lifted up his hand against me. But You, oh Lord, have mercy on me; raise Me up that I may repay them. I know that You are pleased with Me, for My enemy does not triumph over me. In My integrity, You uphold Me and set Me in Your presence forever. *Psalm 41:9-12 NIV*

I told them, 'If you think it best, give me my pay; but if not, keep it.' So, they paid me thirty pieces of silver. And the Lord said to me, 'Throw it to the potter'---the handsome price at which they priced Me!' So I took the thirty pieces of silver and threw them into the house of the Lord to the potter. *Zechariah 11:12 & 13 NIV*

I am the true vine, and my Father is the gardener. He cuts off every branch in me that bears no fruit, while every branch that does bear fruit he prunes so that it will be even more fruitful. You are already clean because of the word I have spoken to you. *John 15: 1-3 NIV*

When he had finished praying, Jesus left with his disciples and crossed the Kidron Valley. On the other side there was a garden, and he and his disciples went into it. Now Judas, who betrayed him, knew the place, because Jesus had often met there with his disciples. So Judas came to the garden, guiding a detachment of soldiers and some officials from the chief priests and the Pharisees. They were carrying torches, lanterns and weapons Jesus, knowing all that was going to happen to him, went out and asked them, "Who is it you want?" "Jesus of Nazareth," they replied. "I am he," Jesus said. (And Judas the traitor was standing there with them.) When Jesus said, "I am he," they drew back and fell to the ground. Again he asked them, "Who is it you want?" "Jesus of Nazareth," they said. Jesus answered, "I told you that I am he. If you are looking for me, then let these men go." This happened so that the words he had spoken would be fulfilled: "I have not lost one of those you gave me." *John 18: 1-9 NIV*

Have you ever taken a walk through a garden after a long strenuous day? It can radiate a *tranquil peace* with sweet aromas that calm the senses. The subtle scents of flowers, trees, shrubs, and the fertile soil fills the evening air with a freshness that soothes the soul. Soft cooing from the morning dove echo throughout the leaves of the tender olive branches, while their melody brings *comfort* and *solace* to the weary heart. The cool breeze greets you like a *refreshing oasis* in a barren land. The shadows cast by the setting sun, as it settles behind the distant hills, seem to engulf you into the garden's mystical ambiance. It's almost as if you become one with the garden, filled to overflowing with its life-giving fruits. You are reminded of God's commandment to *be still and know that I am God!*

In a solitude, that offers comfort within its quiet stillness, the garden *draws you to the Creator.* Here, you are allowed an opportunity to reflect on the events of the day: Time to reflect on your hopes, dreams, and fears of tomorrow. You can sense the nearness of God as you partake of the moment. In the garden you can spiritually walk side by side with God, savoring the *sweet communion of peace,* found within His presence. Truly, that was God's original intent for all mankind when He first created Adam and Eve; placing them in the tranquility of His perfect garden.

I remember reveling in the garden of my maternal grandparent's home as I was growing up. It was there, where I found *solace* from a *family tragedy* when I was thirteen years old. The garden was actually more of an orchard rather than a garden. My grandparents lived on a one-acre lot in a small, prairie town located within the Great Plains of Northeastern Colorado. The back half of their property was encompassed with huge elm trees that provided a great sense of privacy from any neighbor. When I was a mere baby, Grandpa had planted peach trees throughout this half-acre of prairie soil. He spent years tending and nurturing the saplings into a bountiful grove of blossoming splendor. I always loved spending time in the garden; listening to the birds singing from within the branches of the gigantic elm trees. Watching a multitude of butterflies, flitter, and flutter throughout the peach trees and over to Grandma's patch of wildflowers, was always a delightful distraction. Of course, there were also bumble bees galore, toads, a bunny or two, and even a few garter snakes who called the garden home.

One of my favorite activities in the garden involved tending to the daily watering duties that began in early spring. There was an old pump house on the back corner of the lot that fed a small pond, which shared the *life-giving water*, along the small ditches, outward to each of the individual trees. Making sure that the water freely flowed to each tree was a self-appointed task, in which I took great pleasure in supervising. There were actually about a dozen trees in the garden that were tended by Grandpa's nurturing hand. Those trees introduced me to the miracle of God's creation at a very early age. Out of the branches filled with budding leaves, sprouted a full bouquet of blossoming flowers, that literally covered the entire tree. Before long, those blossoms would turn into miniscule buds, and not long after, the branches were so heavy with ripening peaches that Grandpa would have to reinforce the trees with a whole load of lumber. The garden, was truly the first place where I was able to experience the wonder, and the miracle of God's amazing creation.

It was no wonder that when I received the tragic news about losing the baby brother that Mom and Dad were supposed to bring home; my first reaction was to run into the garden. This was the second death that my family had to deal with as just a few months earlier, my beloved Grandfather was suddenly called home to be with the Lord. And yes, it was the same garden that he had coddled and nurtured for all of my life. That was my *sanctuary.* That's where I often found *peace, comfort,* and *solace.* But more importantly, when I ran into this personal sanctuary to find refuge on that particular day, I felt the overwhelming *presence of the Lord.*

I always loved the garden because of the *serenity* and *wonder* that it contained. But that day was completely different. My senses became highly sensitive to the *sovereignty* of God's creation. The birds in the trees sang out with a greater brilliance and clarity. I became keenly aware of the soft whisper of the breeze, gently blowing through the branches of the trees. The coolness of the breeze on that hot summer's day, literally felt like it was the *breath of God.* I talked with Him that day. I opened my aching heart in that moment, and I could *feel*

142

His presence like never before. I felt His comfort. I received His assurance that He was in control. It was an unforgettable moment in my life. That experience allowed me to relate to the stories of Jesus as He made His way into the garden to find *sanctuary* from the overwhelming circumstance of life. It was in the garden where He could quietly focus on an intimate conversation with the Father.

No wonder Jesus often spent time in the *Garden of Gethsemane*! Nestled within the rolling hills between Bethany and the Eastern Gate of Jerusalem, Jesus often escaped to collect His thoughts while seeking the *Father's guidance* and *strength*! His chosen followers would often accompany Him to share in the solitude and in the tranquility of the lush, fertile garden. Really, it was more than a garden, it was a *sanctuary*, a retreat from the demands and rigors of a growing ministry. It provided an escape from the multitudes of people who sought after this Man from Galilee. It was His *prayer closet*. People sought Him for their own selfish gain. They wanted to catch a glimpse of this mighty Prophet; to touch this Man of Miracles. They yearned to witness His magnificent power: Like the wonders when He calmed the sea, cast out demons from those who were possessed, or fed the masses!

On that fateful night, after Jesus shared the *bread* and the *wine* with His chosen lot, Jesus went one last time to pray in the solitude and the tranquility of the garden. He took eleven of the Disciples with Him to the Mount of Olives, but only took Peter, and the two sons of Zebedee, James, and John deeper into the garden. He asked them to watch and pray as He went a bit further to meet with the Father to desperately pray. It probably took some direct encouragement from Jesus, to convince the *eleven* to accompany Him out of the *upper room* and away from the bounty of the Passover meal. It had been a long and eventful week beginning with the *triumphant entry* into Jerusalem, and one that culminated with the celebration of Passover. Surely, all of those men would have much rather remained behind in the comfort of their evening. Even still, they agreed to follow Jesus out, into the shadows of the night.

How serene it must have been that evening as they huddled beneath the shadowed olive trees, watching their *Master* venture deeper into the garden to pray. One can imagine the light of the stars and the radiance of the moon glistening off of the silvery olive leaves. They must have known that Jesus was deeply troubled as they traveled the path into the garden. He must have been unusually quiet and somber on this particular night. Yet, when they found the perfect location deep in the garden, the trio stretched out and reclined in comfort upon the ground. I'm sure that they started off following Jesus' directive to pray, but then you know what I'm talking about. They were too tired to keep their eyes open to keep watch as Jesus had requested. So, they peacefully slipped off into a deep, restful sleep.

Within the secured serenity of the garden, the men just couldn't help but to doze off while Jesus prayed. That is until they were awakened by His words: *Could you not keep watch with me one hour?* These simple words of conviction, must have been forever etched in their memories, as the upcoming events were about to overwhelm them! This was the last moment that they would share with their Master, the beloved Messiah, before His death. Although, they didn't realize it at the time. So, in their blissful ignorance, each time the Teacher came back to check on them, they would quickly fall back to sleep as He returned to the tranquility of the deep garden to pray once again.

The second time Jesus returned; he didn't even bother to wake them. But the third time, was different. His time had arrived.

Returning the third time, he said to them, "Are you still sleeping and resting? Enough! The hour has come. Look, the Son of Man is delivered into the hands of sinners. Rise! Let us go! Here comes my betrayer!" *(Mark 14:41-42 NIV).*

Are you any different than Peter, James, or John? Would you have been able to keep watch as Jesus prayed? Before you answer, all I have to say is; *right, in your dreams.* That is all that can be said about anyone who would infer that they would have responded in a more positive way than the Lord's Disciples. Regardless, on that fateful night, the tranquility and serenity of the garden was about to be lost. Everything was about to change as Judas led an angry mob to apprehend Jesus.

The events that followed that night in the Garden of Gethsemane, forever changed the *spiritual dynamic of humanity*.

Things would never be the same. Over the next *forty-plus days*, (there's that number forty again), all of Jesus' followers would experience and witness the divine power of God's transformational call to *Grace*. It was in the garden; Jesus surrendered Himself in prayer, harnessing the *radiant power* of God's purpose. That is what carried Him through the pain, suffering, and anguish that He was about to endure. He *willingly surrendered* to the Father's plan. He gave Himself to the Father's will; for you and for me! Forty-three days later; after suffering an agonizing death on the cross, before being resurrected from the grave, He ascended into heaven to prepare a place for all who believe in Him. But God's plan is not complete. Jesus will return a second time. It is then that He will begin His *Millennial Reign*. In the meantime, He has given us the same directive that He gave His closest companions that night in the garden, *Watch and pray!*

> But about that day or hour no one knows, not even the angels in heaven, nor the Son, but only the Father. Be on guard! Be alert! You do not know when that time will come. It's like a man going away: He leaves his house and puts his servants in charge, each with their assigned task, and tells the one at the door to keep watch. "Therefore, keep watch because you do not know when the owner of the house will come back—whether in the evening, or at midnight, or when the rooster crows, or at dawn. If he comes suddenly, do not let him find you sleeping. What I say to you, I say to everyone: 'Watch,' *(Mark 13:32-37 NIV)*.

As you contemplate the power within today's devotion, tell me, *where is your place of retreat, that ushers you into God's presence, and facilitates your ability to pray?* Please share a few of the details regarding your personal prayer closet, in the space below.

_____

_____

_____

_____

_____

_____

Gethsemane

The time of betrayal was drawing near;
      Christ knew the hour would come,
For His crucifixion and death on the cross;
      He felt the impending doom.
He gathered together His Disciples,
      unto a place called, "Gethsemane;"
Some He left at the garden gate, while with Him
      went Peter and two sons of Zebedee.
As Peter and James and John with Christ,
      deeper into the garden went,
The soul of our Lord and Savior,
      with sorrow and grief became rent.
Christ spoke gently to His Disciples:
      "Tarry ye here and watch with me;"
Then He walked on a "stone's throw" further;
      fell on His face 'neath the old olive tree.
With eyes lifted up toward heaven,
      and His heart torn with agony,
He prayed, "Oh, God, My Father,
      let this cup-if possible-pass from me."
Yet deep within His heart He knew,
      He was the sacrifice for sin;
So, He prayed His prayer, "Not my will,
      but as Thou wilt, Oh, God, Amen."
He then rose to join the Disciples,
      He left waiting and watching with Him,
But He found them sleeping soundly . . .
      they possessed weakness---as do human men.
He awakened them to watch and pray,
      that temptation they enter not;
For "the spirit, indeed, is willing,"
      but help for the flesh must be sought.
Again, Christ went from them to pray,
      In agony that no man's known;
His sweat fell in great drops of blood to the ground,
      as He prayed in that garden alone.
He prayed three times the previous prayer,
      that "this cup may pass away;"
Including, "not My will but Thine be done;"
      (He fulfilled God's will one day).

146

Three times Christ returned to the Disciples,
        three times He found them asleep;
What great sadness enveloped our Savior,
        when "one hour" they could not keep.
The third time He returned and saith,
        sleep on now and take your rest;
The hour is come---I Am betrayed,
        rise up---let us go; God's way is best.
Christ then was betrayed and delivered,
        into the hands of cruel men;
He died on the Cross of Calvary,
        as the Sacrifice for sin.
He arose again triumphant,
        to become Savior for us all;
He is the way of salvation,
        if only we heed His call.
Won't you tarry with The Master,
        in your own "Gethsemane?"
Come with Him into the garden,
        look to Him . . . He'll set you free!
As the angel strengthened Jesus,
        so, the Savior stands by you;
Out of agony into redemption,
        He is there to help you through.
Through Him, your willing spirit,
        will be strengthened every day;
By prayer, your weakened flesh made strong,
        to cast temptation from the way.
Work and labor for The Master,
        sleep not---while time flies by;
Pray and wait and watch with Jesus,
        the "hour of return" is drawing nigh.
When The Lord again returneth,
        to gather up His own,
May He say, "Your spirit's willing,
        and your flesh, also, is strong."
Your reward will come from heaven,
        at the height of victory---
    If you sleep not through the harvest,
        of today's Gethsemane.

Clarice D. Cook

147

Day 20
Hiding in the Shadows
Scriptural Reflection

Peter answered and said to Him, "Even if all are made to stumble because of You, I will never be made to stumble." Jesus said to him, "Assuredly, I say to you that this night, before the rooster crows, you will deny Me three times." Peter said to Him, "Even if I have to die with You, I will not deny You!" And so said all the disciples.
Matthew 26: 33-35 NKJV

Now as Peter was below in the courtyard, one of the servant girls of the high priest came. And when she saw Peter warming himself, she looked at him and said, "You also were with Jesus of Nazareth." But he denied it, saying, "I neither know nor understand what you are saying." And he went out on the porch, and a rooster crowed. And the servant girl saw him again, and began to say to those who stood by, "This is one of them." But he denied it again. And a little later those who stood by said to Peter again, "Surely you are one of them; for you are a Galilean, and your speech shows it." Then he began to curse and swear, "I do not know this Man of whom you speak!" A second time the rooster crowed. Then Peter called to mind the word that Jesus had said to him, "Before the rooster crows twice, you will deny Me three times." And when he thought about it, he wept.
Mark 14: 66-72 NKJV

Mankind has been hiding in the shadows ever since the day Adam and Eve chose to disobey God's directives. Once they ate of the fruit from the *Tree of Knowledge*, their eyes were opened to the desire of lustful pursuit. That's how they suddenly realized that they were naked. They instantly recognized that things were different, as they were *aroused by lust*, rather than the feeling of deep longing that is only available within the *pure, innocence of love*. That morning when they heard the breath of God entering the garden, they ran within the shadows of the lush foliage to hide, because of their nakedness.

> And they heard the sound of the Lord God walking in the garden in the cool of the day, and Adam and his wife hid themselves from the presence of the Lord God among the trees of the garden. Then the Lord God called to Adam and said to him, "Where are you?" So, he said, "I heard Your voice in the garden, and I was afraid because I was naked; and I hid myself." And He said, "Who told you that you were naked? Have you eaten from the tree of which I commanded you that you should not eat?" *(Genesis 3:8-11 NKJV).*

Running to hide is the most common response to fear. Fear provides a true indication of the intensity and extent involving the *absence of one's faith*. There are other indicators that corelate to either the limit or even absence of faith as you deal with any sort of intimidating challenge, worry, stress, anxiety, outbursts, anger, self-isolation, restlessness, and many more. It is natural to experience any of these reactions within the confines of this existence. But it's when they become *overwhelming* to the degree that you are *consumed* or even *incapacitated* by their force over you, that there becomes a need for concern. The prophet Elijah had such a reaction after standing up against Queen Jezebel and her idol, Baal!

> Now Ahab told Jezebel everything Elijah had done and how he had killed all the prophets with the sword. So Jezebel sent a messenger to Elijah to say, "May the gods deal with me, be it ever so severely, if by this time tomorrow I do not make your life like that of one of them." Elijah was afraid and ran for his life. When he came to Beersheba in Judah, he left his servant there, while he himself went a day's journey into the wilderness. He came to a broom bush, sat down under it and prayed that he might die. "I

have had enough, Lord," he said. "Take my life; I am no better than my ancestors." Then he lay down under the bush and fell asleep, *(I Kings 19:105 NIV).*

Not only did the mighty prophet of God run away to hide, but he crawled under a bush and prayed for the Lord to take his life. He had enough. He was scared, tired, hungry, and *totally intimidated* by the threat against him by the lecherous queen. But above all, he was filled with self-pity. Talk about displaying a total lack of faith by one who should have known better. How could Elijah not totally trust God? How could he run away and hide? How could Israel's great voice, who boldly represented God in such profound ways; how could he be such a coward? The answer to all of those questions is simple. *Elijah was human.*

When challenges arise, and threats come home to roost, it's extremely easy to lock the door and find a corner to hide. Many of us can think of times when we turned tail and ran as we were confronted by a frightening situation. Humanity was designed with a keen *sense of self-preservation.* So, when somebody stands up with courage and strength to face a formidable foe, the world sits up to take notice. I believe our basic instinct is to take flight. I also believe that courage and strength are a pretty good indicator of faith. *Faith* in its simplest form is *trust in action.* When you trust God, you will feel secure, realizing that He is in control. Thus faith, or *trust in God, affords security.* Lack of faith, or trust in God, leads to insecurity.

There's another intense example of fear, recorded in the New Testament. It's worth sharing in today's devotion. It involves, Jesus' arrest in the garden. But specifically, it highlights the overwhelming reaction to fear experienced by Peter.

> Simon, Simon, Satan has asked to sift all of you as wheat. But I have prayed for you, Simon, that your faith may not fail. And when you have turned back, strengthen your brothers." But he replied, "Lord, I am ready to go with you to prison and to death." Jesus answered, "I tell you, Peter, before the rooster crows today, you will deny three times that you know me, *(Luke 22:31-34 NIV).*

I can't even begin to imagine the shock and despair that instantly engulfed Peter's heart at the moment these prophetic words were spoken by his Rabbi. It had been just moments before when Jesus broke the bread, then shared the cup with them, declaring: **This cup is the new covenant in my blood, which is poured out for you.** Talk about a harsh dose of verbal rebuke from the lips of the Lord to top off a reverent, and joy-filled, Passover celebration. It was then when they all joined together to sing a hymn before heading out to the Mount of Olives. They entered a garden known as Gethsemane, where Jesus told some of the Disciples to sit and wait, everyone except the brothers, James, and John, along with Peter. The trio escorted Jesus, deep into the garden, telling them to keep watch as He went alone, further into the garden to pray.

> Returning the third time, he said to them, "Are you still sleeping and resting? Enough! The hour has come. Look, the Son of Man is delivered into the hands of sinners. Rise! Let us go! Here comes my betrayer!" Just as he was speaking, Judas, one of the Twelve, appeared. With him was a crowd armed with swords and clubs, sent from the chief priests, the teachers of the law, and the elders. Now the betrayer had arranged a signal with them: "The one I kiss is the man; arrest him and lead him away under guard." Going at once to Jesus, Judas said, "Rabbi!" and kissed him. The men seized Jesus and arrested him. Then one of those standing near drew his sword and struck the servant of the high priest, cutting off his ear. "Am I leading a rebellion," said Jesus, "that you have come out with swords and clubs to capture me? Every day I was with you, teaching in the temple courts, and you did not arrest me. But the Scriptures must be fulfilled." Then everyone deserted him and fled, (Mark 14:41-50 NIV).

When Judas and his thugs arrived, everyone deserted Jesus and fled for their own personal safety. Even Peter, who had boldly claimed his unwavering allegiance and devotion, ran away to hide in the shadowy darkness of fear. After Jesus' arrest, and as He was led away in chains, Peter followed the mob from a distance, into the courtyard of the High Priest, Caiaphas. It was here, where the Lord, was tried and convicted of blasphemy. Peter *hid in the shadows* of the night, trying to stay out of sight. But he couldn't manage to stay hidden, as he tried to warm himself by a fire. Engulfed within the shadowing flickering of the flames, he was recognized by one of the slave girls who served the

High Priest. *You, you were with the Nazarene,* she loudly declared. *No, I don't know what you're talking about,* Peter cried out before making his way over to the entry way to once again hide, disappearing into the darkness of the shadows. But again, the servant came upon him and blurted out to those in the area, *He is one of them! No! No! You're mistaken!* Peter once again, adamantly denied her accusation. Before long, those who were around Peter, recognized him as a Galilean. *You are a Galilean,* one of them blurted out, before declaring; *Surely, you are one of them.* Peter began to curse and swear at them, *I don't know this man who you're talking about!* Immediately the rooster crowed the second time. Instantly, Peter remembered the words of his Master: **Before the rooster crows twice you will disown me three times. And he broke down and wept,** *(Mark 14:72b NIV).*

When Peter followed Jesus from a distance, to the palace of Caiaphas, I'm sure he was overcome with shock, disbelief, and relentless fear. The world was spinning completely out of control, and it was impossible to make any sense of what was happening. But after *he denied Jesus,* not once, but *three times,* his heart was *consumed with guilt,* while his mind was filled with overwhelming *regret* and deep *remorse.* Peter's fear had triggered the response to run away and hide physically from the world. His guilt and regret exasperated that need, to not only hide from the world, but to hide from God. Just as the first Adam tried to hide from the Creator for disobedience; Peter hid because of his sin of denial against the Word.

It's impossible to imagine the horror that Peter, as well as the rest of Jesus' Disciples were feeling at that moment. Witnessing the horrific events of the Lord's, arrest, scourging, and crucifixion are actually beyond our human comprehension. All of their hopes, dreams, and closely held beliefs died on that cross with their Rabbi. What's worse, even their *faith* in Jesus was completely *crushed.* Is it no wonder that all of them ran away to hide in the shadows of their inconsolable grief and overwhelming despair?

As you try to picture what that would have been like, ask yourself how you would have responded to those events. Would you have denied knowing Jesus as He was led away in chains? *Would you have hidden within the shadows,* silently watching as He was sentenced to die; too afraid to take a stand; too afraid to acknowledge His acquaintance? I'm sure both you and I would have also been too exhausted to even watch and pray! The truth is, none of us are any different than Peter or any of the Disciples. All of us would run off in fear to hide in the shadows; trying to escape our guilt and shame. Yet there would have been nothing you could have done to erase that image of Jesus' suffering out of your mind, heart, and soul. But yet, there was something that God had planned!

> Those who live in the shelter of the Most High will find rest in the shadow of the Almighty. This I declare about the Lord: He alone is my refuge, my place of safety; he is my God, and I trust him. For he will rescue you from every trap and protect you from deadly disease. He will cover you with his feathers. He will shelter you with his wings. His faithful promises are your armor and protection. Do not be afraid of the terrors of the night, nor the arrow that flies in the day.
>
> [8]Just open your eyes, and see how the wicked are punished. If you make the Lord your refuge, if you make the Most High your shelter, no evil will conquer you; no plague will come near your home. For he will order his angels to protect you wherever you go. They will hold you up with their hands so you won't even hurt your foot on a stone.
>
> [14] The Lord says, "I will rescue those who love me. I will protect those who trust in my name. When they call on me, I will answer; I will be with them in trouble. I will rescue and honor them. I will reward them with a long life and give them my salvation," *(Psalm 91:1-5, 8-12, 14-16 NLT)*.

There are many places to hide within the shadows, but there is only one shelter to find refuge and peace. It's under the covering of His wing. *Where do you go for shelter when you are filled with panic and fear? Do you seek protection under the Savior's wing?*

_____

_____

_____

_____

_____

Hiding in the Shadows

(Peter's Song)

I hid within the shadows, as He was led away in chains!
        Watching from the distance, as He suffered through the pain!
I turned my back on Jesus, even though He called me friend!
        Denying that I knew Him, when His life came to an end!

I was hiding in the shadows, when He took His final breath!
        Hiding from my guilt and shame when Jesus met His death!
I'd walked beside the Teacher, as He taught us day by day!
        But I chose to take a different path; I chose to turn away!

Why did I leave Him? Why did He die?
        The anguish is unbearable, for the friend I have denied!
I can't go on, the pain's too great, to live with what I've done!
        Forgive me Lord, for leaving you; I can't believe you're gone!

Now I stand within the shadows; it seems my life's destroyed
        No place to go to find relief, no way to fill the void!
So, I hide within the faces - of the crowds along the way,
        I've turned my back on Jesus; I can't face another day!

This shame will never leave me, for the friend I have betrayed!
        If only I had stood by Him! How I wish I would've stayed!
Now I hide within my torment, as my eyes are filled with tears,
        My life consumed by deep regret – my heart is wrenched in fear!

Why did I leave Him? Why did He die?
        The anguish is unbearable, for the friend I have denied!
I can't go on, the pain's too great, to live with what I've done!
        Forgive me Lord, for all I've done, I cannot carry on!
Forgive me Lord, for leaving you; Please help me carry on!
        Forgive me Lord, for what I've done; I can't believe you're gone!

Lanny K. Cook

Day 21
Shadow of the Cross
Scriptural Reflection

For the law, having a shadow of the good things to come, and not the very image of the things, can never with these same sacrifices, which they offer continually year by year, make those who approach perfect. For then would they not have ceased to be offered? For the worshipers, once purified, would have had no more consciousness of sins. But in those sacrifices, there is a reminder of sins every year. *Hebrews 10: 1-3 NKJV*

How precious is Your lovingkindness, O God! Therefore the children of men put their trust under the shadow of Your wings. *Psalm 36: 7 NKJV*

Then they cried out to the Lord in their trouble, And He saved them out of their distresses. He brought them out of darkness and the shadow of death, and broke their chains in pieces. *Psalm 107: 13, 14 NKJV*

The people who walked in darkness Have seen a great light; Those who dwelt in the land of the shadow of death, upon them a light has shined. *Psalm 109: 2 NKJV*

I offered My back to those who beat Me, My cheeks to those who pulled out My beard; I did not hide My face from mocking and spitting. Because the Sovereign Lord helps Me, I will not be disgraced. Therefore, I have set My face like flint, and I know I will not be put to shame. He who vindicates Me is near. Who then will bring charges against Me? Let us face each other! Who is My accuser? Let him confront Me! *Isaiah 50:6-8 NIV*

I am poured out like water, and all my bones are out of joint. My heart has turned to wax; it has melted away within Me. My strength is dried up like a potsherd, and my tongue sticks to the roof of My mouth; you lay Me in the dust of death. Dogs have surrounded Me; a band of evil men has encircled Me, they have pierced My hands and feet. I can count all My bones; people stare and gloat over Me. They divide My garments among them and cast lots for My clothing. *Psalm 22:14-18 NIV*

Have you ever taken the time to really understand what happened to Jesus at that place called *Calvary*? Let's take a moment and reflect on how Christ suffered for you and for me as He traveled the road to Golgotha! First, He was *betrayed* by the people in this world who were closest to Him. When He was captured and turned over to the Roman authorities, even His *followers fled* in order to ensure their own safety. No one stood up for Him or testified on His behalf at the trial. *He stood alone*, a prisoner in chains, held in bondage! Ridiculed, rejected, mocked, and *despised* by all mankind! He was beaten, whipped, and tortured *without mercy*, by tormentors who took pride in their cruel and brutal treatment of prisoners. They *laughed* with pleasure while viciously ridiculing their victims as they inflicted their agonizing *cruelty* and pain. A *crown of thorns* was first placed upon His head, then beat down onto his scalp with a stick. Continuously, His tormentors *mocked* and taunted the King of the Jews!

Then, He was stripped of His garments and of *all human dignity*. He was brutally lashed to a whipping post, where the soldiers proceeded to lash Him with a whip laced with pieces of bone and pottery shards. Savagely, without mercy, He was *flogged* from the top of His shoulders to His heels. With each lash the flesh was ripped out of His back, shoulders, and legs. Undoubtedly, He convulsed in pain with each torturous blow! His accusers grabbed at His hair, viciously pulling out large strands from His scalp. They *plucked* at His beard, literally ripping it from His face! They *spit* in His face, laughed at Him, kicked Him, punched Him, ridiculed Him, and cursed at Him! With blood flowing from His head and with His back ripped to shreds and beaten raw, they placed a wooden cross beam on His shoulders that weighed more than a hundred pounds. He had to *carry His own cross* through the streets of Jerusalem, as He struggled to reach a hill named Calvary. All along the way, down the Via Dolorosa, the *way of suffering,* mankind cheered the agony and apparent defeat of God's Son, of His precious gift to the world!

When Jesus finally reached His *hill of execution*, they nailed Him to the cross. Yet, in the midst of the conflict and the ovation from the crowd, when the soldier grabbed Jesus' wrist to begin the execution, He didn't struggle - He didn't fight! *He freely opened His hand* to be nailed to that tree! He was *inviting you* into His care. He laid down His life for mankind! Through His hands and through His feet they viciously pounded the *nails of atonement* into the wood. Nailed to that tree, the powers of the world were sending their message of hate-filled tyranny to all of His followers.

The *shadow of the cross* has reached out to the world for over two-thousand years. But it is actually a *shadow of Grace.* Within that shadow we find refuge from the searing heat of a sin-filled world. It provides protection from the elements of a dry and parched land. A wilderness that withers our spirit, and devours the very essence of life from our souls. From within the depths of that shadow, a light shines forth. A *radiance* of hope and peace emanates from the very spirit of grace, as it transcends the world with a message of love, sacrifice, and forgiveness. Under the shadow of grace contained within the reality of Christ's cross, we can once again enjoy *communion* and *fellowship* with God. When we choose to place our burdens, cares, and fears in the midst of that shadow, we will find rest, comfort, hope, and eternal peace. The road which led to the cross was filled with pain and suffering for Jesus Christ. Yet, within that shadow, the *light of grace swallows the darkness, offering salvation to* a lost and broken world.

> He was despised and rejected of men; a man of sorrows, and acquainted with grief; and we hid our faces from Him; He was despised, and we esteemed Him not. Surely He hath borne our grieves, and carried our sorrows; yet we did esteem him stricken, smitten of God, and afflicted. But He was wounded for our transgressions, He was bruised for iniquities: the chastisement of our peace was upon Him; and with His stripes we are healed, *(Isaiah 53:3-5 NIV).*

As you reflect on the relationship you share with Christ, you need to be reminded of the price that was paid for your salvation. You must never forget the suffering He endured to set you free from sin and the sacrifice He made to allow you access into fellowship with the Father. Before He wore *His crown of glory,* Jesus had to endure the *crown of human suffering.* Betrayal, ridicule, rejection, humiliation, affliction, anguish, and death were transformed through the thorns of the crown that adorned His brow as He traveled on the road toward Golgotha! As He agonized on that cross in undeniable torment and exhaustion, He lifted His eyes toward the Father and cried out in Aramaic; *"Eli, Eli, lama sabachthani,"* *that is to say, "My God, My God, why hast thou forsaken me?"* God could not look upon His Son, as the sins of the world came upon Him. For the first time, Jesus was separated from the love of His father as He bore the punishment for sin. His agony and despair defy our human comprehension. As He took His final earthly breath, with His head hanging to His chest in death, the shadow of the cross was forever cast across the face of humanity.

The thought of Jesus hanging from the cross, casting a *lifeless shadow* across the landscape of humanity is a powerful image. But within that reality, we must remember that Jesus served as the Sacrificial lamb for humanity's sin. He died on the cross; shedding His blood and giving His life so that we may live. Jesus didn't deserve to die on the lonely hill of Calvary. He was *spotless, pure, and true!* Yet, He willingly gave His life by shedding His blood to save mankind from eternal damnation. *He freely laid down His life for us!* You and I should have been the ones who had to reap the consequence for our selfish sin, and self-indulgent pleasure. It should have been you and it should have been me nailed to that tree; dying an agonizing and cruel death for the choices we have made. Yet, God loved us so much that He sent Jesus as the atoning sacrifice for fallen humanity. It is Jesus alone that provides a path of salvation for your soul. Through His death on the cross you have been set free! It is His blood that provides forgiveness and washes away your sin! Jesus told His Disciples; **If any man will come after me, let him deny himself, and take up his cross, and follow me. For whosoever will save his life shall lose it: and whosoever will lose his life for my sake shall find it,** (Matthew 16:24, 25).

If you believe that Jesus died to save you from sin, *you are called to take up your cross and follow Him.* He suffered and died so that you could choose life; and have it in abundance! *Do you choose life?*

_____

_____

_____

_____

_____

Shadow of the Cross

Do you see the shadow of the cross upon the ground,
  Do you see the blood of Christ slowly trickling down?
Do you see the agony etched upon His face,
  Oh! What Jesus did that day to save the human race!
Do you see the path He followed, beneath the burdensome tree,
  Do you see where all that weight sent Him down upon His knee?
Do you see the appointed one that helped Him with the cross?
  Oh, Jesus! Begotten Son of God, let man not call it dross.

Do you see Him coming, struggling up Golgotha's hill,
  A hill of death, known as the skull, Redemption's plan to fill?
Do you see the anguish written there within His eyes?
  My Jesus! Savior of the world. Herein redemption lies.
Do you see the stripes and wounds, laid upon His back,
  Shreds of flesh torn from Him, with every brutal whack!
Do you see the mocking crowds, jeering all the way,
  Jesus, precious Son of God. How direful was that day!

Do you see His smitten face, bruised by upraised hands?
  As a lamb led to its slaughter, He stood silent in court stands.
Do you see the innocent blood, pouring from this lamb?
  Oh Jesus! Pure and Blameless. What a wretched soul I am!
Do you see the spittle, dried 'midst blood and sweat,
  Do you see His tormentors, not finished with Him yet?
Do you see the cowering Disciples, leaving Him alone?
  Jesus! Faithful One to all. You are a Friend well known!

Do you see His once full beard, blood-caked, sparse, and thin?
  What ridicule, the pain He felt, as they plucked it from His chin.
Do you see the Savior as He is laid upon the cross so rough?
  Stripped of robe and dignity --- enough was not enough!
Do you see the heavy nails and the hammer in the hand,
  Of a Roman soldier of the day, executioner in command?
Do you see the wounded flesh, where nails were pounded through . . .
  Oh Jesus! Healing hands that blessed and gave men life anew?

Do you see the "crown" of thorns, crammed cruelly on His head,
  Piercing ever deeper . . . Dear Friend, He's there in your stead.
Do you see the mockery of, "I" and "N," "R," "I,"
  Placed above Him on the cross, His shame to magnify?
Do you see that soldier's spear as it was thrust into His side,
  Do you see the gaping wound that cannot be denied?
Do you see the water flowing with His redeeming blood,
  Rushing from His broken heart, cascading like a flood?

161

Do you see His mother's tears as she sadly hovers by,
> Do you see the sun go black in the brightly lighted sky?
Do you see the soldiers as they gamble for His wear,
> Jesus, Sacrificial lamb, unblemished, pure, and fair.
Do you see His tears of mercy, upon that cruel wood?
> "Forgive them, oh, my Father," Yes, His Father understood.
As He took on Himself the sins of all, His sacrifice so great,
> He cried "My God" in anguish, Omniscient love sealed His fate...

Do you see His life now ebbing, while it quietly slips away,
> The end is near, "It's Finished!" A new covenant starts this day!
Oh, Jesus, Our Redeemer, the way of forgiveness He affords.
> One day soon He will return: King of kings and Lord of lords!
Do you see the fading silhouettes, at the close of this long day?
> Do you hear deep silence reigning, as you go along your way?
Do you feel the sullen echoes... resounding all around...
> As a shadow from the Holy cross is cast upon the ground?

Do you see God's plan of salvation, provided by Jesus, His Son?
> The path is laid for sinners . . . to you . . . me . . . and everyone!
Come now to Jesus, the Savior --- Our Redeemer, Lord, and Friend,
> Accept Him to enter His Kingdom---Forever and ever. Amen

Clarice D. Cook

Day 22
The Blood of the Cross
Scriptural Reflection

For the life of the flesh is in the blood, and I have given it to you upon the altar to make atonement for your souls; for it is the blood that makes atonement for the soul. *Leviticus 17:11 NKJV*

Then He took the cup, and gave thanks, and gave it to them, saying, "Drink from it, all of you. For this is My blood of the new covenant, which is shed for many for the remission of sins. *Matthew 26: 27, 28 NKJV*

But when they came to Jesus and found that he was already dead, they did not break his legs. Instead, one of the soldiers pierced Jesus' side with a spear, bringing a sudden flow of blood and water. *John 19: 33, 34 NIV*

For it pleased the Father that in Him all the fullness should dwell, and by Him to reconcile all things to Himself, by Him, whether things on earth or things in heaven, having made peace through the blood of His cross. *Colossians 1: 19, 20 NKJV*

And I will pour out of the house of David and the inhabitants of Jerusalem a spirit of grace and supplication. They will look on Me, the One they have pierced, and they will mourn for Him as one mourns for an only child, and grieve bitterly for Him as one grieves for a first-born Son. On that day the weeping in Jerusalem will be great, like the weeping of Hadad Rimmon in the plain of Magiddo. *Zechariah 12:10-11 NIV*

As the cross of Jesus was raised in place, He hung not only in scornful shame, but in horrendous agony between two convicted thieves! *Excruciating pain engulfed His entire body*, pain unlike any you or I have ever experienced or even imagined. Crucifixion is the most painful form of execution known to man. You don't die from shock, or from a nearly total loss of blood when you're crucified! You die from asphyxiation. You *suffocate*, because the weight of your body won't allow air into your lungs. For every breath, you have to pull yourself up by your arms to inhale. As exhaustion sets in, you no longer have the strength to pull yourself up to breathe! You die from lack of oxygen!

It was a gruesome sight as Jesus gasped for each and every breath! It wasn't like the pictures depict. He was beaten, bruised, and tortured beyond recognition. Even His own mother wouldn't have been able to recognize Him if she hadn't known that it was her Son hanging upon that wooden beam. His face was swollen from the beatings. Blood, mixed with sweat and dirt was caked all over His body, as well as being matted in a tangled mess within His hair and beard. In total exhaustion, while using all the energy He had left, He lifted His eyes toward the Father and cried out, *My God, My God, why hast thou forsaken Me!* As Jesus hung on that cross in undeniable torment, agony, and utter exhaustion, all the sin of the world came upon Him! That was the most personally excruciating pain He experienced that day, as the Father could no longer look at Jesus, when the sin of the world was placed upon the Son.

As if by His command, the sky turned black, and darkness covered the face of the earth. At that very moment, *Jesus took His final earthly breath,* finally allowing His chin to hang limp upon His chest. *It was finished.* Jesus was dead. His mother let out a mournful wail as the tears flowed softly down her cheeks. The handful of Jesus' followers who had the courage to witness the horrific murder of this prophet of God, stood in shocked silence, as they watched the lifeless body of their teacher hang limp upon the cross. But yet, the cruelty of the Roman executioner wasn't finished with his torturous duty. Before the crowd turned their backs to walk away from the horror, a *soldier thrust his spear into the Rabbi's side* to ensure that the death sentence was complete. Instantly, from the side of Jesus, where the spear had been thrust up into His chest, *a river of blood and water gushed free*, covering the ground at the foot of the cross.

There could be no question that Jesus was dead. Even still, His blood continued to *trickle down the cross*. Drop by precious drop, it dripped from His wounded head, oozing out of the wounds from His nail pierced hands and feet. Seeping out from the ripped flesh from His back, and from His pierced side---the *atoning blood of redemption freely flowed* from His lifeless body. Can you picture the life-sustaining-blood flowing from His injuries? Trickling down the rugged wood, staining the dusty soil beneath the cross as it falls, drop by drop, into a puddle of *Divine suffering*? Do you see it? Can you even imagine the horrible sight? Look! Take a good look---right now, in your mind. Allow it to to be forever etched into your memory, heart, and soul. Ask yourself, *why?* Why did Jesus willingly die on that cruel *cross of excruciating suffering*?

The harrowing torture that Jesus endured is beyond human comprehension! His blood freely flowed down that cross, seeping deep into the ground as He was *wounded for your transgression*, and bruised for your iniquity. He shed His blood so that we might live! He was the *Lamb of God*! The *Sacrifice* for mankind's sin! Every last drop of His precious blood was freely shed for you! That blood will set you free! His blood has the power to forgive all of your sins --- past, present, and future! His blood is the *redemption* that provides hope and new life to everyone who accepts its cleansing power!

Trying to understand the need for Jesus to die on the cross is perplexing for many people. In our modern culture, it just doesn't seem to make any sense. In my book, Destiny Defined – The Sons of the Eastern Plains, I addressed this very question. I believe the following consideration will help you better understand the need for Jesus to serve as the atonement for mankind's sin.

> But why did Jesus have to die? Why did God require a blood sacrifice for the forgiveness of humanity's sin? Because of God's sovereignty, or His righteous and "just" nature, sin requires a price to be paid. There is a penalty involved with sin, thus, there is a punishment that must be applied. Sin is actually a death sentence for all of humanity. But because of God's merciful

nature, He provides a means, and a way that none of us could provide for ourselves.

When Adam chose to sinfully disobey God in the Garden of Eden, that choice broke the perfect relationship between the created and the Creator. Relationship was the reason humanity was created in the first place, to share in the fellowship with God the Father. With Adam's sin, humanity was separated from God and death entered into the human equation. What was the first thing the Almighty did when He confronted Adam and Eve in their nakedness as they were trying to hide in the Garden? God shed the blood of an animal in order that the couple could cover themselves with the skins of creatures to protect them from the harsh elements of the world. A world that was no longer perfect. One that was now burdened with the depravity of broken relationship and marred by a death sentence. A sentence that came about by man's free will to choose the path he would follow. Sadly, he chose the path of disobedience.

Most of us can't grasp the severity or the depravity associated with our sinful nature: Especially, how it impacts our relationship with God. Since blood is the sustaining factor in the miracle of life, and without it all life dies; blood became the catalyst for God's forgiveness. The significance of a blood sacrifice first became apparent in the Garden, as recorded in the Old Testament book of Genesis. It was here, when God Himself sacrificed animals to provide Adam and Eve with a covering. Not only the physical covering of garments crafted from the hides of these creatures, but also a spiritual covering for their sin came through the sacrificial shedding of the animal's blood. This was merely a covering of the sin, not a cleansing or a removal of sin. It wasn't a divine forgiveness of sin, but rather a temporary covering for an individual's sinful nature. This is the nature that each of us inherited from Adam and Eve. It is this sinful nature that each of us is born with that demands the need for a personal Savior in our lives.

This is why Jesus Christ had to come into this world, and to die for the sins of all humanity. This sacrifice required the shedding of sinless blood. Not the blood from the arteries of fallen man. Christ's perfect blood served as the propitiation, or payment for our sins. The shedding of Jesus' blood doesn't just provide a covering for our sinful nature. Rather, through His blood our sins are washed away, completely removed from the ledger of sin-based debt. The shedding of blood by His death on the cross, paid the debt we owed. He paid the penalty that we couldn't afford, because of God's divine, unconditional love for His creation; both you, and me. Jesus served as the atoning grace for our death sentence, and all that is asked of any of us, is to simply believe. By accepting Him into your heart you are forgiven and your relationship with God Almighty is restored. All it requires is a child-like faith; just simply believe! When you believe in Him, your sins are removed as far as the east is from the west. Because of God's forgiveness of your sins, you will never stand before Him in judgment. But rather, you will stand beside Him as a joint-heir to His eternal kingdom. That is the promise of your eternal destiny with Jesus. But you must choose to believe![5]

Jesus served as the *propitiation* for humanity's sin, in order that we can gain access to God the Father. Only *His blood was worthy of paying the sacrificial price* that satisfied the *Sovereign's legal requirement* of the *Levitical Law*. The blood of the *Sacrificial Lamb* of God didn't just *cover your sin,* as was the case with the animal sacrifices required within the Mosaic Law. *Christ's blood completely removes the stain of sin from your soul.* His blood doesn't provide a physical covering for your sin, it provides a *divine spiritual cleansing*. The only requirement for you to be cleansed, is to simply put your *trust in Jesus*. Believe on the Lord Jesus Christ and you *will be saved*.

Have you accepted Jesus Christ into your life? Do you believe that He paid the price to free you from your sin? If you do, then who do you know that needs to come to know Jesus? It was Andrew who introduced his brother, Simon Peter to Jesus. Look how Jesus used those two brothers. *Who do you need to share the message of salvation with?* You can't keep it all to yourself. Jesus is calling you to share the message of His love. *Who needs to hear about Him?* Write their names on the lines below. Then go to tell them all about Jesus!

_____

_____

_____

_____

[5]   Lanny Cook, *Destiny Defined-Sons of the Eastern Plains* (Denver, CO: IHS Publishing 2024) pp. 232-233

The Blood of the Cross

Do you see the blood of Christ, shed for all mankind?
      No greater love in heaven or earth could any being find.
The blood of Jesus shed that day takes away your sin,
      No longer just a covering, it's as though they've never been.
"As far as east is from the west," is how sin does become,
      "Never more brought before you. . . it is finished, it is done."
He took upon Himself this day, the sins of all the world,
      Hanging there upon the cross, His grace lay bare, unfurled.

Do you see the love He felt, while dying on that cross,
      His suffering, His anguish, was more than idle dross;
Jesus---perfect---blameless, completely pure within,
      Unblemished Sacrificial Lamb, the One who knew no sin.
Do you see His wounded hands, nail pierced, bloodied, hurt . . .
      As spikes were pounded thru, did you see the life blood spurt?
His feet, too, suffered anguish---these feet that did no harm,
      Only walked to aid the suffering, the weak, the sick, forlorn.

Do you see His curling hair, now blood caked as His beard?
      Why rip out His flowing hair? The Sacrificial Lamb is sheared.
Do you see repulsive spittle, mixed with blood, now dried?
      Upon His face so gentle---for mankind's sake, He cried.
Do you see the piercing thorns, burrow deep into His head?
      Blood coursing down His smitten face; Love's color? It is red.
Do you see His beaten back, from neck down to His feet?
      Gouged out flesh hanging free: Blood covers God's judgment seat.

Do you see that gruesome spear, thrust deep into His side?
      Blood and water bursting forth, as He hung His head and cried,
"Oh, My Father, forgive them, they know not what they do,"
      Beloved, look to Jesus. Dear friend, He died for you!
Do you see His bloodied body---complete from head to toe?
      Savagely mangled, cruelly beaten; Dear One, I want you to know:
The pictures often seen of Him, upon that cruel cross
      Fail to show the depth of agony, great pain, extreme loss.

Do you see a different picture, of this Man of Calvary?
     Do you see the blood He shed; it was shed to set you free?
Free from sin, free from death, free from eternal fire---
               Lift up your heart unto the One who laid upon sin's bier.
Do you see the ultimate sacrifice of this Jesus, God's own Son?
     Undying love, unyielding life, Holy blood... Dear Sinner, Come.
Do you see God's plan of Grace? Jesus *willingly* died on that tree?
     His *blood* takes away the all sins of past, present, future---all three.

Do you now see the way of redemption? Jesus speaks to all,
     "I shed my blood for everyone, if you will only heed My call;
You must believe, My Children, I am the life and the way,
     Come, My blood cries out to you! Now, Come to Me, today!"
Do you see the shadow of the cross, cast upon the ground?
     Do you see the blood of Christ, redemption there is found?
Do you see this Savior, beckoning for you to come...
     "Child, your sins are forgiven---you are that special one!"
                                        Clarice D. Cook

Day 23
The Glory of the Cross!
Scriptural Reflection

Joseph took the body, wrapped it in a clean linen cloth, and placed it in his own new tomb that he had cut out of the rock. He rolled a big stone in front of the entrance to the tomb and went away. Mary Magdalene and the other Mary were sitting there opposite the tomb.
Matthew 27:59-61 NIV

See, My Servant will act wisely; He will be raised up and highly exalted. Just as there were many who were appalled at Him --- His appearance was so disfigured beyond that of any man and His form marred beyond human likeness --- so will He sprinkle many nations, and kings will shut their mouths because of Him. For what they were told, they will see, and what they have not heard, they will understand.
Isaiah 52:13-15 NIV

But we behold Jesus, who was made a little lower than the angels because of His suffering of death, crowned with glory and honour; that He by the grace of God should taste death for every man. ...Forasmuch then as children are partakers of the flesh and blood, He Himself likewise took part of the same; that through death He might destroy him that had power of death, that is, the devil; And deliver them who through fear of death were all their lifetime subject to bondage!
Hebrews 2:9, 14-15 KJV

To him who is able to keep you from stumbling and to present you before his glorious presence without fault and with great joy— to the only God our Savior be glory, majesty, power, and authority, through Jesus Christ our Lord, before all ages, now and forevermore! Amen.
Jude 24, 25 NIV

There are numerous accounts in the scriptures which refer to various forms of linen used to adorn the *earthly body of Jesus*. In His birth, and in His death, the linen which covered His earthly frame provides a profound significance to the story of the Messiah. These descriptions contain a critical message for each and every one of us as we contemplate the life of Jesus, as well as, His impact on our lives. Born into humanity, the Son of God was placed in a manger, *enveloped in swaddling clothes*.

It was the first mention of Jesus' life on this earth began with His mother Mary, wrapping Him in a swaddling band. A square piece of cloth where Mary laid her precious, baby Jesus. His head was placed on one of the four corners which was gently tucked around His neck and the back of His head. His feet were placed at the opposite end of the cloth and the corner folded snugly up over His feet. The two side corners were then folded together across the baby's chest, and strips of cloth were used to wrap around the infant to secure Him within this earthly, linen cocoon.

It wasn't a blanket or a diaper that greeted the Christ child as He emerged out of the womb, but instead, swaddling clothes. As was the custom in those days, *strips of linen served to cover the nakedness of this newborn child*. A covering which provided warmth and protection from the harsh elements of this world. Swaddling clothes bound the Son of God as He took on the form of man, *Confined by flesh*. There was nothing coincidental that at the end of Jesus' earthly, human life, He was once again *wrapped in fine linen*. His *battered, bruised,* and *bloody* remains were bound within a clean, linen burial shroud. His followers gently carried His tortured body to a garden where they placed it in a borrowed tomb provided by Joseph of Arimathea.

> When it was evening, there came a rich man from Arimathea, named Joseph, who also was a disciple of Jesus. He went to Pilate and asked for the body of Jesus. Then Pilate ordered it to be given to him. And Joseph took the body, and wrapped it in a clean linen shroud, and laid it in his own new tomb, which he had hewn out of a rock, *(Matthew 27:57-60 NIV)*.

The Disciple's hearts were obviously filled with overwhelming

173

grief and despair. After all, their greatest hopes, dreams, and ambitions involving Jesus' new earthly kingdom were seemingly destroyed. Reluctantly, they rolled the stone in place, sealing the tomb with a deep sense of harrowing finality. In anguish and dread, they turned their backs on their Master's grave and began to *walk away from the hope of His promise.* He was dead! It was finished! Jesus, His teachings of hope, life, and a kingdom had all come undone. The followers' entire world had come crashing down all around them. Everything that Jesus had shared with them had become meaningless and insignificant. Nothing seemed to matter anymore. The reality of His death consumed every fiber of their being! Yet, His words still lingered in their hearts.

They could *still hear His voice* echoing through their minds - laughing with them, sharing with them, teaching them, blessing them. The image of His face and His smile overwhelmed their thoughts as they fought to purge the shocking events of the past few days from their minds. All of Jesus' followers must have been consumed in *debilitating confusion.* They couldn't help but to be lost in their own personal solitude as they each attempted to deal with nightmarish emotions of horrific proportions. One by one, they slowly walked away from the tomb of their Master. Not a word was spoken as a haunting silence filled the scene as they each turned their back on the hope and dream of their Rabbi's promise. Burned within their mind was the *last image of their Lord* as they wrapped His broken body in the shroud.

Within the solemn trepidation contained within every step, moving away from the tomb, their hearts longed for rest from their torment. But they couldn't escape the reality of the anguish as each of their *minds whirled with personal regret* for the loss the Master. But even worse; was the remorse they felt for their own choice to *hide in the shadows* as they abandoned their Lord. There were too many regrets to count as the tragedy decimated their entire world. They were completely consumed with anguish; they couldn't begin to imagine how they could ever move on with their own lives or find a new reason to live. For the moment, they could do nothing more than *wallow in the depth of despair* as they mourned the tragic death of their beloved friend and teacher.

The fine linen that bound Jesus in death was from the same

human weave that originally bound Him at birth. *Life and death were both embodied within the confines of swaddling cloth.* Jesus was bound by *human flesh and frailty at His birth*, while death attempted *to eternally bind Him* through the crucifixion on the cross. Yet, the *glory of the cross* shone forth when on the third day, the Power of God declared that Jesus be resurrected from the chains of death and from the bondage of human flesh.

> Now upon the first day of the week, very early in the morning, they came unto the sepulcher, bringing spices which they had prepared, and certain others with them. And they found the stone rolled away from the sepulcher, and they entered in, and found not the body of the Lord Jesus. And it came to pass as they were perplexed thereabout, behold, two men stood by them in shining garments: And as they were afraid, and bowed down their faces to the earth, they said unto them, Why seek ye the living among the dead? He is not here, but is risen: remember how He spoke unto you when He was yet in Galilee, saying, The Son of Man must be delivered into the hands of sinful men, and be crucified, and the third day rise again! And they remembered His words, *(Luke 24:1-8 NIV).*

Like a *dormant seed* lying lifeless in the cold stone tomb, the dead Christ was merely waiting for the warmth of God's new glorious day. Within that glorious day, Jesus was to become the glory of the Risen Son. At the appointed time, the lifeless body of Jesus erupted in *radiance, power,* and *glory* as God's Almighty hand reached down, lifting the *Redeemer out of the clutches of death.* Like a butterfly emerging from a lifeless cocoon, Jesus *conquered the shroud of death* and destruction when He overcame the stronghold of Satan's grip.

> Then Peter arose, and ran to the sepulcher; and stooping down, he beheld the linen clothes laid by themselves, and he departed, wondering in himself at that which was come to pass, *(Luke 24:12 NIV).*

The entire foundation of Christianity is established upon the *radiant glory of the Resurrected Jesus.* If there was no resurrection, than the entire Gospel of Jesus Christ is a scam. The Apostle Paul made this very declaration in his first letter to the church in Corinth.

If there is no resurrection of the dead, then not even Christ has been raised. And if Christ has not been raised, our preaching is useless and so is your faith. More than that, we are then found to be false witnesses about God, for we have testified about God that he raised Christ from the dead. But he did not raise him if in fact the dead are not raised, *(I Corinthians 15:13-15 NIV)*.

It is true! The *grave was conquered!* In *magnificent splendor, majesty, power,* and *glory-Jesus lives!* That is the message that these followers took to their grave. They were eye witnesses to the truth of the Resurrected Christ. Their faith never wavered regardless of the personal attacks and even the torturous deaths that confronted each of them. They confirmed that Jesus is the King of kings and Lord of lords. He reigns forevermore! He has power over life, and He has been given dominion over death! How many times have you allowed the *shroud of human frailty* to serve as an excuse for your lack of commitment, or for your lack of obedience and service to the Lord?

How long will worldly desires interfere with your personal relationship with Jesus? Is your soul bound by the constraints of the flesh? Through the *glory* of Christ, you can be set free. You are not condemned to live in spiritual bondage. God's power and anointing is unlimited and eternal. The *glory of the cross* allows your spirit to fly free from sin and shame! However, you must choose to accept the *radiance of God's glory* for yourself! *Are willing to do that?* On the lines below, share your thoughts regarding the *radiance of God's glory.*

_____

_____

_____

_____

_____

_____

_____

_____

The Glory of the Cross

Do you see the shadow of the cross upon the ground?
      Do you see the blood of Christ, still pooling all around?
Do you see His body---battered, bruised, and dead?
      Oh! What Jesus did for man! To Calvary was led!
Do you see the setting sun, sinking low into the night?
      They come for the body of Jesus, crucified upon this site.
Do you see the grave cloth, folded o'er the body of One
      That knew no sin, who was perfect---God's only begotten Son!
Do you see the grieving women, His mother, with Mary's two,
      The hour grew late to anoint Him, as was the custom to do;
Do you see Joseph of Arimathea taking charge of His body then?
      "We'll take Him to the garden, where is hewn my own tomb den."
Do you see them gather the linen, the shroud of death 'round Him,
      Place over His head the napkin, wrapping all flesh and skin?
Do you see the friends lift His body, gently carry Him away?
      Oh, Jesus, precious Jesus! What pain you suffered this day!
Do you see them enter the garden, with the body of Jesus, oh so dear?
      The way grows faint in the twilight, as the tomb is looming near.
Do you see the soldiers following, with drawn sharp spears held high?...
      While the fear of God overtakes them, and fills the darkened sky.
Do you see the tomb in the shadows as they slowly enter in?
      They place the body of Jesus on the hand-hewn ledge therein.
Do you see the women weeping, each disciple bowing his head?
      This Son of God, Messiah---their Hope---lies before them dead!
Do you see them in deep sorrow---frightened, confused, and lost?
      Losing their Rabbi, they're scattered, bewildered, wind-tossed.
Do you see His many companions---Mother, brethren, friend,
      Now backing toward the exit? . . . . Expectations at an end.
Do you see the mighty, heavy stone rolled across the tomb?
      Sealing in this Man of Hope, there is no greater doom.
Do you see the Roman soldiers, placed to guard this site?
      As figures all around them, simply fade into the night...
Do you see the Sabbath, during this time of ages past,
      Come and go in fashion---of prayer, and rest, and fast?
From the evening of this Friday 'til the sun again goes down
      Upon the coming seventh day---then a new week will abound.
Do you see the dawning morning, of this another week,
      Do you see the women coming, for Jesus' tomb they seek?
Do you see the rays of sunshine, to show the dreary way?
      As they hurry to the garden at the early break of day;

177

Do you see their broken hearts, deep sorrow mixed with grief?
>With Jesus' death came anguish, profound---beyond belief!
Do you see the borrowed cavern, in the early morning light?
>The gravesite looks quite different than when they left that night;
They do not see the soldiers that they had planned to ask,
>To move the heavy stone away, into the grave to pass!
Do you see the shocked astonishment, as gladness fills the air,
>When they see the tomb is empty, Dear Jesus is not there!
Do you see the mighty, heavy stone, rolled over to the side?
>"He is not here, HE'S RISEN!" The happy voices cried!
Do you see the radiant angel, standing watch beside the tomb?
>"Indeed, the Lord has risen! He's conquered death and doom!"
A mighty earthquake of the Lord, has rolled away the stone,
>As Jesus burst forth the victor, now immortal flesh, and bone!
Do you see God's VICTORY, which the tomb could never hold?
>The Living, Loving, Son of God, broke the bonds quite bold!
Do you see those fetters fall, as the grave He overcame?
>Sin and death are conquered, In Jesus' Precious Name!
Throughout the garden echoes resound, over and over again,
>Jesus is Conqueror over all---Death, all evil, and sin!
"He is Risen, He is Risen, Christ Jesus lives today;
>He is the Life, He is the truth, He is the only way!"
Do you hear the angels sing, gathered all around;
>"He is Risen, He is Risen!" It is the sweetest sound.
"He is Risen, He is Risen, Christ Jesus lives today;
>He is Risen, He is Risen." Yes! Jesus paved the way!
Heaven and Earth both proclaim, the wonderful, glorious news:
>"He is Risen, Jesus Lives." Life is ours to gain---not lose;
Do you have that message, written on your heart?
>"He is Risen, Our Jesus lives, never to depart!"
Do you see the shadow of the cross upon the ground?
>Do you see the broken fetters, lying all around?
Do you see the Risen Savior, Jesus Christ, our Lord?
>Do you see the Cross of Glory, He is alive forever more.

>Clarice D. Cook

Day 24
The Power of the Cross!
Scriptural Reflection

The Lord will lay bare His holy arm in the sight of all the nations, and all the ends of the earth will see the salvation of our God. *Isaiah 52:10 NIV*

And if the Spirit of Him, who raised Jesus from the dead is living in you, He who raised Christ from the dead, will also give life to your mortal bodies through his Spirit, who lives in you... because those who are led by the Spirit of God, are sons of God. For you did not receive a Spirit that makes you a slave of fear, but you received the Spirit of sonship. And by Him we cry 'Abba Father.' The Spirit Himself testifies with our spirit that we are God's children. Now if we are children, then we are heirs---heirs of God and co-heirs with Christ, if indeed we share in His sufferings in order that we may also share in His glory. *Romans 8:11, 14-17 NIV*

For I am not ashamed of the gospel, because it is the power of God that brings salvation to everyone who believes: first to the Jew, then to the Gentile. For in the gospel the righteousness of God is revealed—a righteousness that is by faith from first to last, just as it is written: "The righteous will live by faith." *Romans 1: 16-17 NIV*

In the past God spoke to our ancestors through the prophets at many times and in various ways, but in these last days he has spoken to us by his Son, whom he appointed heir of all things, and through whom also he made the universe. The Son is the radiance of God's glory and the exact representation of his being, sustaining all things by his powerful word. After he had provided purification for sins, he sat down at the right hand of the Majesty in heaven. So he became as much superior to the angels as the name he has inherited is superior to theirs. *Hebrews 1: 1-4 NIV*

You can't even begin to imagine the vast multitude of miracles and wonders that the *Disciples witnessed* as they journeyed throughout the countryside with Jesus. However, you can almost picture them becoming somewhat callous to the everyday wonders that they experienced within the demands of the Master's ministry. After all, crowds followed Jesus everywhere in an effort to catch a glimpse of Him, to hear His words, to experience His wonder, and to benefit from His miraculous power. The *demands of the ministry must have been exhaustive* as Jesus, with His chosen, fought their way through the mobs of lost and afflicted humanity. The masses relentlessly sought after this mighty Prophet and Teacher. Begging that He would reach out and silence the cries of affliction which emanated from the very essence of their broken lives.

These followers, defined by their *human nature*, must have become overwhelmed by the daily task of assisting Jesus in feeding the *spiritual, emotional,* and *physical* needs of the people. Undoubtedly, they too would be completely drained in various ways at the end of each encounter. One can almost envision them waking up in the morning and feeling a sense of dread over the thought of dealing with another mob of desperate beggars. But of course, there were times that even the weary followers would have been in complete awe, like when Jesus raised Lazarus from the dead.

Truly, that was something out of the ordinary, and it undoubtedly provided an emotional *resurgence of commitment* to the ministry they had been called to pursue. Obviously, Jesus reached out and harnessed everybody's attention with that wondrous act. After all, that particular miracle was of the highest personal concern to the Disciples since Lazarus was a close friend of all. So, when *Jesus commanded Lazarus to come forth from* the grave, there was without question, an added sense of excitement and jubilation from the followers of the Man from Galilee.

But could it be that after following Jesus for three years, these men had come to expect even greater things from Jesus? Their attention began to drift towards their own understanding; clouded by their own desire for what they thought God's purpose should be. Is it possible that the everyday occurrence of performing miraculous healings and transforming lives could have become just a *distraction* to their *personal purpose, glory,* and *influence* within the ministry? Possibly, they had become numb to the eternal significance of their calling and began to focus and consider their own *humanly defined ambitions* over this amazing Jesus movement.

If these twelve men were anything like you and me, it could be that the demands of the ministry had become more of a burdensome chore rather than one of *pleasure, wonder,* and *divine surrender* that they had first experienced. As time went on, they had to wonder where Jesus' ministry was heading and we can see that they began to speculate where it would all lead. We know that they argued over such things as where they would sit within the Kingdom of their Lord and Master. However, nothing that they had experienced or learned over the three years of Jesus' ministry could have prepared them for what was about to happen. They were all caught off guard by the events of the Passover Celebration that had resulted in Jesus' crucifixion.

In the grave where the followers placed their Master's body, the death of all *hopes, dreams, understanding,* and *aspirations* were bound in silence when the stone sealed the darkened tomb. For *two nights, they anguished over their loss.* In terrified confusion, they struggled with their doubts, consumed with fear, regret, and guilt. They were lost in a barrage of personal memories of precious moments spent in communion with their Lord.

But then, on the *third day,* the *Power of God* descended upon the cold, lifeless body of Jesus, and new life burst forth into the being of the Son. He was *transformed through the Power of the Spirit of God* into the *Living Sacrifice* for the sins of humanity. The Power of God, through His Spirit, raised Jesus from the grave. This Power is beyond any human comprehension. If it wasn't for this Power, the *story of Jesus Christ would have ended* within the confines of the cold, darkened tomb.

God had a different plan, knowing that in our human frailty, we would need a Power to tell us where to go and what to do! When the resurrected Christ gathered the remaining Disciples together, He promised them a *Comforter.* He told them of One whom God would send to show them the way and to light their paths. One who would provide them strength, encouragement, and wisdom beyond their own human understanding. The *Power of God would flow through His Spirit* to settle upon the newly anointed Apostles. The Spirit of God would provide them with courage and faith necessary to persevere when the ground they trod became shaky and unstable.

> And when they had prayed, the place where they were assembled together was shaken; and they were all filled with the Holy Spirit, and they spoke the word of God with boldness, *(Acts 4:31 NKJV).*

> But when the Holy Spirit has come upon you, you will receive power and will tell people about Me everywhere---in Jerusalem, throughout Judea, in Samaria, and to the ends of the earth, *(Acts 1:8 NIV).*

> But the Helper, the Holy Spirit, whom the Father will send in My Name, He will teach you all things, and bring to your remembrance all things that I said to you, *(John 14:26 NIV).*

Through the Power of God, the *Disciples boldly delivered* the message of the One True God, and His gift of salvation to a lost and hurting world. Through this Power, the *Body of Christ was born and the Age of Grace arrived.* By the grace of God and through the Power of the Holy Spirit, believers have been nurtured, protected, guided, and called to faith in the Lord, Jesus Christ. *To reject the Power of the Spirit of God, is to reject the resurrection of the crucified Christ*, as well as deny the very existence of God the Father. It was through the Power of God that Jesus was able to touch the hearts, souls, and lives of all who seek after Him. The Power is completely embodied within the *Triune God* through the person that Christian's refer to as the Holy Spirit.

When the woman reached out and touched the hem of His garment, it was *God's Power* that released the healing energy through the cloth. When Peter responded, *You are the Messiah, the Son of the Living God!* it was *God's Spirit* who revealed this revelation to him. When Jesus cried out, *Lazarus come forth!"* It was the *Power of the living God* which filled His words, transforming the corpse with new life! It was the *Power of God's Spirit* that descended into the grave, upon the broken remains of the Son, shrouding His body with the essence of *new life* and a *resurrected glory*. God's plan of redemption for mankind came to life at the moment the miracle of the resurrection occurred.

You too can *access this Power* when you choose to accept Christ's sacrifice by allowing Him into your life. The Power of God through His Spirit is available for your *edification and transformation into the likeness of Christ*. It is available to lead you and protect you. It is there to fill you with God's bountiful blessings and to anoint you with the fruits of His Spirit. In that way, you too can become a useful servant and disciple to the Living God. By accessing His power, you will be able to bask in the goodness and prosperity contained within His purpose and plan for your life. An often-overlooked reality of the cross, involves the reality that the Power of the Holy Spirit was fully released into the world when Jesus took His final breath on that old, splintered beam of wood. The Holy Spirit will remain until that moment **when in a twinkling of an eye, the dead in Christ shall rise, and those who remain will ascend into the clouds to meet Jesus in the air**, as is recorded in 1 Thessalonians chapter 4.

> **For as many as are led by the Spirit of God, these are the sons of God,** *(Romans 8:14 NIV).*

> **Your ears shall hear a word behind you saying, 'This is the way, walk in it,' whenever you turn to the right hand or whenever you turn to the left,** *(Isaiah 30:21 NIV).*

When your way grows weary and the days seem long, *seek God in His sanctuary*. When the world turns against you and the storms of life engulf you, make the effort to hang on tight to His promise. You must turn to Him for guidance and direction when making any decision in your life. In good times or in trying times, you need to acknowledge God and the Power of His Spirit. It is then that you will *find solace* and *strength* through the *Power of the living God!*

> Is anyone among you suffering? Let him pray. Is anyone cheerful? Let him sing psalms. Is anyone among you sick? Let him call for the elders of the church, and let them pray over him, anointing him with oil in the name of the Lord. And the prayer of faith will save the sick, and the Lord will raise him up. And if he has committed sins, he will be forgiven. Confess your trespasses to one another,

184

and pray for one another, that you may be healed. The effective, fervent prayer of a righteous man avails much. Elijah was a man with a nature like ours, and he prayed earnestly that it would not rain; and it did not rain on the land for three years and six months. And he prayed again, and the heaven gave rain, and the earth produced its fruit, (James 5: 13-18 NKJV).

So, the question that I'm sure you're asking involves how can you access that power? What can you do to find it? It's simple. Just pray! Lift your eyes to the Master and pour out your heart to Him: **Ask and it will be given to you; seek and you will find; knock, and it will be opened to you,** (Matthew 7: 7 NKJV).

The intensity of Jesus' prayer in the Garden before His betrayal caused him to sweat droplets of blood. But the intensity of that prayer completely *engulfed Him with the power of the Holy Spirit*, that not only *accompanied* Him to the grave, but *delivered* Him from the grave, on the third day. The same power that raised Jesus out of the tomb is available to you. It's at your fingertips. Or, maybe I should say it's at the tip of your tongue. In fact, prayers don't even need to roll off your tongue to be heard by God. You can petition Him through your spirit. To engage the power of God that brings life to the dying, hope to the downhearted, faith to the doubters, and promise to the desperate, just pray in the name of Jesus. After all, Jesus is the Mediator between you and God. When you pray, the *power of God will meet you* at that very moment and within your personal circumstance.

> I urge, then, first of all, that petitions, prayers, intercession, and thanksgiving be made for all people— for kings and all those in authority, that we may live peaceful and quiet lives in all godliness and holiness. This is good, and pleases God our Savior, who wants all people to be saved and to come to a knowledge of the truth. For there is one God and one mediator between God and mankind, the man Christ Jesus, who gave himself as a ransom for all people. This has now been witnessed to at the proper time, (I Timothy 2: 1-6 NIV).

As we close today's devotion, it's important to reflect back on a few of the previous topics, all of which involved the cross. Each of these lessons are intertwined with one another. In ways, they are similar to the Parables of Jesus, as they are relevant by their own merit, but they also provide deep insight when considered from a spiritual perspective. The *shadow of the cross* presents the depth of *sacrifice*, required for *grace* to arrive in this lost and broken world. Jesus' *blood on the cross* paid the *price* for mankind's *redemption*. Because of that great price, *forgiveness* of sin was offered to anyone who believes in the Lord, Jesus Christ. The *glory of the cross* conquered death through *God's glorious radiance*, projected onto the *Resurrected Son*. Through the *Spirit of God's power*, Jesus was raised from the dead. Afforded by the *power of the cross*, mankind received access to the *Holy Spirit,* or Comforter. It was the Comforter who filled Jesus with the power of God's Spirit as the Son humbled Himself to pray in the Garden, seeking the Father's will. Within that same power, as believers in Christ, we are provided guidance, strength, and power to gain *eternal access* to God's Kingdom.

No one can fully realize the depth of power available through prayer. But when you *pray to Jesus*, the *Mediator* between you and God; the *power of God's Spirit is released*. God always hears your prayer, but He won't always answer them according to your desired outcome. They will be answered in *His way*, in *His timing*, and according to *His will*. Today's question involves Jesus' prayer in the Garden as He ended it with: **Not My will, but Thy will be done!** *Do you trust God enough to end every prayer the same way?*

_____

_____

_____

_____

_____

_____

_____

_____

_____

The Power of the Cross!

Do you see the shadow of the cross upon the ground?
      Do you see the blood of Christ? Redemption there is found;
Do you see that Jesus---now sitting on His throne?
      Oh, the Resurrected Son of God! Man's sin, He did atone!
Do you see His followers, still gazing toward the sky,
      Mouths agape in wonderment, they do not quite know why,
The Messiah had to leave them; to Heaven He must go,
      But He left with them a message, He wanted them to know.

Do you see Him speaking softly, as He continues on,
      His heart is filled with love for them, it sings Redemption's Song;
"I go to prepare for you a place, that where I am you'll be,
      My house holds many mansions; One day soon you'll see."
Do you see the angel's wings, forming clouds above?
      As Jesus keeps on speaking with a rich, deep voice of love.
Do you see His Disciples, He speaks unto them now,
      Their work is yet to continue and He is saying how.

"Go ye into all the world, and preach to everyone
      The greatest story ever told---The Gospel of God's Son;
For this is the plan of the ages, promised in days of yore,
      To Abraham, Isaac, and Jacob---to Adam and Eve before."
Do you see them listening, intent on every word,
      This is the "great commission," no soul before had heard,
"Preach redemption's message: 'salvation's now at hand;'
      Let man believe, be baptized, then he shall not be damned."

Do you see His children, reaching out to Him,
      Eagerly awaiting redemption, forgiveness from their sin?
Jesus said unto them, "observe all things I've taught,
      What I've commanded, do ye; then goodness shall be wrought."
Do you see them turn toward heaven, as the angels cluster near,
      Jesus speaks yet once more to them, they gather close to hear,
"Lo, I am with you always, you'll not be left alone,
      Even unto the end of the age, then you'll be gathered home."

Do you see the band of angels, as they anxiously await,
      The return of their Beloved, for God has set the date;
Do you see their joyful faces, radiating light and cheer,
      The Lord of lords returneth; they've missed His presence there.
Do you see the feet of Jesus, as they start to leave the ground?
      He's rising, rising upward; Homeward He is bound.

Do you see the wistful faces, of those He leaves behind?
　　　He'll give them peace and comfort---The "Holy Spirit" kind.
Do you see the hand of Jesus, as He waves His last "good-bye"?
　　　Now He'll soon rise, out of sight, taken up into the sky;
Do you see one final glimpse, that was theirs upon that day,
　　　Of the One who softly told them, "I am the Life---the Way."
Do you see the cloud enfold Him, within their angel wings?
　　　If you listen very closely, you may hear as heaven sings,
For they are all awaiting the return to heaven from earth,
　　　Of Jesus Christ, Son of God. How great---Celestial mirth!

Do you see the joy in Heaven, at the return of God's own Love?
　　　Do you see the celebration that was held that day above?
Do you see your own dear Savior, sitting on the right of God?
　　　Oh, Dear One, lift your praise that He once walked earth's sod!
Do you see the shadow of the cross upon the ground?
　　　Do you see the blood of Christ? Redemption there is found!
Do you see the glory of the cross of Calvary?
　　　You then can know the power of the cross that sets you free!

Do you see the angel, as he greets His Disciples there?
　　　"Why stand ye still now gazing, for Jesus is not here?
But I will tell you something, that I think that you should know,
　　　This Jesus will return to you in the way you saw Him go."
Do you yet see believers, still gazing toward the clouds?
　　　Keep your watch, keep waiting---a hopeful heart enshrouds
The hope the angel promised, "This Jesus will return" . . .
　　　The power of the cross of Christ within our hearts will burn.

Do you see the many redeemed, through all the ages of time?
　　　From Adam and Eve, until today. God's glorious grace sublime.
Do you see the "souls for Jesus," gathered 'round God's throne,
　　　Where Jesus waits to welcome, His own dear children home.
Do you see the Power, of the cross of Calvary?
　　　The cross of Love---love divine, it sets the sinner free;
No greater sacrifice for love is there, than from the Holy One,
　　　He laid down His life for mankind---This Jesus, God's own Son.

Do you see the shadow, of the cross upon the ground?
　　　Do you see the blood of Christ? Redemption there is found;
Do you see the Glory, of the Cross of Calvary?
　　　Do you see the Power, that hereby sets you free?

Clarice D. Cook

Day 25
The Shadow, Blood, Glory, and Power
Scriptural Reflection

A voice of one calling: 'In the desert prepare the way of the Lord; make straight in the wilderness a highway for God. Every valley shall be raised up, every mountain and hill made low; the rough ground shall become level, the rugged places a plain. And the glory of the Lord will be revealed, and all mankind together will see it. For the mouth of the Lord has spoken. *Isaiah 40:3-5 NIV*

From the west, men will fear the name of the Lord, and from the rising sun, they will revere His glory. For he will come like a pent-up flood that the breath of the Lord drives along. 'The Redeemer will come to Zion, to those in Jacob who repent of their sins.' Declares the Lord. *Isaiah 59:19, 20 NIV*

There is an evil which I have seen under the sun, and it lies heavy upon mankind: those to whom God gives wealth, possessions, and honor, so that they lack nothing of all that they desire, yet, God does not enable them to enjoy these things, but a stranger enjoys them. This is vanity; it is a grievous ill. A man may beget a hundred children, and live many years; but however many are the days of his years, if he does not enjoy life's good things, or has no burial, I say that a stillborn child is better off than he. For it comes into vanity and goes into darkness, and in darkness its name is covered; moreover it has not seen the sun or know anything; yet it finds rest rather than he. Even though he should live a thousand years twice over, yet enjoy no good---do not all go to one place? All human toil is for the mouth, yet the appetite is not satisfied. For what advantage have the wise over fools? And what do the poor have who know how to conduct themselves before the living? Better is the sight of the eyes than the wandering of desire: this also is vanity and is chasing after the wind....... For who knows what is good for mortals while they live the few days of their vain life, which they pass like a shadow? For who can tell them what will be after them under the sun? *Ecclesiastes 6:1-9, 12 NIV*

Since the days of Adam and Eve when they chose to disobey God's commandments, a *darkness covered* the inhabitants of this world. Engulfed within this darkened hideaway is an evil that lurks within the shadows, attempting to hide itself from the presence of God. It struggles to control the lives of those it encounters, devouring all who fall prey to worldly temptation, desire, and sinful passion. It comes to kill, steal, and destroy everything within its path. The *shadow of death* and evil has been cast across the earth, and nothing in mankind's power or control can stop its reign of terror. The shadow of evil is like a wide *chasm that separates you* from the love of God, denying access to the blessing of *His love*, and the warmth of *His light*.

Trapped within the shadow of darkness, mankind's destiny is sealed. This shadow separates you from everything that is good and righteous. You are trapped within the confines of Satan's evil intent. Yet, God devised a plan to save the souls of mankind, allowing us fellowship and communion once more within the Light of the world. The Light radiates from behind the cross, casting a *shadowed image; illuminated in brilliance* across the chasm of darkness. It is a bridge that transcends a dangerous ravine. It is the passage that allows access from the *darkness into the light.* The light of Christ emanates from the very heart of the Father as He desires an intimate relationship with His children.

The *shadow of sin* separated us from the love of our Creator. And yet, the shadow of the cross offers protection from the glaring heat contained within the desert of humanity's Godly disobedience. Sin required a Sacrificial Lamb in order that your sins could be forgiven. By the *blood of the cross*, the legal requirement of atonement was replaced by grace. Jesus' blood has set us free and we are no longer captive to sin or the grave. His blood brings new life to a lost and hopeless world, as Jesus' sacrifice was made on behalf of all mankind. The biblical story was consummated on the cross; as the *Son of God*, who arrived as the *Son of Man*, became the *Intercessor* between the Father and humanity. Jesus became the *Deliverer* for all of mankind. Jesus served as the atonement for your sin. He gave His life so that you may choose life for yourself.

Jesus didn't deserve to die on the cross in torturous agony. You

191

and I are the ones deserving of such a fate. As the Messiah's blood trickled down the wooden beams of the cross, pooling upon the ground below, the course of human history~ of mankind's destiny; was forever changed. Christ was spotless, pure, and true! Yet, *He willingly gave His life* in order to complete God's plan of salvation. His death on the cross provided an opportunity to once again bask in the light of God's righteousness. Out of the *darkened shadows* the *cross opened the door to the Light of God.* The Gospel of Luke records the very first person to be saved by the *Light of Grace.* It was the thief who was crucified with Jesus.

> One of the criminals who hung there hurled insults at him: "Aren't you the Messiah? Save yourself and us!" But the other criminal rebuked him. "Don't you fear God," he said, "since you are under the same sentence? [41] We are punished justly, for we are getting what our deeds deserve. But this man has done nothing wrong." Then he said, "Jesus, remember me when you come into your kingdom." Jesus answered him, "Truly I tell you, today you will be with me in paradise," (Luke 23:39-43 NIV).

When you lift your eyes toward the heavens in search of redemption, you see the *silhouette of the cross, illumined by the brilliant light, radiating out of the Father's love* for you. Through the blood of the cross, you have been given an opportunity to enter into fellowship and communion with God the Father. You are afforded a means to enter into relationship with the Creator of your soul.

The true *glory of the cross* became apparent in the early morning hours on the third day after Jesus was crucified. Several of His followers had decided to go to the grave at the break of dawn in order to properly prepare Jesus' body for burial. The air was cool and crisp as they walked along the path in the garden toward the tomb which contained the beaten, bloodied remains of their Master. The trees within the garden engulfed the narrow path that led to the tomb. The leaves of the sycamore and olive trees glistened in the morning light while the golden rays of a new morning filtered through the dense foliage, lining the path toward the tomb. The birds in the trees were waking to the new dawn as their joyful songs welcomed a bright and glorious day.

The stillness of the garden was disturbed only by the shuffle of the women's feet along the path as they silently made their way toward the place where Jesus lay. Their voices were silenced and their minds numbed by the events of the previous days. The women's movements mirrored the brokenness of their hearts as they trudged toward the borrowed grave to perform the grueling task of preparing the body for its final rest. The joy of the Passover was no longer prevalent within their hearts and souls. The anticipation of the celebration had turned to heartbreaking terror and anguish as they quietly approached the place where His body had been placed. The women found themselves in a haunting, lifeless, and foreboding garden. It had become a garden of death.

When they arrived at the tomb, they were met by an astonishing, almost unbelievable sight. An angel of the Lord appeared before them asking: *Why do you look for the living among the dead? He is not here; He is Risen as He said!* Their hearts leaped with joy while they instantly rejoiced with an uninhibited chorus of praise and adoration to God! "HE is Risen! HE is Risen!" Yes, HE is Risen, indeed! Thousands of years later, the echo of their voices can still be heard as the message of joyous redemption continues forward through millions of voices who follow the risen Lord! Yes, it is true, *HE IS RISEN! INDEED!*

How can these voices still be heard after the passing of nearly two-thousand years of history? Wouldn't the *annals of antiquity silence their cries and devour their joy*? If it were left up to human means to deliver the message of the resurrected Jesus, the story would have ended in just a matter of years. Within a few generations the story would have been lost within the pages of antiquity. Forever sealed within the shadow of mankind's sinful nature. However, within God's plan of salvation, through the *power of the cross* the story lives on. Thousands of years after Jesus walked the face of this earth, *the Spirit of the Living God provides the force* that continues to change lives and save the lost souls of humanity. His strength provides conviction, wisdom, guidance, and direction, even before a person accepts the resurrected Jesus into their lives.

But once you open up your heart and receive God's perfect gift of salvation into your life, the *Comforter whom Jesus promised*, will fill you with His peace and an assurance that transforms you into the likeness and the image of the living God. That is the promise of the power of the Holy Spirit. This is the reality of living your life with Christ. Never again will you have to rely on your own strength, ability, or power to manage your way through this life. You have been empowered to be more than you could ever be on your own. Through the ages the testimonies have accumulated; stories of *ordinary people doing super-ordinary things in the name of Jesus*. The power of the living God is an integral part of the salvation message.

The power of the cross was realized when Jesus took His final, earthly breath. At that moment, the day sky became completely black and the world shook with the grieving power of God. *And Jesus cried out again with a loud voice, and yielded up His spirit. Then, behold, the veil of the temple was torn in two from top to bottom; and the earth quaked, and the rocks were split, and the graves were opened; and many bodies of the saints who had fallen asleep were raised; and coming out of the graves after His resurrection, they went into the holy city and appeared to many. So when the centurion and those with him, who were guarding Jesus, saw the earthquake and the things that had happened, they feared greatly, saying, "Truly this was the Son of God!"* (Matthew 27:50-54 NKJV). The power of the cross tore the Temple veil in half; allowing access for anyone to enter into the Holy of Holies to share in the fellowship of the Father. That is, you can enter into the Father's presence if you accept Jesus into your life by believing in Him.

It is through the **power of the cross** that you are *transformed* into a living sacrifice for God, made holy and acceptable for His service. To *accept Jesus, is to gain the power* that raised Him up out of the grave. It is this power that provides the ability to live a sanctified life. That is, a life that is set-apart for God's purpose and for the dream in which you were created. When you accept Him for Who He is, you will discover that His dream for your life becomes a reality. Through Him you will find your purpose, and your destiny. Through His power you will become more than you could ever become on your own. For Jesus told us: **All Power is given unto me in heaven and in earth. Go ye** therefore, and teach all nations, baptizing them in the name of the Father, and of the Son, and of the Holy Ghost: Teaching them to observe all things whatsoever I have commanded you; and lo, I am with you always, even to the end of the world. Amen, *(Matthew 28:18-20 NIV).*

Through Jesus' sacrifice on the cross of Calvary, you have been offered a gift of life. Jesus - the *Living Water*, will wash away your sin. You are cleansed through the Messiah's blood, and robed in His righteousness. It is through the *glory* of *Christ's resurrection*, that you will walk in His light. By the *Power of God's Spirit*, you can bask in the *promise* of an *eternal relationship* with the Lord. Proclaimed within the *shadow, blood, glory,* and *power of His cross*, you can find access to the Father. It is yours for the asking if you simply believe! *Do you believe?* Is Jesus the Lord of your life? After coming to this point of our devotional study, *how has your perspective on Jesus changed?* Do you see Him in a different light? *Do you feel as if you're closer to Him now than before you started?* Take a moment to share your thoughts in the space below.

_____

_____

_____

_____

_____

_____

_____

_____

_____

_____

_____

_____

_____

_____

_____

_____

The Shadow, Blood, Glory, and Power

Do you see the shadow of the cross upon the ground?
>Do you see the blood of Christ? Redemption there is found!
Do you see the Glory of the Cross of Calvary?
>Do you see the Power that hereby sets you free?
Do you see the reason of the cross where Jesus died?
>Why He shed His precious blood ..., as He was crucified;
He became the Sacrifice, God had promised years before,
>The Sacrificial Lamb of God, who could ask for more?

Do you see the glory of the cross of Calvary?
>Do you see the meaning it holds for you and me?
The sting of death He overcame, victory o'er the grave;
>That direful tomb can never more our bodies to enslave!
Do you see the power within that wooden tree?
>Do you know that yet today it sets believers free?
Alters lives of those who come, who give their hearts to Him,
>Changes evilness to good, forgives man's earthly sin!

The shadow of the cross of Christ still lingers on and on,
>"While earth remains," He promised, "it never will be gone;"
Until the day of His return, to gather up "His bride,"
>Seed-time and harvest, winter, spring, summer, fall will abide.
Come beneath the shadow of that old rugged cross,
>Partake of the blood of salvation, no longer to be lost;
Revel in the glory of the great resurrection day,
>The power of the Cross of Christ is the only way!

The shadow and blood and glory, is beckoning you today,
>Do not wait any longer, come now, please---don't delay;
The power of God is waiting, to give you life anew,
>The arms of Jesus are open, He's waiting in heaven for you!
There are four that bear witness, of God's infinite love,
>Great joys await the believer, in that precious home above;
The Cross of Jesus, the Savior, provides the open door---
>The Shadow, Blood, and Glory, along with the Power, these four.
>>In the name of the Lord, Jesus Christ. Amen & Amen
>>>Clarice D. Cook

Day 26

The Savior's Eyes

Scriptural Reflection

But the eyes of the Lord are on those who fear him, on those whose hope is in his unfailing love, to deliver them from death and keep them alive in famine. *Psalm 33: 18, 19 NIV*

My frame was not hidden from You, When I was made in secret, and skillfully wrought in the lowest parts of the earth. Your eyes saw my substance, being yet unformed. And in Your book, they all were written, the days fashioned for me, when as yet there were none of them. How precious also are Your thoughts to me, O God! How great is the sum of them! *Psalm 139: 15-17 NKJV*

"To the angel of the church in Thyatira write: These are the words of the Son of God, whose eyes are like blazing fire and whose feet are like burnished bronze. I know your deeds, your love and faith, your service and perseverance, and that you are now doing more than you did at first. *Revelation 2: 18, 19 NIV*

Jesus said to him, "I am the way, the truth, and the life. No one comes to the Father except through Me. "If you had known Me, you would have known My Father also; and from now on you know Him and have seen Him." *John 14: 6,7 NIV*

Before we move forward with today's devotional consideration, it's important to recognize some *doctrinal* information that is relevant to to better understand the main topic of this discussion. Because of *God's glory*, no man can look upon Him and live to tell about it. Even Moses, the mighty deliverer of Israel was not allowed to look upon the face of God the Father. Literally, within our human form, we would be totally vaporized if we dared look upon the Father's glory. According to the scriptures, it's not just mankind who can't look upon the overwhelming radiance of God, neither can the angelic hosts of heaven. In the Gospel of John 1:18, we are reminded of Jesus' words involving this very topic. No one has ever stood face to face with the Father other than Jesus. His glory; His radiance; His brilliance; even His very nature is completely beyond our human comprehension. God the Father is Spirit and He is Power. Is it no wonder that Jesus took on human form in order for mankind to finally be able to relationally access the Almighty?

> And the Lord said, "I will cause all my goodness to pass in front of you, and I will proclaim my name, the Lord, in your presence. I will have mercy on whom I will have mercy, and I will have compassion on whom I will have compassion. But," he said, "you cannot see my face, for no one may see me and live." Then the Lord said, "There is a place near me where you may stand on a rock. When my glory passes by, I will put you in a cleft in the rock and cover you with my hand until I have passed by. Then I will remove my hand and you will see my back; but my face must not be seen." *(Exodus 33:19-23 NIV).*

The Trinity is a rather difficult concept for mankind to wrap their brain around. *God is three in one – Father, Son,* and *Holy Spirit.* One God, in *three distinct persons.* Some folks like to think of it as three different forms as a means to better understand this miraculous wonder. But make no mistake, to consider them a mere form, not only limits, but completely minimizes the truth as to Who each of these persons, (three yet one), really are. Of course, that's the part which makes this concept so difficult for any of us to understand.

But, for explanatory purpose, let's move forward in agreeing that in a sense, the three in one concept is similar to the way humans are created. We have a *physical nature* with a *spiritual form* contained within a *soul*, which is maintained through a *mind* that operates with an *intellectual capacity*. Each of these attributes are independent in nature, while also contained and connected within the same form. These distinct capacities collaborate in order to make us who we are. Without our mind, body, and soul we would never exist and since we've been told that we have been created in the image of God, we too are designed with three distinct attributes that are reflective of the Triune God. However, it is important to bring all of this back to the realization that somehow, in God's miraculous capacity each of these distinct attributes are defined as persons; not roles, attributes, or forms.

The Triune God is embodied within the designation of the Father. He is the *omniscient* (all-knowing), *omnipresent* (all-encompassing in all places), *omnipotent* (all-powerful); Spirit of benevolent glory, grace, love, and mercy. The conduit that shares these miraculous attributes with humanity is contained within the form of the *Holy Spirit*. It is through the Holy Spirit that all of God's blessings flow into the world and over our lives. God's glory is revealed through the work of the Holy Spirit. God's power is released through the gifts of the Holy Spirit. God's holiness is recognized through the touch of the Holy Spirit. His mercy is manifested through the diligence of the Holy Spirit.

That brings us to the third person of the Trinity. The *expression of the Father's voice* comes to us through the *Word of God*, Jesus, the Son of God. It is the Word that spoke all of creation into existence. It is the Word that brings light into the world. It is the *Word that became flesh* and dwelt among us. It is the Word that shares *God's grace* with the world. It is the Word that *provides access* to the Father through relationship.

The first chapter of John's Gospel provides deep insight into the *pre-eminence of Jesus*, that is He has *always been* and *will always be*. It also helps to understand the truth regarding the Trinity that God was, is, and will always be three in one as verse seventeen and eighteen reinforce the notion that no one has ever seen God, but the Son comes from the Father and it is God that has declared the name of Jesus. The Bible often refers to Jesus as the Word. The first chapter of John is probably one of the most notable passages in the New Testament and it clearly declares the miraculous wonder involving the intimate details, defining the Word of God.

> In the beginning was the Word, and the Word was with God, and the Word was God. He was in the beginning with God. All things were made through Him, and without Him nothing was made that was made. In Him was life, and the life was the light of men. And the light shines in the darkness, and the darkness did not comprehend it.

> [10] He was in the world, and the world was made through Him, and the world did not know Him. He came to His own, and His own did not receive Him. But as many as received Him, to them He gave the right to become children of God, to those who believe in His name: who were born, not of blood, nor of the will of the flesh, nor of the will of man, but of God. And the Word became flesh and dwelt among us, and we beheld His glory, the glory as of the only begotten of the Father, full of grace and truth.

> [16] And of His fullness we have all received, and grace for grace. For the law was given through Moses, but grace and truth came through Jesus Christ. No one has seen God at any time. The only begotten Son, who is in the bosom of the Father, He has declared Him, *(John 1:1-5, 10-14, 16-18 NKJV).*

Since Jesus is the Word, that became flesh and dwelt among us, we can now experience God's *grace and truth in tangible ways*. Because of the Word, we can experience God through our human senses. We can hear, touch, feel, and see God's grace in profound ways. That is the very essence of today's topic. When Jesus was crucified on the cross, Joseph of Arimathea went to the Roman authorities and requested to have the Teacher's body released to him to bury the Lord in the newly chiseled tomb within the confines of a lush, nearby garden. After Jesus was taken down off of the cross, He was wrapped in a burial shroud and placed in the newly hewn tomb, one intended to be used for Joseph after his own death.

It was in this solemn place that the body of the Lord was laid to rest. The stone was rolled in front of the tomb opening, just moments before the setting sun ushered in the Sabbath. As soon as the tomb had been sealed, and the Roman Guard assumed their position to watch over the dead body of Jesus, all of the followers of Jesus scurried home in order to comply with the Levitical Law that forbid the breaking of the Sabbath. From the setting sun on what we refer to as Good Friday, until the sun set on the following day, the Jews were required to rest, and to not engage in any sort of work-related duties. So, there they were, no place to go and nothing to do except wait for the longest of nights, and the passing of the day to mournfully reflect on the tragedy of the Teacher's death.

Painfully, Jesus' followers endured their overwhelming suffering throughout this unforgettable *Sabbath* from Friday at sunset, through Saturday, and continuing into the early morning hours of Sunday. Their agony was reminiscent of the prophetic words of Jeremiah regarding the events immediately following Jesus' birth when Herod ordered the killing of the innocent male babies, two-years old and younger in the region surrounding the peace filled town of Bethlehem.

> A voice was heard in Ramah,
> Weeping and great mourning,
> Rachel weeping for her children;
> And she refused to be comforted,
> Because they were no more, *(Matthew 2:18 NASB).*

All of the followers of Jesus, along with His mother Mary, were filled with unconsolable heartbreak. It's easy to imagine that they were completely exhausted after enduring several days of relentless horror that involved the arrest, trial, scourging, and crucifixion of their Lord. But a new morning was about to dawn. With the arrival of that new day came a new age. The *Age of Grace was about to be revealed*. Within the fellowship of Jesus' most devoted followers was a woman named Mary of Magdala. If you and I were to be honest, we'd probably say that we could relate to Mary and the challenging circumstance of her life. She was a great sinner who had made a mess out of her tormented existence. That is, until she encountered Jesus and her life was changed forever. She *found forgiveness in the loving eyes of her Lord*, and she became one of His most fervent followers. In fact, she was one of the few who wasn't too afraid to make her way to Golgotha to stand by the side of Mary, the mother of Jesus and the disciple whom the Teacher loved throughout the horrific experience of the crucifixion.

Mary of Magdala was just one of thousands of people that encountered Jesus in such a way that their life was completely changed during His three-year ministry. The Bible is filled with a multitude of miraculous stories similar to hers. But her capstone experience within the biblical narrative comes in the early morning hours of the Sunday that followed Jesus' death. *Mary was the first* of the followers to encounter the resurrected Jesus. In fact, the scripture shares that at first, she didn't even recognize the Lord. She mistook Him for the gardener. Take a moment to carefully reflect on the following passage:

> But Mary stood outside facing the tomb, crying. As she was crying, she stooped to look into the tomb. She saw two angels in white sitting there, one at the head and one at the feet, where Jesus' body had been lying. They said to her, "Woman, why are you crying?" "Because they've taken away my Lord," she told them, "And I don't know where they've put Him." Having said this, she turned around and saw Jesus standing there, though she did not know it was Jesus. "Woman," Jesus said to her, "why are you crying? Who is it you are looking for?" Supposing He was the gardener, she replied, "Sir, if you've removed Him, tell me where you've put Him, and I will take Him away." Jesus said, "Mary." Turning around, she said to Him in Hebrew, "Rabbouni! — which means "Teacher." "Don't cling to Me," Jesus told her, "For I have not yet ascended to the Father. But go to My brothers and tell them that I am ascending to My Father and your Father—to My God and your God," *(John 20:11-17 HCSB).*

Maybe it was the depth of despair that had consumed Mary from the events of the last few days. Could that have been what limited her ability to realize she was talking to the resurrected Jesus? As an eye-witness to His death, it was possible that her mind couldn't equate the gardener to actually being her Lord. After all, she witnessed all of the horror. She saw the soldier thrust the spear into her Lord's chest, that allowed a river of blood and water to rush out of His side. She was there when they lowered her Master off the cross, wrapped Him in the burial cloth, before carrying Him off to be placed in Joseph's tomb. She witnessed the sealing of that tomb, and knew beyond a shadow of a doubt that the Teacher was dead.

Personally, I believe that Mary didn't acknowledge Jesus because of the *glory of His resurrected body*. The reality of His magnificent transformation must have blinded her ability to recognize the earthly image of the Jesus that she had come to know. Regardless of why she didn't initially identify Jesus; there is a significant point that is hidden within the context of the previous passage involving Mary. She turned around to look at Jesus the instant after He called her by name, *Mary!* There can no denying that when Jesus calls your name, and if you choose to turn around to see Him for who He truly is, your *eyes will be opened to the glorious splendor of His mercy and grace.* When you finally heed His call, turn toward Him and stare into the eyes of the resurrected Savior, your life will be changed forever!

So, I close with a few questions regarding today's devotion. *Have you gotten close enough to actually look into the eyes of Jesus? If you have, what have you seen, felt, or experienced? If you haven't, what do you need to do to draw closer to Him so that you can look into His eyes and realize His love?* Remember, if you diligently seek after Him, He will draw near to you! Take a moment to write down your thoughts regarding those questions.

_____

_____

_____

_____

_____

_____

_____

_____

_____

_____

_____

_____

_____

The Savior's Eyes

I had seen Him from a distance, as I lived from day to day,
      But I never really knew Him, as I walked along my way,
I had listened to the stories of His mercy, grace, and love,
      He came to us from heaven . . . Redemption from above.
Yet, I really never knew Him, I never heard His call,
      I never knew He loved me. How could He care at all?
But then one day I heard His voice - calling out my name,
      As I struggled in this lonely world, embarrassed by my shame;
My life was scarred by failure - cloaked in a shroud of brokenness,
      I was weary from my journey, and I longed to find sweet rest!

My eyes rested upon the Savior, as I wallowed in deep pain,
      He told me that He loved me! I would never be the same!
I looked into the Savior's eyes; I found forgiveness through His grace,
      He saved me from my sin and shame; He chose to take my place.
I glanced into His mournful eyes as He died upon that tree,
      When He paid the price for my broken life, on a cross at Calvary.
Miraculously, I saw the Light of the Resurrected Lord,
      Who conquered death! He's alive today, and lives forever more!
I stared into My Savior's eyes as He said "I love you child,
      Now take My hand and let Me come - sit with you awhile."

I looked into my Savior's eyes, as I chose to ask Him in,
      His eyes were filled with tenderness, with forgiveness for my sin.
I've gazed into my Savior's eyes, as we've walked along our way,
      I've found His strength, and wisdom would guide me every day.
I've glanced away from my Savior's eyes, when I have failed the test.
      Yet, He merely says "I love you - I know you've done your best."
I've peered into my Savior's eyes, and I've seen God's glory shine,
      Redemption offered freely, through God's grace and love divine.

      Lanny K. Cook

The angel said to the women, "Do not be afraid, for I know that you are looking for Jesus, who was crucified. He is not here; he has risen, just as he said. Come and see the place where he lay. Then go quickly and tell his disciples: 'He has risen from the dead and is going ahead of you into Galilee. There you will see him.' Now I have told you."
(Matthew 28:5-7 NIV).

Day 27
Salvation's Hand
Scriptural Reflection

Immediately Jesus made the disciples get into the boat and go on ahead of him to the other side, while he dismissed the crowd. After he had dismissed them, he went up on a mountainside by himself to pray. Later that night, he was there alone, and the boat was already a considerable distance from land, buffeted by the waves because the wind was against it. Shortly before dawn Jesus went out to them, walking on the lake. When the disciples saw him walking on the lake, they were terrified. "It's a ghost," they said, and cried out in fear. But Jesus immediately said to them: "Take courage! It is I. Don't be afraid." "Lord, if it's you," Peter replied, "tell me to come to you on the water." "Come," he said. Then Peter got down out of the boat, walked on the water, and came toward Jesus. But when he saw the wind, he was afraid and, beginning to sink, cried out, "Lord, save me!" Immediately Jesus reached out his hand and caught him. "You of little faith," he said, "why did you doubt?" And when they climbed into the boat, the wind died down. Then those who were in the boat worshiped him, saying, "Truly you are the Son of God."
Matthew 14:22-33 NIV

A man with leprosy came and knelt before him and said, "Lord, if you are willing, you can make me clean." Jesus reached out his hand and touched the man. "I am willing," he said. "Be clean!" Immediately he was cleansed of his leprosy. Then Jesus said to him, "See that you don't tell anyone. But go, show yourself to the priest and offer the gift Moses commanded, as a testimony to them." *Matthew 8:2-4 NIV*

Now when they had left the multitude, they took Him along in the boat as He was. And other little boats were also with Him. And a great windstorm arose, and the waves beat into the boat, so that it was already filling. But He was in the stern, asleep on a pillow. And they awoke Him and said to Him, "Teacher, do You not care that we are perishing?" Then He arose and rebuked the wind, and said to the sea, "Peace⌐ be still!" And the wind ceased and there was a great calm. But He said to them, "Why are you so fearful? How is it that you have no faith?" *Mark 4:36-40 NKJV*

Within the topic of today's lesson, when I take a moment to reflect on the concept of Salvation's hand, my mind immediately wanders to the life of Simon Peter. I think of him as a rough and tumble kind of guy. Truly *Peter was a man's man!* When I think of Peter, I think of the movie, Fiddler on the Roof. I think of Tevye the milkman! A simple, hard-working family man whose softer side is always finding a way to have a conversation with God! Within those many conversations, he asks a multitude of perplexing questions, trying to find answers to the difficult challenges of life and the circumstances that he finds himself in within his small, quaint, village. Now when I find myself pondering the character of Tevye the milkman, my mind can't help but wander to the music shared within that classic Broadway Musical. Of course, the theme song *Fiddler on the Roof* is unforgettable, but the two songs that literally strike a chord in my heart, and cause me to burst out in song (at least when nobody else is around), are *Traditions*, and *If I Were a Rich Man*.

So, in my mind, Tevye and Peter are kindred spirits. Even though Peter was an uncultured, Jewish fisherman who was more than a bit ragged around the edges; I think that both could have been cut from the same batch of Jewish cloth. Refinement was not part of Peter's genetic makeup, although he was obviously strong-willed, impulsive, and overly brash. The Gospel accounts of Peter provide evidence that he most often engaged his mouth before engaging his brain. He was a man of action, and he was never afraid to be the first of Jesus' men to stand up in any situation.

But behind that brash, bold exterior I think that maybe Peter lacked a bit of self-confidence. If you could take a look into the heart of this rock of a man, you'd probably see some serious self-doubt. Even though it was Thomas who earned the title of being the "doubter" out of the gaggle of Jesus' original twelve chosen, Simon Peter seemed to be the one who was always being called out or corrected by Jesus. The continued rebuke of Peter for his brash behaviors and careless words must have created at least some sense of doubt deep inside him.

It was Peter who took Jesus aside to rebuke Him for speaking prophetic words concerning His upcoming suffering and death.

> From that time Jesus began to show to His disciples that He must go to Jerusalem, and suffer many things from the elders and chief priests and scribes, and be killed, and be raised the

third day. Then Peter took Him aside and began to rebuke Him, saying, "Far be it from You, Lord; this shall not happen to You!" But He turned and said to Peter, "Get behind Me, Satan! You are an offense to Me, for you are not mindful of the things of God, but the things of men," *(Matthew 16:21-23 NKJV)*.

It was Peter, along with James and John who fell asleep while Jesus prayed in the garden, and it wasn't just once that they they couldn't stay awake as Jesus went deep into the garden to pray. Even after coming back the first time and rebuking them for falling asleep, they couldn't manage to keep their eyes open. When Jesus came back the second time, all three were still sleeping so He quietly retreated back into the garden to pray for the third time.

> Then Jesus came with them to a place called Gethsemane, and said to the disciples, "Sit here while I go and pray over there." And He took with Him Peter and the two sons of Zebedee, and He began to be sorrowful and deeply distressed. Then He said to them, "My soul is exceedingly sorrowful, even to death. Stay here and watch with Me." He went a little farther and fell on His face, and prayed, saying, "O My Father, if it is possible, let this cup pass from Me; nevertheless, not as I will, but as You will." Then He came to the disciples and found them sleeping, and said to Peter, "What! Could you not watch with Me one hour? Watch and pray, lest you enter into temptation. The spirit indeed is willing, but the flesh is weak." Again, a second time, He went away and prayed, saying, "O My Father, if this cup cannot pass away from Me unless I drink it, Your will be done." And He came and found them asleep again, for their eyes were heavy. So He left them, went away again, and prayed the third time, saying the same words. Then He came to His disciples and said to them, "Are you still sleeping and resting? Behold, the hour is at hand, and the Son of Man is being betrayed into the hands of sinners. Rise, let us be going. See, My betrayer is at hand," *(Matthew 26:36-46 NIV)*.

Peter was also the one who boasted that he would never forsake the Lord, even if everyone else ran away in fear. Once again, Jesus had to put him back into his place by rebuking him; informing Peter of his upcoming denial. But even then, Peter responds to the Lord with that boastful pride that seemed to be his personal trademark.

> Peter answered and said to Him, "Even if all are made to stumble because of You, I will never be made to stumble." Jesus said to him, "Assuredly, I say to you that this night, before the rooster crows, you will deny Me three times." Peter said to Him, "Even if I have to die with You, I will not deny You!" And so said all the disciples, (Matthew 26:33-35 NKJV).

Just a few verses later in the same chapter of Matthew's Gospel, we read that the Lord's prediction came true as Peter denied knowing Him three times before the rooster crowed. Surely, this was the overwhelming, culminating circumstance that caused Peter to run and hide, doubting everything he had learned over the past several years.

> Now Peter sat outside in the courtyard. And a servant girl came to him, saying, "You also were with Jesus of Galilee." But he denied it before them all, saying, "I do not know what you are saying." And when he had gone out to the gateway, another girl saw him and said to those who were there, "This fellow also was with Jesus of Nazareth." But again he denied with an oath, "I do not know the Man!" And a little later those who stood by came up and said to Peter, "Surely you also are one of them, for your speech betrays you." Then he began to curse and swear, saying, "I do not know the Man!" Immediately a rooster crowed. [75] And Peter remembered the word of Jesus who had said to him, "Before the rooster crows, you will deny Me three times." So he went out and wept bitterly, (Matthew 26:69-75 NKJV).

Finally, on the night Jesus was betrayed, it was Peter who pulled out his sword and cut-off the ear of the High Priest's servant before Jesus rebuked him yet again. Apparently, Peter had forgotten that Jesus was the One to calm the waters. At the time, he never imagined that his Master would attempt to try to calm him down. After all, Peter was fighting for their lives and simply trying to protect his Rabbi. That wasn't God's plan or purpose, and Peter had yet to understand any of that. Of course, as seemed to always be the case, Jesus had to clean up Peter's mess as the Man of Miracles reattached the servant's ear.

Then He asked them again, "Whom are you seeking?" And they said, "Jesus of Nazareth." Jesus answered, "I have told you that I am *He.* Therefore, if you seek Me, let these go their way," that the saying might be fulfilled which He spoke, "Of those whom You gave Me I have lost none." Then Simon Peter, having a sword, drew it and struck the high priest's servant, and cut off his right ear. The servant's name was Malchus. So Jesus said to Peter, "Put your sword into the sheath. Shall I not drink the cup which My Father has given Me?" *(John 18:7-11 NKJV).*

All of these examples show the inadequacies of Peter, and the blundering mistakes that seemed to follow him nearly everywhere, I can't help but to relate to the kind of person that he was. I think you probably can as well. All of us have doubts, insecurities, and most often simply muddle our way through life. But hope arrives when I reflect on the days of preparation that carried Peter into his calling to be the Rock on which Jesus built His Church. The time of preparation that these chosen ones endured is what built their faith, and taught them to place their complete trust in their Teacher.

As I take the time to ponder the faith that was developed in Peter over the course of time spent with Jesus, I'm reminded of the passage I shared in the scriptural reference at the beginning of today's devotion. The one contained in Matthew 14:22-33, if you want to go back and read it again to refresh your memory. When Peter jumped out of that boat during the horrendous storm to answer his Master's call; I am encouraged and inspired regarding the amount of faith that must have taken on Peter's part.

With Jesus approaching their vessel, as the thunder rumbled all about and the waves were crashing at His feet, Peter was fine as long as he kept his eyes focused on Jesus. But when he became distracted by the wind, the waves, and the thunder that surrounded him; he sank like a rock. Maybe that was part of the Lord's sense of humor. Maybe not. But regardless, Jesus was right there to save Peter from his distracted, lack of faith. Jesus reached down into the watery abyss that threatened to become Peter's grave, grasped his hand and pulled him out of the waves and drew him close to the safety and protection of His own chest. It was

Salvation's hand that reach down to save Peter from his doubting plight on that momentous occasion.

Jesus saw Peter for who he was created to be. The very first time they met; Jesus called Simon "Peter." The rough and reckless fisherman was, in Jesus' eyes, a firm and faithful rock of devotion. Because Peter was willing to leave all he had to follow the Rabbi, God used him in great ways. Just as Jesus had proclaimed, Peter became the Rock on which He built His Church. And the gates of hell have not prevailed against it. As Peter shared the Gospel message around the land, people were amazed at his bold and sound teaching, especially since he was "unschooled" and "ordinary" when compared to all of the recognized teachers in Israel. The Rock, became the first Pope of the organized Catholic Church.

Spending years following Jesus made all the difference in Peter's life. He was called by the Lord's grace, and justified by Salvation's hand. The same strong, powerfully gentle hand that lifted Peter out of the torrential waters, is reaching out to you. Right now, at this very moment. If you are immersed in the depths of a personal storm, all you need to do is reach up and allow Salvation's hand to lift you out of the despair of your circumstance. *Do you see the hand of Jesus reaching down to save your life? Will you take His hand, or will you take your chances and try to swim to safety under your own power?* Take a moment to share a time when you were caught in a storm and Jesus took you by the hand.

_____

_____

_____

_____

_____

_____

_____

_____

Salvation's Hand

The journey of a lifetime, is filled with many trials,
    As you seek to find life's answers, as you trek across the miles.
Scan the far horizon, in search of distant dreams,
    Without a light to guide your path, you drift through stormy seas.
So, reach out to stroke the precious hand, of God's perfect, baby boy,
    Who was sent into this dreary world, to fill your heart with joy.
Touch the hand of this Holy Child, and behold a wondrous sight,
    As His mother draws Him close to her, on a cold and starry night.
He was born amidst the hay and straw, in a lowly manger stall,
    Angel's glory spread the light, while shepherds heard the call.
The stillness of that glorious night, would change earth's destiny,
    While shepherds watched with wonderment, upon a bended knee.
Reach out and touch the hand of One, who keeps watch upon the fold,
    Who tends His sheep and keeps them safe, as in the days of old.
He is the Shepherd to God's children, His staff protects each one,
    As He reaches out and draws you close, He is God's Only Son!
The innocence of the Holy Child, would shine throughout His life,
    He touches hearts of sinful men, and frees them from their strife.
Reach out and touch the hand of One, known as the Carpenter,
    His callused hands are cut and bruised, yet perfect, true, and pure.
Hands made strong through endless days, of working in His trade,
    With hammers, saws, and chisels, crafted wonders He has made.
An artisan, whose love is wood, He chisels, planes, then sands,
    To smooth each piece of lumber, with rugged, craftsman's hands.
Reach out and touch the hand of One, whose miracles proclaim,
    His love for those lost in sin.... the blind, the sick, the lame.
His healing hands reach out to those, who cannot find their way,
    Those who walk in darkness, and struggle through each day!
He blessed the bread and broke it, as the multitudes were fed!
    He is the door to eternal life; He raised men from the dead!
Reach out and grasp the hand of One, who calms the raging sea,
    His word can calm the torrent, when you seek Him prayerfully.
With His hand He draws you to Himself, He wipes away your tears,
    He knows your pain and suffering, and calms your many fears.
His gentle touch, His calming voice, calls you to seek His face,
    To choose the path that leads to Him, to accept God's gift of grace.
Reach out and touch the hand of One, who died upon that tree,
    He was born to be the sacrifice.... He arose to set you free!
His nail-scarred hands reach out to you, beckoning from above,
    So, take His hand and follow Him, May He fill your heart with love.
Let Him lead you on His path, as you walk along the way,
    May His light forever guide you, as you travel day by day!

Lanny K. Cook

213

Day 28
The Promise of His Word
Scriptural Reflection

In the beginning was the Word, and the Word was with God and the Word was God. He was in the beginning with God. All things were made through Him and without Him nothing was made that was made. In Him was life, and the life was the light of men. And the light shines in the darkness, and the darkness did not comprehend it. And the Word became flesh and dwelt among us, and we beheld His glory, the glory as of the only begotten of the Father, full of grace and truth. *John 1:1-4 & 14 NIV*

The tempter came to him and said, "If you are the Son of God, tell these stones to become bread." Jesus answered, "It is written: 'Man shall not live on bread alone, but on every word that comes from the mouth of God.'" *Matthew 4: 3-4 NIV*

What advantage, then, is there in being a Jew, or what value is there in circumcision? Much in every way! First of all, the Jews have been entrusted with the very words of God. *Romans 3:1,2 NIV*

In the past God spoke to our ancestors through the prophets at many times and in various ways, but in these last days he has spoken to us by his Son, whom he appointed heir of all things, and through whom also he made the universe. The Son is the radiance of God's glory and the exact representation of his being, sustaining all things by his powerful word. After he had provided purification for sins, he sat down at the right hand of the Majesty in heaven. So he became as much superior to the angels as the name he has inherited is superior to theirs. *Hebrews 1:1-4 NIV*

Now that you have purified yourselves by obeying the truth so that you have sincere love for each other, love one another deeply, from the heart. For you have been born again, not of perishable seed, but of imperishable, through the living and enduring word of God. *1 Peter 1:22, 23 NIV*

Israel's purpose was divinely inspired and centered on being a spiritual blessing to humanity. That blessing was manifest in the mystery of the incarnation of God—*Emmanuel*, translated as *God with us*, as He took on the flesh of humanity in the form of the one named Jesus. Philip Yancey, in his book *The Jesus I Never Knew*, said this about the Messiah who made His arrival in Israel 2,000 years ago: "Jesus did not come close to satisfying the lavish hopes of the Jews. The opposite happened: within a generation Roman soldiers razed Jerusalem to the ground. The young Christian church accepted the destruction of the temple as a sign of the end of the covenant between God and Israel, and after the first century very few Jews converted to Christianity."[6]

The realization of this Messianic blessing was the initial earthly step in the establishment of God's Kingdom. But *God's plan of salvation would take thousands of years for this initial stage to be realized* and thousands more for the plan to come into full fruition. According to the *Life Application Study Bible*, "Paul had a vision of a church where all Jews and Gentiles would be united in their love of God and in obedience to Christ. While respecting God's law, this ideal church would look to Christ alone for salvation. A person's ethnic background and social status would be irrelevant—what mattered would be his or her faith in Christ. But Paul's vision has not yet been realized. God chose the Jews, just as he chose the Gentiles, and he is still working to unite Jew and Gentile in a new Israel, a new Jerusalem, ruled by his Son."[7]

Paul's vision will find fulfillment, but not during this age. It will only be realized within the Millennial Reign of Christ. As previously discussed during the Day 28 devotion, in Romans 11, he provides insight into the mystery of God's plan for the nation of Israel and the Jewish people. I believe this passage of Scripture has profound insight into Israel's role during the last days, which, of course, actually began with the advent of the Church Age after the resurrected Christ's ascension to heaven and the pouring out of the Holy Spirit on the Day of Pentecost.

---

[6] Phillip Yancey, *The Jesus I Never Knew* (Grand Rapids, MI: Zondervan, 1995), p. 53.

[7] *Life Application Study Bible: New International Version* (Wheaton, IL: Tyndale House Publishers, Inc., 1998, 1989, 1990, 1991), p. 2428.

Did God reject his people? By no means! I am an Israelite myself, a descendant of Abraham, from the tribe of Benjamin. God did not reject his people, whom he foreknew. . . Again I ask: Did they stumble so as to fall beyond recovery? Not at all! Rather, because of their transgression, salvation has come to the Gentiles to make Israel envious. But if their transgression means riches for the world, and their loss means riches for the Gentiles, how much greater riches will their full inclusion bring,
(Romans 11:1–2, 11–12 NIV).

It is necessary to highlight several points in these verses that could easily be skimmed over and ignored. Israel's transgressions brought riches to the world when they rejected Jesus, which was of great benefit to the rest of us, as the *Gospel was proclaimed first to the Jews and then the Gentiles.* This is a pretty straightforward point that was accepted in Paul's ministry and the early beginnings of the Church. However, Paul makes a bold and deeply profound statement in the final verse when he states, *there will be even greater riches involved when God's chosen race is brought into full inclusion.* He also states, *how much greater riches will their full inclusion bring.* Paul specifically shares that God's chosen race will be included in the *glory of God's promise* through the *grace* of the Lord Jesus Christ. Paul's letter to the church in Ephesus is a sound inference to this *mystery regarding Israel* and the Church, together as one for the purposes of God, which, of course, can only happen through the blood of Christ.

Therefore, remember that formerly you who are Gentiles by birth and called "uncircumcised" by those who call themselves "the circumcision" (which is done in the body by human hands)—remember that at that time you were separate from Christ, excluded from citizenship in Israel and foreigners to the covenants of the promise, without hope and without God in the world. But now in Christ Jesus you who once were far away have been brought near by the blood of Christ.

For he himself is our peace, who has made the two groups one and has destroyed the barrier, the dividing wall of hostility, by setting aside in his flesh the law with its commands and regulations. His purpose was to create in himself one new humanity out of the two, thus making peace, and in one body to reconcile both of them to God through the cross, by which he put to death their hostility. He came and preached peace to you who were far away and peace to those who were near. For through him we both have access to the Father by one Spirit.

Consequently, you are no longer foreigners and strangers, but fellow citizens with God's people and also members of his household, built on the foundation of the apostles and prophets, with Christ Jesus himself as the chief cornerstone. In him the whole building is joined together and rises to become a holy temple in the Lord. And in him you too are being built together to become a dwelling in which God lives by his Spirit, *(Ephesians 2:11–22 NIV)*.

The illustration of a structure in this passage provides an interesting analogy to the **architectural design of God's plan** of salvation. Christ, who is the visible image of the invisible God, is the Chief Cornerstone. The dynamic of that insight is actually something that is worth pondering for a moment before moving forward. Within the concept of constructing a building, the **cornerstone** is the first stone that is set. The rest of the stones are placed in relation to this specific stone. The cornerstone is the determining factor for the position and the integrity of the entire structure. According to Paul, the foundation of God's holy temple is built on the apostles and prophets of Israel. The rest of the building—Jews and Gentiles—are joined together through Christ.

God's promise is intricately wrapped within numerous covenants which He entered into with Israel. Ultimately, His plan of redemption doesn't just involve just the Church, but also His Chosen people, the Jew. This reference involves Jesus' words regarding Jerusalem's destiny as found in the Gospel of Matthew. But now, this takes us back to Israel. Reflect on the message that I shared from the 2nd edition of The Mystery of Zion – Israel and the Last Days.

In essence, this was not only the Messiah bidding His beloved city of peace farewell, it was a parting, prophetic word declaring that He would see them again, at a future date. His final words indicate the necessity for the elder son (remember the parable of the prodigal son?) to recognize and then declare that the Messiah, *is* the blessed One who returns in the name of the Father.

Jerusalem, Jerusalem, you who kill the prophets and stone those sent to you, how often I have longed to gather your children together, as a hen gathers her chicks under her wings, and you were not willing. Look, your house is left to you desolate. For I tell you, you will not see me again until you say, 'Blessed is he who comes in the name of the Lord,' *(Matthew 23:37-39 NIV).*

The aforementioned scriptures provide undeniable, biblical evidence that address at least part of the mystery, involving Israel's continued existence; not just for today, but through the end of the ages. Jesus' prophetic words involving the descendants of Abraham, divinely confirm the authenticity regarding Israel's promised hope.

The dependability and inerrancy of scripture demands the existence of Israel not only for a future time but also through the end of time. Why? Because they are foretold within the Word of God. Since God is sovereign, there is no denying His purpose or plan. Not even the gates of hell can prevail against them! Neither can the misinterpretation of scripture by the finite mind of humanity stand against the divine appointment of Israel.

To bring this section to a close as it relates to the Mystery of the Kingdom, it's important to connect Israel's role to the Day of the Lord. If you accept the concept of this "Day" being the reference to the Millennial Reign of Christ, followed by the end of the ages, then it is easy to recognize Israel's part within that time frame.

But do not forget this one thing, dear friends: With the Lord a day is like a thousand years, and a thousand years are like a day. The Lord is not slow in keeping his promise, as some understand slowness. Instead he is patient with you, not wanting anyone to perish, but everyone to come to repentance. But the day of the Lord will come like a thief. The heavens will disappear with a roar; the elements will be destroyed by fire, and the earth and everything done in it will be laid bare, *(2 Peter 3:8–10 NIV).*

Israel is completely woven throughout the tapestry of God's purpose, leading up to the Day of the Lord. In fact, when the "Day" arrives, His plan of salvation will be complete. It all started with the Abrahamic Covenant, which ultimately birthed the nation of Israel. It continued on through the remaining Covenants; the Mosaic, Palestinian, Davidic, New Covenant of Grace, and finally, the New Covenant with Israel. Through it all, Israel was intricately written into the promises of God Almighty. Just as the "Day of the Lord" brings God's plan of redemption to completion, so does Israel's role in the salvation of humanity come back around full-circle. Israel has always played a leading role on the stage of God's redeeming love.[8]

The Promise of God's Word involving His plan for the redemption of mankind is both intimately and intricately contained within *His Covenants*. Israel has always been the recipient of those agreements, but she was never intended to be the sole beneficiary to the blessing of God's promise. However, Israel served as the conduit that brought the Jewish Jesus, (the Word), into this world. Jesus became the *fulfillment of the Levitical Laws*, while those very same Laws became the instrument of condemnation; causing the Sacrificial Lamb of God to be executed on the cross. However, God has not abandoned Israel, as she holds the key to Jesus' Second Coming.

To close out today's devotion, it's important to leave with this one main point written upon your heart. Jesus' death produced a new promise, a *New Covenant* that was offered to both *Gentiles, and Jews*. That Promise, is literally spelled out in probably the most infamous scripture within the entire Bible, found in the Gospel of John.

> For God so loved the world that He gave His only begotten Son, that whoever believes in Him should not perish but have everlasting life. For God did not send His Son into the world to condemn the world, but that the world through Him might be saved, (John 3:16, 17 NKJV).

Too often as Christians, we throw out the sixteenth verse of this profound proclamation of God's promise, like candy in a big parade; but we are reluctant to consider the seventeenth verse. So, let's simply end today's lesson with a few simple questions. First, do you completely agree with verse sixteen? *Do you believe in God's only begotten Son*

---

[8]   Lanny K. Cook, *The Mystery of Zion – Israel and the Last Days, 2nd Edition* (Denver, Co: IHS Publishing, 2024), pp. 132, 133

and know for certain that everlasting life with Him awaits you at the end of your journey here on earth? Second, *do you see Jesus as a Lord who condemns you, or is He the One that offers forgiveness, salvation, acceptance, and life-everlasting?* That question is profound. The answer cannot be both. The Promise of the Word is that Jesus came to save you, not to condemn you! He didn't come to destroy the Law, but rather, that through Him the Law would be fulfilled. *Jesus is the reason* you are no longer under the Law of legalistic works. Because of Jesus, you can have life more abundant through His grace. It is grace through Christ that fulfilled the requirements of the Law, by the shedding of His perfect, spotless, blood. I recommend you to take a moment to fully digest this truth before moving on with today's devotion! **As you ponder your thoughts, take a moment to briefly make note of the insight that caught your attention or any questions that came to your mind involving today's study.**

_____

_____

_____

_____

_____

_____

_____

_____

_____

_____

_____

_____

_____

_____

_____

_____

The Promise of His Word ~ John 1

In the beginning was the Word, and the Word was with God and the Word was God...

Lift your eyes to heaven, for the coming of the Lord,
    He's the Promise of the ages, proclaimed within His Word.
From the dawn of all Creation, the Word contained the key -
    Redemption from man's sinful state, His Word will set you free!

Through Him all things were made, without Him was not anything made that was made.

The Lord of all creation – Spoke the heavens into place.
    Then by His Word, upon the earth, He made the human race.
As the heavens declare His glory – His creation is on display;
    We hear the voice of the living Word, as we go from day to day!

In Him was life, and the life was the Light of men.

The Light of the world is dawning – on this bright and glorious day,
    His Word is Life and the Light of men, the Truth and only Way!
The Word provides forgiveness, His Word provides the Light,
    Now bask within His Promise - redeemed from sin's dark plight!

The Light shines in the darkness, and the darkness has not overcome it.

His Light consumes all darkness, when you trust His holy Word,
    Freedom from the grip of death, thru hope in Christ the Lord!
To walk within the brilliance of His mercy and His grace...
    The gift that He provides you, will guide you thru life's race.

And the Word became flesh and dwelt among us, and we have seen His glory...

The Word was sent from heaven, to fulfill salvation's plan,
    The Lamb of God – the sacrifice – to atone the sins of man!
"For unto us a child is born," God's glory from above.
    "And to us a Son is given" - the mercy of God's love!

...Glory as of the only Son, from the Father, full of grace and truth.

The Savior of the world was born long ago on Christmas Day,
    From the glory of the Father's grace, - the Life, Truth, & Way
The Word of God redeems you, if you merely take a chance,
    The love of God heals your heart, and moves your soul to dance!

For from His fullness, we have all received grace upon grace.

"Amazing grace, how sweet the sound that saved a wretch like me,
    I once was lost, but now I'm found, was blind but now I see."
As you celebrate salvation, may you praise His Holy Name;
    Accept God's gift of amazing grace, you will never be the same!

Lanny K. Cook

222

Day 29
The Light of the World
Scriptural Reflection

Arise, shine, for your Light has come, and the Glory of the Lord rises upon you. See, darkness covers the earth and thick darkness is over the peoples, but the Lord rises upon you and His Glory appears over you. Nations will come to Your Light, and kings to the brightness of Your dawn. *Isaiah 60:1-3 NIV*

Who among you fears the Lord and obeys the word of His servant? Let him who walks in the dark, who has no light, trust in the name of the Lord and rely on his God. But now, all you who light fires and provide yourselves with flaming torches, go, walk in the light of your fires and of the torches you have set ablaze. This is what you shall receive from My hand. You will lie down in torment. *Isaiah 50:10-11 NIV*

For God sent His Son not into the world to condemn the world; but that the world through Him might be saved. He that believeth on Him is not condemned: but he that believeth not is condemned already, because he hath not believed in the name of the only begotten Son of God. And this is the condemnation, that light is come into the world, and men loved darkness rather than light, because their deeds were evil. *John 3:17-19 NIV*

The people who walked in darkness
Have seen a great light;
Those who dwelt in the land of the shadow of death,
Upon them a light has shined.
Isaiah 9:2 NKJV

Imagine being summoned to court for a *major indiscretion* you inadvertently committed. You are being tried for a crime that you never intended to happen. You were a victim of circumstance; in the wrong place at the wrong time, perchance you associated with the wrong crowd. Your lawyer has done his best to present a case on your behalf, but things are looking grim and the consequences will inevitably be severe. You need to prepare yourself for the worst, since he's not sure that the jury has been convinced of your innocence. Sitting at the front of the courtroom, behind your table of defense, you realize that your *life is no longer in your control*, someone else holds the key to your future, your hopes, your dreams, and your destiny. Your life's ambitions and prosperity lay in the balance of the upcoming verdict.

The bailiff cries out *All Rise!* bringing you to your feet with your head bowed in shameful humility. Before another word is uttered, the judge calls out your name, commanding you to step toward the bench. Your heart beats with uncontrolled terror as you reluctantly move forward. While you stand before the judge, a hush descends upon the courtroom. The silence magnifies your fear. The judge's voice thunders across the courtroom as he begins, *I see according to these records that you are a follower of the One called Jesus! Is this true?"* he asks, as his eyes penetrate to the very depths of your soul. *Yes, your honor, it is true!* you reply with a trembling voice. The question itself multiplies your guilt as you realize that your sins have not exemplified a life befitting of your faith or the One you profess to follow and serve.

The judge replies: *Yes, I know that this is true, for on these documents Jesus Himself has placed His seal of protection!* He continues: *This seal provides immunity from my judgment! Christ has intervened on your behalf. He accepted the punishment for you! You are forgiven! Case dismissed! Court adjourned!* You can't believe your ears! You grab your lawyer and shake his hand as your loved ones run forward to hug and kiss you! Your heart leaps with joy as you realize that you received a pardon from your indiscretions, and life has been restored. You have been set free! You have been the recipient of grace.

Such was the case for the woman who had been caught in the act of adultery and was brought before Jesus by the religious leaders of those days. They weren't bringing this woman before the Rabbi in order for her to receive justice. But rather, she was merely a pawn in their cunning plan to find fault with Jesus, regardless of His' response to her shameful situation.

> At dawn He went to the temple complex again, and all the people were coming to Him. He sat down and began to teach them. Then the scribes and the Pharisees brought a woman caught in adultery, making her stand in the center. "Teacher," they said to Him, "this woman was caught in the act of committing adultery. In the law Moses commanded us to stone such women. So what do You say?" They asked this to trap Him, in order that they might have evidence to accuse Him. Jesus stooped down and started writing on the ground with His finger. When they persisted in questioning Him, He stood up and said to them, "The one without sin among you should be the first to throw a stone at her."
>
> Then He stooped down again and continued writing on the ground. When they heard this, they left one by one, starting with the older men. Only He was left, with the woman in the center. When Jesus stood up, He said to her, "Woman, where are they? Has no one condemned you?" "No one, Lord," she answered. "Neither do I condemn you," said Jesus. "Go, and from now on do not sin anymore."
>
> Then Jesus spoke to them again: "I am the light of the world. Anyone who follows Me will never walk in the darkness but will have the light of life." *(John 8:2-12 HCSB).*

The Law required punishment for sin. The religious legalists of Jesus' day were calling for judgement on this woman. But the Rabbi spoiled their plans. *Legalism says God will love you if you change.* But *grace says God loves you,* so much that He sent His only Son to serve as the atonement necessary to secure your liberty, completely and forever! *Grace trumps Legalism* – Christ came not to destroy the law, but that through Him the Law would be fulfilled. Legally, God looks at you as if you died with Christ, since your sins were buried with Him after you accept Him into your life. Because of His sacrifice, through the blood that He shed, you are no longer condemned. Jesus served as the propitiation – He served as the appeasement for sin's condemning consequence - death. Through His resurrection, you are offered new life by His grace. Because of God's grace, you can discover forgiveness for your sin. Forgiveness is the only path to a life free from shame and regret.

Because of grace, through Jesus Christ, your freedom is guaranteed. You are able to live for a greater purpose and a greater hope. *Liberty requires a sacrifice and Jesus paid the price for you.* He took your judgement upon Himself. He willingly became the sacrifice for your sin so that you can live. The One Who knew no sin, became sin on the cross so that you could live free.

. If you do not accept and live in the liberty provided by the sacrifice of Jesus, then you are guilty of rejecting God's grace. That is the only unforgivable sin; to blaspheme the Holy Spirit by rejecting God's free gift of salvation into your life – by rejecting Jesus' sacrifice for you! When you accept Jesus as your Savior you become one with Him and the old life has died away. But the focus of a relationship with Christ is not about dying, it's about living. It's all about enjoying a life free from bondage, free from the burden, free from the penalty of your sin. It's about living in Liberty – through God's Grace!

> At one time we too were foolish, disobedient, deceived and enslaved by all kinds of passions and pleasures. We lived in malice and envy, being hated and hating one another. But when the kindness and love of God our Savior appeared, he saved us, not because of righteous things we had done, but because of his mercy. He saved us through the washing of rebirth and renewal by the Holy Spirit, whom he poured out on us generously through Jesus Christ our Savior, so that, having been justified by his grace, we might become heirs having the hope of eternal life, *(Titus 3:3-7 NIV).*

So many times, in life, you lose sight of what is really important. You often feel more comfortable hiding in the darkness because it shadows our sinful nature and deceptive ways. Too often it's easier to stay locked up in the bondage of sin's pleasure than walk in the Light of life. Even though the darkness of the world causes us to stumble and fall as we trudge along the path of life in search of the lustful desires of our heart. It's pretty scary to be exposed in the light. But that's not true when it comes to Jesus' light. You don't have to stumble around in the darkness, tripping and falling, as you hopelessly trudge along. You have been given a Light! He is the Light that dispels the darkness! The Light that illuminates your path. **But the path of the just is like the** shining sun, that shines ever brighter unto the perfect day. The way of the wicked is like darkness; They do not know what makes them stumble, *(Proverbs 4:18-19 NKJV).*

As you travel along the path of this life, you not only need to equip yourself with that Light, but you need to let it shine. Turn it on. Don't hide it under a bushel. If you continue to walk in darkness, sooner or later you're going to fall off the cliff known as "destruction."

> Then Jesus spoke to them again, saying, "I am the light of the world. He who follows Me shall not walk in darkness, but have the light of life," *(John 8:12 NIV).*

We have been given a Light, and the Light of the world is Jesus...

> You are the light of the world—like a city on a hilltop that cannot be hidden. No one lights a lamp and then puts it under a basket. Instead, a lamp is placed on a stand, where it gives light to everyone in the house. In the same way, let your good deeds shine out for all to see, so that everyone will praise your heavenly Father, *(Matthew 5:14-16 NLT).*

Let Him shine out of your life! But For His Light to shine, you must first repent of your sinful ways and ask for His forgiveness. *What regrets or shame do you carry that you need to ask forgiveness?* Confess those transgressions to Him and then reflect on ways you can allow His Light to shine out brighter in your life.

_____

_____

_____

_____

_____

_____

_____

_____

_____

_____

_____

The Light of the World is Jesus!

Oh, come to the Light, He's calling today,
  The Light of the World will show you the way;
The Word became flesh one night long ago,
  Because God the Father loves you so!

Oh, come to the Light, He died on the cross,
  That the souls of mankind would suffer not loss,
To the evils and sin and the throes of hell,
  God gave His own Son, for the gospel to tell.

The Gospel of Light, the good news proclaimed:
  Jesus rose from the grave, where His body was lain;
The Victor o'er death arose from the dead,
  Redemption is free, He was there in our stead!

The Light of the World, oh, come one and all,
  He's beckoning, waiting, please heed His soft call;
The time is now fleeing, the night draweth nigh,
  When the age of forgiveness fast passeth by.

Then only those ones who said, "Yes," to the Light,
  Will pass with the Savior through the dark night
Into the bright morning that waiteth beyond,
  Where sin can no longer hold saved souls in bond.

There with the Savior, the redeemed will be free,
  The Joy of all Heaven awaits you and me,
If only we now give our hearts to that One,
  The Light of the Ages, God . . . Father and Son!

Eternal life we then will know,
  Perfect bliss, He will bestow,
No sin, no darkness, no black of night,
  For Jesus our Lord will be the Light;

Forever and ever and evermore,
  Oh, the marvelous wonders He holds in store
For all who now come and simply believe;
  Oh, Dear One, the Light of the World receive!

Clarice D. Cook

Be Still to Find His Promise
Scriptural Reflection

Very early in the morning, while it was still dark, Jesus got up, left the house and went off to a solitary place, where he prayed. Simon and his companions went to look for him, and when they found him, they exclaimed: "Everyone is looking for you!" *Mark 1: 35-37 NIV*

One of those days Jesus went out to a mountainside to pray, and spent the night praying to God. When morning came, he called his disciples to him and chose twelve of them, whom he also designated apostles. *Luke 6:12, 13 NIV*

Now it came to pass, about eight days after these sayings, that He took Peter, John, and James and went up on the mountain to pray. As He prayed, the appearance of His face was altered, and His robe *became* white *and* glistening. And behold, two men talked with Him, who were Moses and Elijah, who appeared in glory and spoke of His decease which He was to accomplish at Jerusalem. But Peter and those with him were heavy with sleep; and when they were fully awake, they saw His glory and the two men who stood with Him. Then it happened, as they were parting from Him, *that* Peter said to Jesus, "Master, it is good for us to be here; and let us make three tabernacles: one for You, one for Moses, and one for Elijah"—not knowing what he said. While he was saying this, a cloud came and overshadowed them; and they were fearful as they entered the cloud. And a voice came out of the cloud, saying, "This is My beloved Son. Hear Him!" When the voice had ceased, Jesus was found alone. But they kept quiet, and told no one in those days any of the things they had seen. *Luke 9:28-36 NKJV*

Jesus went out as usual to the Mount of Olives, and his disciples followed him. On reaching the place, he said to them, "Pray that you will not fall into temptation." He withdrew about a stone's throw beyond them, knelt down and prayed. *Luke 22:39-41 NIV*

Immediately Jesus made the disciples get into the boat and go on ahead of him to the other side, while he dismissed the crowd. After he had dismissed them, he went up on a mountainside by himself to pray. Later that night, he was there alone, and the boat was already a considerable distance from land, buffeted by the waves because the wind was against it. Shortly before dawn Jesus went out to them, walking on the lake. *Matthew 14:22-25 NIV*

The scriptures are full of insight regarding the *need for rest*, as well as the importance of taking time to get away from the crowds. It takes some effort to learn to deal with the chaos of life and discover your effective means to still your heart. The reality of finding rest, will have miraculous results as it opens the door to draw closer to your Maker and Creator. Most people would never admit it, or even recognize this natural phenomenon, but the Lord's power and strength is most often realized and afforded to you when you take the time *to still your heart*. Jesus modeled this truth throughout His ministry on earth.

The concept of this truth, actually comes from the *Ancient of Days,* Himself. It took the *Word of God* six days to speak the entire universe and all that we know into existence. In the first chapter of Genesis, Moses records that during those days of creation, God created light and separated the darkness with it. He designed the firmament to separate the water covered void of earth, from the great expanse of the heavens. From there He distinguished the land from the seas and commanded a rich, lush vegetation to cover the earth.

It was then that He spoke the sun, moon, and stars into existence as He assigned them to their appointed place throughout the universe. They would serve as signs, seasons, days, and years for the life He was about to create. Living creatures, both great and small, entered the life cycle of God's earthly splendor as fish, birds, cattle, beasts, and even creepy, crawly things took their place within the confines of God's miraculous wonder of paradise. God was about to place His crowning achievement in the center of that lush *Garden, known as Eden.* He created man in His *own image.* As the *Triune God*, man was designed as a reflection of the Almighty's nature; a body, mind, and spirit.

At the end of each of these six-days of creation, when evening came and the Lord was finished with the day's chores, He would reflect back and say it is *Good.* On the sixth day, as the sun was setting in the east, the Lord looked over His completed work and exclaimed, *it is very Good.* Creation was complete. There was only one thing left for the Lord to do; that was to *rest* from His work. He took the next day off from His labor, and declared that day to be *holy.*

> So the creation of the heavens and the earth and everything in them was completed. On the seventh day God had finished his work of creation, so he rested from all his

work. And God blessed the seventh day and declared it holy, because it was the day when he rested from all his work of creation, *(Genesis 2:1-3 NLT).*

Not to get distracted from moving forward with the main topic of today's devotion, but many people get hung up on believing that the Lord could have created everything in a mere six days. But just to provide some context to that thought before we move on, it's important to share Peter's words from the third chapter of the book that shares his name: But, beloved, do not forget this one thing, that with the Lord one day is as a thousand years, and a thousand years as one day, *(2 Peter 3:8 NKJV).*

Regardless of the actual amount of time required for God to complete creation, there remains a significant point to remember from the Genesis account. Since we are created in the *Triune image of God*, we too need to take time to *rest*. The reality of entering into a restful state requires you to *calm* your mind, *quiet* your heart, and *relax* in *His presence*. You will never be able to accomplish any of that if you don't have *peace*. True peace will only arrive if you learn to *be still and know that He is God*. Only then, will you find the restful peace that *passes all understanding*.

As I mentioned at the beginning of today's devotion, Jesus modeled this concept throughout His earthly ministry. Numerous passages of scripture from the Gospel records, refer to Jesus going off on His own somewhere to pray. *He needed time to Himself*. He needed time to *focus*, to *re-energize*, to *clear* His mind, and to *hear* His father's voice. His ministry demanded that He find time to not only be still, but enter into the presence of the Father to find *guidance*, *strength*, and *power* to continue forward. There's no better place to do that, at least for me, than within the beauty and glory of God's natural creation.

The heavens proclaim the glory of God. The skies display his craftsmanship. Day after day they continue to speak; night after night they make him known. They speak without a sound or word; their voice is never heard. Yet their message has gone throughout the earth, and their words to all the world, *(Psalm 19: 1-4 NLT).*

I'm sure you have a favorite spot; a go-to place where you can run when you need a break. All of us have times when you need some alone time, some peace and quiet; a break from the chaos, and a reprieve from the world. Where is this place for you? When was the last time you were there? As I mentioned earlier, that place for me has always been found in the great outdoors. That is where I can always go to get closer to God and feel His presence in a profound way.

As an adolescent, I learned to relax and *be still under the stars.* Well, at least in the summer months. My Dad modeled this practice, and in ways it became a deeply engrained tradition for me. In fact, during those years at home, in the evenings after the sun would set behind the glorious Rocky Mountains just west of Denver, I would anticipate the chance to go out with my father to sit on the front porch and gaze into the heavenly expanse of God's firmament. I have fond memories of sharing that cement step with Dad, sometimes one of my brothers, and even occasionally Mom would join us on the porch, just out the front door. I can still tell you where each of the visible constellations were from my front porch perspective, nearly sixty-years later.

My father was a quiet, introspective man, and as such, there was never really any conversations involved while we sat together on those steps. But I was able to share in my *father's presence*, while also basking in the very *essence of God' glory.* I learned how to *be still* on those nights; to be *comfortable* in the silence, and to be able to *listen* to God's voice as I embraced the magnificent wonder of His celestial message. I learned to contemplate the miraculous creation story and actively imagine the heavenly glory that spoke to Jesus during the time He spent praying in the Garden or out in the wilderness. I could only imagine the conversations He had with His Father, whether spoken or unspoken, during those quiet moments of serene fellowship. I felt that same serenity sitting with my father, contemplating the glory of God's craftsmanship.

We would usually sit there with our eyes lifted to the heavens, for a good thirty to forty minutes before heading into the house to get ready for bed. I never had any trouble falling asleep after my time under the stars with Dad. As I look back on those special moments, especially now since my father has passed, I realize that those times shared beneath the Lord's heavenly glory, prepared me for life in many ways. I discovered how to be still and *humbly* enter into the presence of the Lord's glory. I also realized the importance of *lifting my eyes* to Him, while pondering the magnificence, beauty, and power of His nature. But most importantly, I came to realize not only the need and benefits of entering into His rest but also the means to acquire it.

Where is your retreat that allows you to enter into the presence of Jesus? Where do you go to find your rest and peace? Maybe it's the great outdoors as well. Or, maybe you find it by getting into the Word. Possibly, you find His presence by turning on the good ole, southern-gospel music and entering into His presence through worship and praise. Regardless, *when was the last time you were there?* If it's been a while, maybe it's time to return; right now, at this very moment. The older I get, the more I realize that I can't ever get enough of God's heavenly rest. *What about you?* As you ponder these questions, briefly share a few of your thoughts in the space below.

_____

_____

_____

_____

_____

_____

_____

_____

_____

_____

_____

_____

_____

_____

_____

_____

Be Still to Find His Promise

This life is but a journey as we walk from day to day,
    Living through each moment, searching to find a way.
Working to achieve our goals, in search of meaning for this life,
    A job, a house, a fancy car --- dear children, and a wife.
We search, we dream, we carry on; the chaos seems to build;
    While, a void down deep inside, is yearning to be filled!
Accomplishments seem shallow – as the treasures pile up,
    Nothing that we gather seems to fill this empty cup!

We seek the many answers, to the questions that arise,
    The hectic pace of life itself has caught us by surprise.
Life is much too busy, as we rush throughout each day;
    To recognize the answer, we will pass it on the way!
Be "Still" and find the answer, be "Still" to find the Way,
    That leads to life eternal, and the never-ending day!
Silence your ambition, and the chaos of life's race,
    Lift your eyes to heaven, to find God's loving, grace!

Be "Still" to find His promise; declared from long ago,
    Foretold throughout the scriptures - the Bible tells us so;
God so loved His children, that He offered up a plan,
    He sent Salvation to this world – to save the souls of man.
Listen to the Promise, as He whispers to your heart;
    The Love He shares for all of us, will never, ever part!
Reach out to claim the Promise; He gives us each a choice,
    Be "Still" and listen closely, to His peaceful, calming voice.

Decide to claim the Promise, offered through His grace,
    A gift that's freely given - He came to take our place.
Accept Him at His Promise, He became our sacrifice,
    As a sheep led to the slaughter, He paid the final price!
Proclaim the message of the Promise, death no longer reigns,
    Jesus conquered sin's hold; He broke those dreadful chains!
Now be "Still" to find the Promise, be "Still" to feel His Love,
    Redemption, freely given, 'tis God's blessing from above!

Stand Firm upon the Promise, His love will never end;
    Master, Savior, Teacher, He's our Comfort and our Friend!
The Holy One of Israel sent from heaven to this earth;
    Be "Still" to find the Promise; as you realize His worth!

Lanny K. Cook

Day 31
The Cross in the Floor
Scriptural Reflection

Then the King will say to those on His right, 'Come, you who are blessed by My Father; take your inheritance, the kingdom prepared for you since the creation of the world. For I was hungry and you gave me something to eat, I was thirsty and you gave Me something to drink, I was a stranger and you invited Me in, I needed clothes and you clothed Me, I was sick and you looked after Me, I was in prison and you came to visit Me.' Then the righteous shall answer Him, 'Lord, when did we see you hungry and feed You, or thirsty and give You something to drink? When did we see You a stranger and invite You in, or needing clothes and clothe You? When did we see You sick or in prison and go to visit You?' The King will reply, 'I tell you the truth, whatever you did for the least of these My brothers of Mine, you did for Me.
Matthew 25:34-40 NIV

Just as a body, though one, has many parts, but all its many parts form one body, so it is with Christ. For we were all baptized by one Spirit so as to form one body—whether Jews or Gentiles, slave or free—and we were all given the one Spirit to drink. Even so the body is not made up of one part but of many. Now if the foot should say, "Because I am not a hand, I do not belong to the body," it would not for that reason stop being part of the body. And if the ear should say, "Because I am not an eye, I do not belong to the body," it would not for that reason stop being part of the body. If the whole body were an eye, where would the sense of hearing be? If the whole body were an ear, where would the sense of smell be? But in fact God has placed the parts in the body, every one of them, just as he wanted them to be. If they were all one part, where would the body be? As it is, there are many parts, but one body. The eye cannot say to the hand, "I don't need you!" And the head cannot say to the feet, "I don't need you!" *I Corinthians 12:14-21 NIV*

Growing up each of us had people we admired and at times maybe actually worshipped, in a child-like, adoring sense. Personally, I admired a few professional athletes, along with a few movie stars, as well as a few entertainers who could dance like Ginger and Fred, or those who could sing with angelic voices, like Andy Williams, Nat King Cole, or Ella Fitzgerald. There were teachers, as well as coaches through my school days whom I totally respected and admired. And, of course, as children, it's natural to acquire a deep love for your mother. You can't help but to think she's the tops. For those who had a gentle, loving, selfless father; you loved him, but it was more like a deep respect for him and you dreamed to follow in his footsteps. That's the way it was for me. Dad truly was the one I admired most through those wonder years of childhood.

As I reached my teens, all of that changed, but not in the sense that I became disillusioned with any of the original folks that I loved and admired. I finally realized the difference between admiration and worship as my *eyes began to open* to the reality of a much bigger world; one outside of the isolating influence within the simple structure of family and heroes. Being raised in the church, the stories of the Bible were instilled in my heart from the earliest recollections of my life. But as I grew out of adolescence, my perspective began to change, and my view on who I wanted to fashion my life after, *was also transformed.* That point arrived, around fifteen years old, when I attended my first, week-long church camp in the mountains west of Denver.

It was at camp, where the Bible stories of my early years led to the realization involving my need, for a *personal connection* to the true message of Scripture. I realized the significance of going beyond a basic understanding of God's Word, into the *intimacy of fully embracing a relationship* with the true Author of the faith. It was at camp, where my *spiritual eyes opened.* I wanted to go beyond simply knowing about God's love, as presented in all of the biblical stories. I needed to *accept the purpose of His Word* into my life. Simply stated, my world view had changed as I realized there was a deeply intimate aspect of personally, accepting God's love. At that point, I came to understand that there is only *One* who I needed to fashion my life after.

How many times do we think to ourselves, *if only I could be more like Jesus?* He lived His life for thirty-three years on this earth while experiencing many of the same emotions, needs, trials, tribulations, and temptations each of us have endured. He knew what it was like to be hungry, and to be thirsty; to laugh and smile; to suffer and cry. He experienced the warmth of the morning sun as it rose in the eastern sky, as well as the sweet smell of freshened earth, emanating from the life-giving, spring rains. He inhaled the fragrant bouquet of wild flowers in the field as the butterflies fluttered overhead. He knew what it was like to feel pleasure and pain; happiness and strife; to seek the assurance of His earthly parents as well as the blessing and guidance of His heavenly Father.

As a young man working in His earthly father's carpenter shop, He undoubtedly knew what it was like to be cut and bruised while enduring the pain of physical exertion. He must have had times when the mallet missed its intended target and landed squarely on His thumb, or His measurements weren't quite right and another timber had to be measured and cut. He worked long, strenuous hours as He struggled to help his family survive within their meager existence. He learned to use the tools of His trade to meticulously craft the works for this ancient society. Saws, mallets, nails, draw knives, and planes were all part of His everyday life as He grew up amidst the shavings and dust that collected within the family enterprise. Undoubtedly, He was called upon to craft wagons, carts, wheels, tools, doors, yokes, and even farmer's plows. He probably was required to construct the wooden crosses which were in major demand by the Roman government as they continued to perform their grotesque, grizzly daily executions along the roads leading to Jerusalem.

Isn't it amazing that before Jesus became a teacher and a prophet, He first learned how to be a *craftsman* under the watchful eye of Joseph. Joseph was a skilled laborer, a master craftsman who knew how to measure, cut, and fit the many pieces required to build an essential necessity to accommodate the demands of life in those days. So, Jesus was taught how to shave and sand the shape of the yoke for a perfect fit of the oxen team in order that the team would not suffer from the wear of an abrasive and misfit burden. He learned how to gather and fit together the inanimate, unrelated parts necessary to create a tool that was useful for mankind's existence and prosperity. He apprenticed as a young man in a shop where the natural beauty of wood was *bridled into a purposeful and essential form.*

Is it no wonder that as Christ's ministry transformed, He was able to bridle the *emotional* and *spiritual* nature of twelve men's souls, and transform them into the greatest Church the world has ever known. It was in His early years, working with Joseph that Jesus became a *Master Builder.* It's no wonder that He needed a thorough understanding involving the intricacies of architectural design as He was about to unveil the *Kingdom of God* to all the world. Actually, since He was the Word who spoke all of creation into existence, I'm pretty sure that He had a *natural knack* for the projects He built in Joseph's carpenter shop.

Christ is the Master of *transforming lives* and turning them into useful tools that are necessary for the furthering of God's Kingdom. Each individual part outside of the whole is nothing more than a timber or a nail. But when Christ meticulously cuts, trims, shaves, then sands His work to refined perfection, He is able to fit each of us together, to serve as a significant component of the body as a whole. Once you accept Jesus into your life and choose to follow Him, you are joined together as a unique part of the body, and you become a *significant part of His purpose.* No single component is more important for its *function* - no single part will receive more *recognition or honor.*

As servants of the Master, you have a *calling;* you have a *function* to perform for His service. You are called to contribute to His Kingdom and in the process glorify the One who you have chosen to follow; Jesus. Each of us are called to serve Him through the use of our *talents* and through the *examples* of our lives, after He calls out for us to follow Him. So, no matter whether you sing, preach, or teach the word, He has called you unto His own. No matter whether you cook, or clean, build the walls, or plumb the pipes, He has called you unto Himself in order to use your talents in service towards the *glory of God* and the *building,* as well as the *edification* of His Kingdom. You will be rewarded unto your own measure of active devotion. You will be rewarded according to the extent you contributed toward His service. I'm not talking about how much money you give to the church. I'm talking about how much of yourself you give to the Lord. One day you will *stand before Jesus!* At that time, as He looks directly into your eyes, I pray He says, *good and faithful servant, in you I am very pleased!*

My father, Gordon, possessed what I like to refer to as a *gentle, quiet faith*. He was a man of few words, but the depth of his faith was vividly evident through his actions, and the sharing of the carefully selected words that he was willing to offer in a conversation. My father was also gifted as a craftsman with a keen sense of constructing projects and maintaining all things mechanical. His mechanical aptitude was truly a gift. When the pastor of his church needed someone to install flooring in the foyer of their new building, he knew who to ask, and my dad graciously agreed. With his God-given talent inspiring him, my father completed the task. In the midst of the elegant marble tiled floor, he crafted a beautiful wooden cross made of oak. He stained it with a dark color to create a contrast that immediately drew your attention to the *image of the cross* when you entered the front door.

These were the ways that Dad, shared his faith. Through his talents, the Light of Jesus was evident in his life. His love for the Lord moved him to share his gifts and talents for *God's glory* as he journeyed through this world. Not long after he finished the cross in the floor of the foyer, my mother wrote the poem contained at the end of today's devotion. I felt compelled to share it as a means of encouragement for you. I admired my father for his ability to share his God-given talents in simple ways that truly served his Lord. Too many believers feel inadequate in their ability to share their *faith*, in a *natural way*. Since only a few are gifted to preach or teach the Word of God, what else is there to do? Not everyone is called to share their faith in such ways. Actually, you are called to share your faith, not only through your natural talents, but by the way you live your life. That is how the Light of Christ shines out for the world to see. Just remember, it's not about you. It's all about getting out of the way so that Christ's light can shine in a manner that attracts others to Him. *How can you get out of your personal limelight so that Jesus' Light will shine brighter?* That is the simple question on which today's devotion is founded. What talents do you have to share with those around you? *What simple gifts have you been blessed with to share Jesus' light to a lost and hurting world?*

> You are the light of the world. A town built on a hill cannot
> be hidden. Neither do people light a lamp and put it under
> a bowl. Instead, they put it on its stand, and it gives light to
> everyone in the house. In the same way, let your light shine
> before others, that they may see your good deeds and
> glorify your Father in heaven, *(Matthew 5:14-16 NIV).*

Take the next few minutes and record in the space below, *how your gifts, talents, and life allow the Light to shine out for the world to see.* If you honestly examine your life through that perspective, you will learn how to let Him shine out brighter than ever before.

_____

_____

_____

_____

_____

_____

_____

_____

_____

_____

_____

_____

_____

_____

_____

_____

_____

_____

The Cross in the Floor

What can I do for Jesus, He did so much for me;
How can I serve the Savior, He set my spirit free?
I cannot sing, I cannot teach, nor can I preach the word,
Yet I want to share His love, with those who've never heard.
I long to sing, to preach, to teach, to do some noble deed;
To touch the lives of sinners, Help fill their aching need.
Oh yes, I long to do these things --- That's the least that I could do,
But Jesus gently tells me, I have other plans for you!
"You do not speak with eloquence, nor did you learn to sing,
You cannot preach, nor can you teach, that's simply not your thing.
But, child, you have a special gift, I gave to only you,
An artisan, whose love is wood, great things your hands can do.
You know I gave my very life, on Calvary that day ---
Crucified, nailed to the cross, to take all sin away.
To give eternal life to those, who will believe and come,
For God so loved this sin-filled world, He gave His only Son.
To serve as a reminder, of my sacrificial death,
Seek your talents, use your skills, draw in the craftsman's breath.
Measure, cut, fit, and piece, true craftsmanship is rare,
The beauty taking form and shape, shows loving hands that care.
The nailing, sanding, final touch, it's all a work of art ---
The perfect gift from you to me, done from your loving heart.
Piece by piece, and peg by peg --- This work you did for me,
You placed my cross within this floor, for all the world to see.
It says to those who view it, 'see what they did to Me,
Mocked me, beat me, scourged me, then nailed me to the tree!'
It gives my simple message, to all who may pass by:
'I, Jesus..., crucified, buried, dead, arose to live on high,
That whosoever enters through, God's own holy door,
May comprehend my Father's plan, that's why man's sin I bore!'
Acceptance then is in their hands, what will they do for me?
My child, you laid the groundwork, to help set their spirits free!
You may not teach, you may not preach, you may not sing my praise,
Yet others you may lead to me, through humble simple ways.
Pure of heart, pure of mind, you gave your best I see,
With loving, gentle hands you formed, the cross of love for Me!"

Clarice D. Cook

Day 32
The Bethlehem Way
Scriptural Reflection

But you Bethlehem Ephratah, though you are small among the clans of Judah, out of you will come for me one who will be ruler over Israel, whose origins are from old, from ancient times. Therefore Israel will be abandoned until the time when she who is in labor gives birth and the rest of His brothers return to join the Israelites. He will stand and shepherd His flock in the strength of the Lord, in the majesty of the name of the Lord His God. And they will live securely, for then His greatness will reach to the ends of the earth. And He will be their peace. *Micah 5:2-5 NIV*

If you then, though you are evil, know how to give good gifts to your children, how much more will your Father in heaven give good gifts to those who ask Him! So, in everything, do to others what you would have them do to you, for this sums up the Law and the Prophets. Enter through the narrow gate. For wide is the gate and broad is the road that leads to destruction, and many enter through it. But small is the gate and narrow the road that leads to life, and only a few find it. *Matthew 7:11-14 NIV*

The Lord is my shepherd; I shall not want. He makes me to lie down in green pastures; He leads me beside the still waters. He restores my soul; He leads me in the paths of righteousness For His name's sake. Yea, though I walk through the valley of the shadow of death, I will fear no evil; For You are with me; Your rod and Your staff, they comfort me. You prepare a table before me in the presence of my enemies; You anoint my head with oil; My cup runs over. Surely goodness and mercy shall follow me All the days of my life; And I will dwell in the house of the Lord Forever. *Psalm 23: 1-6 NKJV*

Throughout the history of this world, the battle between *good and evil* has been fought on the forefront of people's lives. All the while the *souls* of mankind lie in the balance. You risk not only losing your earthly life in this battle, but you also risk condemning your soul to *eternal separation* from God if you don't accept His gift of salvation. So often it appears that evil forces are the victors of these personal skirmishes that rage in our hearts; those that pit right against wrong. However, that doesn't need to be the case if you choose to follow the *path of redemption!*

When you choose to follow the *road less traveled*, which is the path that leads to salvation – you'll find that it is paved with abundant blessings from God. As a follower of the Lord Jesus Christ, you can break free from the strongholds of evil through His strength and power. You will be able to overcome the *temptation of darkness* when you whole heartedly seek after Jesus and surrender your life into His care. Only through Jesus Christ, will you find the victory over the personal battles of sin that try to distract and destroy you. You are not destined to become another victim in Satan's snare of destruction. He continually devises plans and strategies to distract, cripple, and limit your eternal potential.

> I am the door. If anyone enters by Me, he will be saved, and will go in and out and find pasture. The thief does not come except to steal, and to kill, and to destroy. I have come that they may have life, and that they may have it more abundantly, *(John 10:9, 10 NKJV).*

In spite of Satan's desperate attempts to destroy your *relationship* with God, the Almighty has a plan to save you from the *destructive force* of sin and death. That plan comes through Christ, who not only offers life, but He brings hope, peace, and joy back into your life when you accept Him as your Savior. Even though at times it appears that evil has overcome God's grace and mercy, you can rest in the assurance that Jesus Christ *will prevail* in all things.

Even during the most difficult times of life, Jesus will be victorious. At those times when it appears that Satan has won another skirmish in your life, if you choose to trust the Lord, and totally surrender control of your circumstance to Him, you will ultimately find the victory through His strength, mercy, and grace! Even if the outcome isn't what you think it should be, or even what you prayed it would be, Jesus Christ has never lost a battle to the forces of darkness. Regardless of the outcome, within the Lord's sovereign plan for your life, when you prayerfully submit any situation into His care, it will eventually turn, for your good, and within His purpose. That is a lesson that all of us need to realize. When the storms hit, and they will without a doubt, you can *rest in the promise* of His assurance that He will turn all things into good, for His glory and purpose.

A great passage that highlights this promise is found in the Gospel of John. It's the *story of Lazarus*, a close friend and follower of Jesus who had died while the Lord was in another town. In fact, within His infinite divinity, Jesus realized that Lazarus was dead, even before the news arrived. Within His divine purpose, and His mercy to turn all things into good, Jesus delayed His return to tend to the grieving sisters of Lazarus. He prolonged His return for ninety-six hours, to place an exclamation point on the miracle He was about to perform. After four days, the human body begins to decompose, and everyone knew that Lazarus was dead, because in southern slang, *he stinketh!*

> Then Jesus said to them plainly, "Lazarus is dead. And I am glad for your sakes that I was not there, that you may believe. Nevertheless, let us go to him." Then Thomas, who is called the Twin, said to his fellow disciples, "Let us also go, that we may die with Him." So, when Jesus came, He found that he had already been in the tomb four days. Now Bethany was near Jerusalem, about two miles away. And many of the Jews had joined the women around Martha and Mary, to comfort them concerning their brother. Then Martha, as soon as she heard that Jesus was coming, went and met Him, but Mary was sitting in the house. Now Martha said to Jesus, "Lord, if You had been here, my brother would not have died. But even now I know that whatever You ask of God, God will give You." Jesus said to her, "Your brother will rise again." Martha said to Him, "I know that he will rise again in the resurrection at the last day."
>
> Jesus said to her, "I am the resurrection and the life. He who believes in Me, though he may die, he shall live. And whoever lives and believes in Me shall never die. Do you

believe this?" She said to Him, "Yes, Lord, I believe that You are the Christ, the Son of God, who is to come into the world," *(John 11:14-27 NKJV).*

Throughout Jesus' ministry there are numerous accounts recorded in the Gospel record, where the Lord *raised the dead* back to life. These miraculous wonders served to seal His words that He is the *resurrection and the life*. But each of those miracles brought these individuals back to life in the same form as they were before. At the time of Jesus' resurrection, He *conquered the grave*, unlocking the chains of death that separated humanity from eternal fellowship with the Creator. Jesus wasn't just brought back to life, but rather, He was resurrected from the grave with an *incorruptible, body*. One that is now immortal and can never be touched by death again. All of those whom Jesus raised from the dead during His ministry, all died a second time, as they still inhabited a *corruptible body of flesh*. Jesus was transformed into His heavenly form through the resurrection. That is the *promise* of redemption; each of us will receive an incorruptible heavenly form when we leave this world and enter into eternal fellowship with Him.

As you walk the trail of this life, you will struggle through the debris and undergrowth that covers your path. It's easy to get caught up in the tangled mess that often obscures the route that you have chosen to follow. At times, you'll find yourself venturing out from the safety of the trail. You'll end up *traversing across unstable ground*, maybe even losing your footing in those treacherous and dangerous conditions. In a panic, you'll struggle to find your way back to the solid footing of the *Lord's straight and narrow path*.

But then as you finally get back on the right course, you'll encounter an unmarked fork in the road that tempts you to wander off in a new, uncharted direction. Many times, these forks come from God, as He allows you to once again make your own choice as to the direction you want to take. But, so often, they come from the world's influence, or even your own wandering desires. Those forks appear appealing at first, yet after a short time, you'll realize that the dangers are not worth the agony of the trek. Throughout life, you must *constantly re-evaluate* your direction and decisions in this life. At times, you may unwittingly take the split in the road that leads to destruction, rather than stay on the path that leads to life. Regardless, your *free will* allows you to choose for yourself the continued setting of your course.

Jesus tells us, **I am the way, the truth and the life, no man comes unto the Father, but by me!** What road have you chosen to follow? Is it a road that brings peace, joy, hope, and contentment to your life; while also providing eternal security? Or is it a road that brings stress, anxiety, frustration, and guilt into your circumstance? Do you find yourself overwhelmed within the struggles associated with the path that you're following? You don't have to continue traveling down the road of worldly pleasure and selfish gain; along the road of stress, discontent, tension, or relentless danger. You can choose to follow the only path that leads back to the presence of your Creator. By His side you will encounter the blessing that is offered to those He calls His own.

While the gate is narrow that leads to life, it is also very simple to pass through that entrance. To ask Jesus to come into your life, or to rededicate your life to Him, all you have to do is say this simple prayer:

Dear Jesus, I know that have lived in sin and I don't want to continue down a path that leads to destruction. I have heard about how you died on the cross for my sins; and how you rose from the grave by the Power of the Living God! Lord Jesus, I pray for your forgiveness. Please come into my heart and save my soul from my sinful nature! I freely choose to walk away from that broken path, and turn to You. Lord, I pray that you will take control of my life, and that You will guide my paths in order that I may live every moment for You! Lord, I pray that Your light will shine out in my life, that others may see You in me! Lord, I thank You for the sacrifice that You made for me! I accept Your gift of Salvation! Now, I pray that You will take my life and transform it into a vessel that is pleasing to you. I offer my life as a living sacrifice to You! I pray all these things in the name of Jesus Christ, Amen!!

The Bethlehem Way!

I followed the road less traveled, and encountered the Bethlehem way,
  I followed a star to the stable, where Mary and Joseph did stay.
A child was born so long ago, to a virgin who called Him, "Son,"
  A promise was given to the world, He was the Chosen One!
I followed the road less traveled, past a carpenter's shop one day,
  A boy learned a skillful trade, from one who was aging and gray!
The shop was filled with chiseled works, made by the sweat of the brow,
  A cross for Rome, an oxen yoke, even doors and a farmer's plow.
I followed the road less traveled, to a gentle river, running wide,
  The place was known as Jordan, where a mighty prophet did abide!
"I say, 'repent and be baptized, For the kingdom of heaven is at hand,'"
  "The Son of Man is coming you must choose to take a stand."
I followed the road less traveled, to a place called Galilee,
  Where Jesus had found the Disciples, casting nets upon the sea.
"Follow me," He cried to them, along that wind swept shore,
  "I will make you fishers of men! If you give up your earthly chore!"
I followed the road less traveled, to where miracles abound,
  The lame now walk; blind can see, the lost have now been found!
Amidst the throng of doubters, were the temples favored ones,
  Whose jealousies for Jesus' power, were quick to cast their stones.
I followed the road less traveled, past a fertile garden fair,
  The Son of Man had come to pray, for the burdens He had to bear!
"Let this cup pass from me," Were the words He prayed that night,
  As He anguished in the torment, from the disciple's watchful sight.
I followed the road less traveled, facing a place where death was found,
  To a hill they called Golgotha, where the sins of man were bound.
I gazed upon this broken man, He was punished for my sin,
  And realized how great the price, when He died for sinful men.
I followed the road less traveled, as I walked past an empty tomb,
  The Son of Man conquered death, and left that stone-cold room.
Jesus Christ is alive once more; of this you can be sure.
  He will reign throughout eternity, He is sovereign, true, and pure.
I followed the road less traveled, as I wandered through this life;
  I found a friend who walks with me, In good times and in strife.
That baby born so long ago, was sent to set men free,
  He lived and died, yet rose again, and now lives eternally.
I followed the road less traveled, it was a narrow, rocky way,
  But it's the road that leads to heaven, to a never-ending day.
For Christ has come to save our souls, if we choose to follow Him;
  He stands before the door and knocks; I pray you'll let Him in!
I will follow the road less traveled, throughout each and every day...
  In remembrance of my Savior, He lights the narrow way.

Lanny K. Cook

251

Day 33
In the Twinkling of an Eye
Scriptural Reflection

And in that day a great trumpet will sound. Those who were perishing in Assyria and those who were exiled in Egypt will come and worship the Lord on the holy mountain in Jerusalem. *Isaiah 27:13 NIV*

After the suffering of His soul, He will see the light of life, and be satisfied; by His knowledge my righteous servant will justify many, and He will bear their iniquities. Therefore I give Him a portion among the great, and He will divide the spoils with the strong, because He poured His life unto death, and was numbered with the transgressors. For He bore the sin of many, and made intercession for the transgressors. *Isaiah 53:11-12 NIV*

At that time the sign of the Son of Man will appear in the sky, and all the nations of the earth will mourn. They will see the Son of Man coming on the clouds of the sky with power and great glory. And He will send His angels with a loud trumpet call, and they will gather His elect from the four winds, from one end of heaven to the other. *Matthew 24:31-35 NIV*

We are living in an exciting time! In an age that was prophesied thousands of years ago by the prophets of God. Daily, prophecies continue to be fulfilled as described in the Bible. Evangelists around the world agree that the *Rapture of the Church* could happen at any moment. What is the *Rapture* you may ask? It is that time when Jesus Christ will return to the earth to take His children home, as He promised in Acts 1:9-11. The clock continues to wind down toward the appointed time described in the Scriptures. It is highly probable that we are the generation appointed by God to witness the *glorious and unprecedented return* of the Lord Jesus Christ with our own eyes. It is highly possible that we may be the eye-witnesses to the most triumphant spectacle ever seen by mankind. On that bright and cloudless morning, we will lift up our eyes at the sound of the trumpet and we will all be changed as we stand in awe-struck wonder! We will behold the *splendid glory of the Lord* as He reaches down to gather together His children and take them home!

> Behold, I show you a mystery; we shall not all sleep, but we shall all be changed, in a moment, in the twinkling of an eye, at the last trump: for the trumpet shall sound, and the dead shall be raised incorruptible, and we shall be changed, (*1 Corinthians 15: 51, 52 NIV*).

Christ will come so quickly that the decision to accept Him as Savior and Master must have already been made before His sudden return - before the *first sound of His trumpet call!* Oh, what a glorious day that will be for all of those who are ready and waiting. For those who have lifted their eyes to the heavens in anticipation of His return. Will you be ready? Or, will you be caught off guard as in the days of Noah?

> But as the days of Noah were, so shall also the coming of the Son of man be. For as in the days that were before the flood they were eating and drinking, marrying, and giving in marriage, until the day that Noah entered into the ark. And knew not until the flood came, and took them away; so shall also the coming of the Son of man be. Then shall two be in the field; the one shall be taken, and the other left. Two women shall be grinding at the mill; the one shall be taken, and the other left. Watch therefore: for you know not what hour the Lord doth come, (*Matthew 24: 37-41 NIV*).

Are you ready to meet the Master? Have you accepted Christ as your Savior? It's not enough to know who this Jesus is! You are required to make a choice! To take a stand and accept God's gift of Love and Salvation into your heart. Do you believe that Christ was born into this world, unto the Virgin Mary; that He lived among us on this earth; was crucified on the cross, as the redemption for our sins; and He conquered death through the resurrecting power of God the Father? If you believe these things, then all you have to do is say a prayer and accept God's sacrifice for your sins, by asking Jesus to come into your heart. Ask Him to take over your life and to forgive you of your sins. Only through simple faith can you allow Jesus to come into your life and transform you into His likeness. Once you have taken this simple step you will be ready to greet our Lord and Master when that trumpet sounds and He calls us Home. It's true that no one but the Father knows the hour of Christ's return. But Jesus Himself told us; **"Now learn this lesson from the fig tree: As soon as its twigs get tender and its leaves come out, you know that summer is near. Even so, when you see all these things, you know that it is near, right at the door. Truly I tell you, this generation will certainly not pass away until all these things have happened.,** (*Matthew 24: 32-34 NIV*).

Several years ago, I completed a dissertation addressing God's plan for Israel within the confines of the *End Times*. The reality of Israel's purpose, as well as that of the collective body of Christian believers, is intricately connected. God called Israel to serve as the path for the Messiah to enter into the world. After the death, resurrection, and ascension of Jesus, He appointed the Church. or the body of believers to share the Good News of the Messiah with a lost and hurting world. *Israel was reborn* as a nation in 1948 to once again play a *significant role in God's plan*. After the *Church is Raptured* out of this world, Israel will serve as the key that opens the door for the Second Coming of Christ. Consider what I share about Israel's rebirth as a nation signifying a major prophetic sign that the End Times are upon us. This reference comes from a study out of my book, *The Mystery of Zion - Israel and the Last Days*.

The majority of biblical scholars agree that the fig tree in this parable has always been representative of Israel. Throughout

Matthew 24, Jesus is speaking specifically about the "end times" or the "signs of the age." When He speaks of the fig tree, the disciples are surely aware of whom He is speaking about. Allen M. Barber writes, "Christ's Parable of the Fig Tree without doubt refers to the presence of the nation of Israel in the Middle East during the last days. It also warns Christians to heed the 'sign of Israel' in the land as evidence God's time clock is racing forward for the Lord's return. Despite clear evidence the last days have arrived, many Christians remain ignorant of the signs of the times and their prophetic significance."[9]

Matthew, Mark, and Luke record two other references that Jesus made regarding the fig tree. The first, in Matthew and confirmed in Mark, appears to be an inconsequential side note of a story when Jesus came across a barren fig tree. But as always with the recorded words of Jesus, they all hold profound significance. Allen Barber notes, "Jesus used figurative language in cursing the barren fig tree to teach the disciples that He came to Israel in His first advent looking for spiritual fruit but found none. A fig tree with leaves but no fruit symbolized the blindness of Israel's religious leaders. Given their devotion to the Torah, they should have recognized that Jesus filled the Scriptures concerning the Messiah; however, they were blinded by their own traditions."[10] In 70 AD, right around the time of the Passover celebration when the Romans destroyed Jerusalem, the curse of the fig tree was realized. One thousand, eight hundred and seventy-eight years later that curse was lifted as a second prophetic word of Jesus came to fruition; the nation of Israel was reborn on May 15, 1948.[11]

This prophetic sign involving Israel, denotes the time frame known as the End of the Age. It provides a pretty solid starting point for expecting Christ's return, along with anticipating the Rapture of the Church. Even within the Church body, there is a lot of misunderstanding, as well as confusion within the concept of the *Rapture*, and the *Second Coming of Christ*. They are two separate

[9] Allen M. Barber, *The Day of the Lord* (Mustang, OK: Tate Publishing, 2011), p. 114.
[10] Ibid., p. 106.
[11] Lanny Cook, *The Mystery of Zion*, p. 104

events, and both have their own, distinctly divine purpose. But many Christians, have never studied the scriptures to be able to differentiate between the two. For today's devotion, I will only share insight into the *prophetic nature of the Rapture*. As Christian believers, it's essential to understand what this unparalleled, glorious event, entails. Once again, I'll refer to The Mystery of Zion - Israel and the Last Days, where it speaks about the Rapture.

> The multitude of prophetic events that have been fulfilled during the past century lead God's timetable to a point where the rapture of the Church could come at any moment. Of course, there are skeptics, along with "doomsday" enthusiasts, who provide vocal commentary both in agreement and in opposition to such a prophecy. But if biblical prophecy has any merit (and I contend that it does), we have no other option than to believe this event could happen at any moment within the next few years. Of course, it's impossible to come to an agreement even within the confines of biblical scholars as to the exact time of this event. Many a sermon and many a dissertation, along with many personal convictions, have been focused on the possibilities as to the timing of this event.

> What I am sure of is that only God knows the timeline, and whatever He chooses, I can trust it will be to His glory and purpose. Therefore, rather than speculate, it's safe to just say that according to Scripture, there will be a Rapture and the Church will be taken out of this world. There are two main passages that cite this event—a miraculous event that brings an end to the "Church Age." The first is found in Paul's letter to the church in Corinth:

> Listen, I tell you a mystery: We will not all sleep, but we will all be changed—in a flash, in the twinkling of an eye, at the last trumpet. For the trumpet will sound, the dead will be raised imperishable, and we will be changed. For the perishable must clothe itself with the imperishable, and the mortal with immortality. When the perishable has been clothed with the imperishable, and the mortal with immortality, then the saying that is written will come true: "Death has been swallowed up in victory" (1 Corinthians 15:51–54 NIV).

This event will signal the end of the Church Age, or Age of Grace, and the end of the New Covenant of salvation that is offered freely to anyone who accepts it through the atoning blood of Jesus Christ. Ron Rhodes writes, "The rapture is a sign-less event that can occur at any moment. This is in contrast to the second coming of Christ, which is preceded by many events that transpire during the seven-year tribulation period (see Revelation 4–18)."[12]

Clarence Larkin, in his book *Dispensational Truth* (which was written nearly a century earlier), speaks of this event as "the most startling 'event' of this Age and Dispensation." He continues to share this thought: "On the morning of that glorious day the air will be filled with the 'spirits' of the 'Dead in Christ,' come back to earth to get their bodies, raised and glorified."[13]

The second reference to the Rapture is found in Paul's epistle to the church in Thessalonica: After that, we who are still alive and are left will be caught up together with them in the clouds to meet the Lord in the air. And so we will be with the Lord forever (1 Thessalonians 4:17 NIV).[14]

Behold, the hour is at hand! Time is getting short. Each year, each week, each day, each hour, in fact, every passing minute brings eternity that much closer. *You cannot afford to be caught unaware!* You must be prepared for that *glorious day*! Once the time of the *Gentiles is fulfilled*, the Rapture will come. Keeping the promise of *Christ's Last Trumpet Call* that initiates the very *End Times* at the forefront of your thoughts; you must realize that it is time to reach out to share the gift of salvation with those all around you.

---

[12] Ron Rhodes, *The End Times in Chronological Order* (Eugene, OR: Harvest House, 2012), p. 48.

[13] Clarence Larkin, *Dispensational Truth* (Philadelphia, PA: Rev. Clarence Larkin Est., 1918), p. 13.

[14] Lanny Cook, *The Mystery of Zion*, pp. 152, 153

For the time is drawing nigh; it is coming ever so quickly! I leave you with a simple question before I share this final scriptural truth for you to ponder: *Are you ready to meet Jesus, face to face?*

> According to the Lord's word, we tell you that we who are still alive, who are left until the coming of the Lord, will certainly not precede those who have fallen asleep. For the Lord himself will come down from heaven, with a loud command, with the voice of the archangel and with the *trumpet call* of God, and the dead in Christ will rise first. *(I Thessalonians 4:15-16 NIV).*

Are you ready for Jesus to rapture you home into eternity? What do you need to do in order to be prepared for that great and glorious day? Take a moment to record your thoughts regarding Jesus' return in the clouds at the time of the Rapture.

_____

_____

_____

_____

_____

_____

_____

_____

_____

_____

_____

_____

_____

_____

_____

_____

_____

_____

_____

_____

_____

The Trumpet Call

The Trumpet clearly calls me, to a realm beyond this place;
   I am raised to meet my Savior; I have longed to see His face!
We are caught up all together, to meet Him in the air,
   A mighty cloud of witnesses, forever in His care!

He softly bids me; *Enter, come kneel before My throne,*
   Come sit with Me forever, for child you are My own!
I bask within His presence - He draws me closer to His breast,
   This weary soul is finally home, in Him I find sweet rest!

I take my place before Him - as I nestle at His feet,
   He lays His hand upon me – His promise is complete!
He shares with me His pleasure, as a Father with His child;
   My good and faithful servant, your soul's been reconciled.

With earthly trials behind me, I found the narrow Way,
   To the courtyard of His Temple, to a never-ending day!
Now I live within His presence, complete in perfect peace,
   A blessing from the Father, that will never, ever cease!

Eternity together, forever sealed within His grace,
   I marvel at the wonder; the *radiant glory* of His face.
In the twinkling of an eye, I now stand before the King,
   I join with heaven's chorus; all praise to Him, we sing.

To forever reign with Jesus, He is the righteous Lord,
   He prepared a place for anyone, who lives by His accord.
Raptured into heaven, transformed by God's own Son,
   Abundant life forever more, the chains of death undone.

Lanny K. Cook

Listen, I tell you a mystery: We will not all sleep, but we
will all be changed— in a flash, in the twinkling of an eye, at
the last trumpet. For the trumpet will sound, the dead will
be raised imperishable, and we will be changed. For the
perishable must clothe itself with the imperishable, and the
mortal with immortality, (*I Corinthians 15: 51-53 NIV*).

Day 34
What Will Your Answer Be?
Scriptural Reflection

Swing the sickle, for the harvest is ripe. Come, trample the grapes, for the winepress is full and the vats overflow --- so great is their wickedness! Multitudes, multitudes in the valley of decision! For the day of the Lord is near in the valley of decision. The sun and the moon will be darkened, and the stars will no longer shine. The Lord will roar from Zion and thunder from Jerusalem; the earth and the sky will tremble. But the Lord will be a refuge for His people, a stronghold for the people of Israel. *Joel 3:13-16 NIV*

When the Son of Man comes in His glory, and all the angels with Him, He will sit on His throne in heavenly glory. All the nations will be gathered before Him, and He will separate the people one from another as the shepherd separates the sheep from the goats. He will put the sheep on His right and the goats on His left. Then the King will say to those on His right, 'Come, you who are blessed by My Father; take your inheritance, the kingdom prepared for you since the creation of the world. *Matthew 25:31-34 NIV*

For this very reason, Christ died and returned to life so that He might be the Lord of both the living and the dead. You, then, why do you judge your brother? Or why do you look down on your brother? For we will all stand before God's judgment seat. It is written: "As surely as I live, says the Lord, every knee will bow before me; every tongue will confess to God.' So, then, each of us will give an account of himself to God! *Romans 14:9-12 NIV*

The Bible shares insight into two separate avenues of *formal judgement* that Christ will administer over the lives of anyone who has ever lived. The first is referred to as the *Bema Seat Judgement*, while the second is known as the *Great White Throne Judgement*. Each of which are distinctly different and are applied with a totally separate purpose. In biblical terms it's applied to either the *sheep or the goats.* One is an assessment of your life after your name was written in the *Book of Life*. The other is a judgement of *condemnation* for rejecting the grace of the Messiah.

The Bema Judgement happens *immediately following the Rapture* of the Church. It is here where each believer will have to provide an account for their faith in the Lord, and the way in which they lived their life for Christ. There is *no condemnation* associated with the Bema Judgement, as you will give an account directly to Jesus, for the way you lived after accepting Him as Lord and Savior. Jesus will assess your life according to actions that let His light shine through you. You will be rewarded for the fruits of your devotion to Him.

The only way to participate in this event is if you are a believer in the Lord Jesus, the Christ. This is an exclusive ceremony and non-believers are not allowed entrance under any circumstance. If your name is not written in the Book of Life, you'll still either be in your grave, or hanging out on earth, struggling through the traumatic challenge of the Great Tribulation. Remember, that the Bema Seat Judgement occurs immediately following the Rapture of believers, and includes both the *living and dead who accepted Jesus* into their hearts.

Many Bible scholars believe that the following passage of scripture contained within Paul's letter to the church in Corinth refers to this particular event. Make note of the reference to the term, Day, which suggests the Bema Seat Judgement, as well as the *endurance* of your work. Pay close attention to the language regarding what happens if you work is burnt. Even still, *you will be saved*. This passage clearly refers to the examination of a believer's life.

> For no other foundation can anyone lay than that which is laid, which is Jesus Christ. Now if anyone builds on this foundation with gold, silver, precious stones, wood, hay, straw, each one's work will become clear; for the Day will declare it, because it will be revealed by fire; and the fire will

test each one's work, of what sort it is. If anyone's work which he has built on it endures, he will receive a reward. If anyone's work is burned, he will suffer loss; but he himself will be saved, yet so as through fire, *(1 Corinthians 3:11-15 NKJV).*

The Great White Throne Judgement on the other hand happens after the completion of the *Millennial Reign* of Christ. This is truly a trial that ends in judgement for everyone who *rejected God's free gift of salvation* as offered through the Son, Jesus. I won't share any of the details regarding this event, as I believe you won't be in attendance. Especially, since you're devoting yourself to this forty-day journey of discovering Jesus.

None of us can even begin to imagine what it will be like to stand before either the Bema Judgment Seat, or the Great White Throne Judgement of Christ. Having to provide an accounting for your life is an extremely intimidating thought. In Matthew, Jesus himself tells us; **But I tell you that everyone will have to give account on the day of judgment for every empty word they have spoken. For by your words, you will be acquitted, and by your words you will be condemned,** *(Matthew 12:36, 37 NIV).*

I honestly believe that Christ is referring to both of the judgements within this reference, even though they aren't interchangeable between the sheep and the goats. Christians will have to give an account of their faithfulness and devotion to the Lord. Non-believers will have to provide an account for rejecting the free gift of God's grace and mercy, as offered through the Lord, Jesus Christ. What Christ makes clear in that passage is *that everyone will have to give an account* for their lives.

What could you possibly say to the King of kings, and Lord of lords that will convince Him to allow you to enter His heavenly Kingdom; where you will be honored to reign with Him forever and ever? One thing is for certain, He will know both the truth and the deceit that has rolled across your lips. He has seen and heard all that you have done while living your life here on earth. He also completely understands the true condition of your heart. Nothing you say at that instant will be able to change the course of your destiny.

At that moment when you stand before the Christ; the One whose blood was shed for your sins as the *Sacrificial Lamb* of all humanity; He will either *take you by the hand* and reward your faithfulness, if you're standing before the *Bema Seat Judgment*, or if you're standing before Him at the *Great White Throne Judgement*, He will simply turn you away by saying, *I never knew you.*

The names of all believers have been written in the *Lamb's Book of Life!* Those who recognize the need for His forgiveness and who have accepted Him as their Savior, will at that moment be Raptured into His presence. That is the *Only Way* to gain access into His Kingdom. Remember His words, *I am the way, the truth and the life, no man cometh unto the Father, but by me!* For those individuals who rejected the sacrifice of God's Only Son, their *fate is sealed* when they pass from this life. Only the individuals whose names are contained within the pages of the *Lamb's Book of Life,* will be allowed to enjoy the eternal paradise that affords communion with God the Father within the *radiance of His glory!*

> Then I saw a great white throne and him who was seated on it. Earth and sky fled from his presence, and there was no place for them. And I saw the dead, great and small, standing before the throne, and books were opened. Another book was opened, which is the book of life. The dead were judged according to what they had done as recorded in the books, *(Revelation 20:11-12 NIV).*

At the time when you stand before either of the two seats of judgement, the recorded account of your life will serve as the only *admissible evidence presented* on your behalf. At that point, it cannot be altered. The recorded acts of your days will either condemn you to eternal damnation or allow you to walk through the heavenly gates wearing a crown of righteousness. That crown is is only available through the *coronation of spiritual re-birth* when you accept Jesus as your Lord and Savior. Your reward from the Bema Seat Judgement will be a *crown of righteousness*. Your crown of glory will be adorned with the jewels of your faithfulness, symbolizing any work, words, and devotion that *glorified God* throughout your days! Your faith and devotion to Him, will be the only thing that prevails! Do you remember the saying that I shared on the Dedication page of this devotion by C. T. Studd? *Only one life, will soon be past. Only what's done for Christ will last.*

Before we close today's devotion, it's critical that you reflect on one final passage of scripture. Make sure to ponder these words before moving on to the last reflection of today's study.

> But God, who is rich in mercy, because of His great love with which He loved us, even when we were dead in trespasses, made us alive together with Christ (by grace you have been saved), and raised us up together, and made us sit together in the heavenly places in Christ Jesus, that in the ages to come He might show the exceeding riches of His grace in His kindness toward us in Christ Jesus. For by grace you have been saved through faith, and that not of yourselves; it is the gift of God, not of works, lest anyone should boast. For we are His workmanship, created in Christ Jesus for good works, which God prepared beforehand that we should walk in them, (Ephesians 2:4-10 NKJV).

Your faith in the Lord is the only thing stands the test of time, allowing you to be raptured into heaven when the Lord returns. For those individuals who have accepted Christ as their Savior, they will be rewarded according to their faithful devotion to Him. You are His hands and feet in this world for such a time as this. *What lives have you touched through His love?* How have you shared His words of encouragement and hope with a soul who was broken and lost? As a believer, those are the works that will justify your heavenly reward! Jesus said, *lay up for yourself treasures in heaven... for where your treasures are, there your heart will be also!*

There is a day of reckoning coming soon. You will stand before Jesus and provide an account for your life. *How will you respond as you stand before God's throne? What might the Lord say to you?*

_____

_____

_____

_____

_____

_____

What Will Your Answer Be?

When before God's throne you stand?
How many souls bear your witness,
Once you reach that promised land?
Christ will ask the question,
"Whom did you tell of Me?"
How many did you lead to salvation,
By my death on that cruel tree?
For you knew I came to save sinners,
You knew I died for each one,
You knew I am your redemption,
For I am God's crucified son!
I put on the cloak of a human,
When I became as one of you---
I came as that babe in a manger,
And into manhood I grew.
I thirsted and hungered no different,
Than anyone else on earth,
I experienced sorrow and sadness,
I also knew joy and mirth.
I felt pain and heartache and suffering,
Inside this human form;
I, too, grew tired and weary,
Dejected, weak, and forlorn.
Dear One, I was no different,
As I suffered and bled for you!
I felt the great pain of heartache,
When rejected by friends I knew.
I lived the humiliation,
That can only be known by one
Who has been mocked, scourged, beaten,
Even cursed and, yes, spat upon!
My back nearly broke 'neath the burden,
Of the weight of that old rugged cross
As I struggled to reach Golgotha,
To save the souls that are lost.

The crown of thorns cruelly pierced me,
They bore deep into my head;
The blood ran freely down my face;
Beloved, I was there in your stead.
I writhed in raging torment,
As the nails were pounded through
My hands and feet; Oh, the anguish!
Beloved, I did it for you!
Oh, the searing pain that engulfed me,
When they raised that cross in place,
Agony became my companion,
As I hung suspended in space!
I hung on that cross many hours.
I suffered! I bled! I died!
But I rose again triumphant,
In heavenly splendor to abide!
I love you, Dear Sinner, immensely,
For I willingly died on that tree
So, I could provide the salvation,
That's yours throughout eternity!
As I meet you here, Dear Christian,
Before this throne of grace,
I draw you close in tender love,
And greet you face to face.
Now I ask of you Believer,
Whom did you tell of me?
Did you bring one soul to repentance,
Help set one sinner free?
Beloved, I am the Redeemer,
I emptied myself for thee!
I became the Hope of the ages,
Now, what have you done for Me?

Clarice D. Cook

Day 35
How Do You Know Him?
Scriptural Reflection

He has rescued us from the domain of darkness and transferred us into the kingdom of the Son He loves. We have redemption, the forgiveness of sins, in Him. He is the image of the invisible God, the firstborn over all creation. For everything was created by Him, in heaven and on earth, the visible and the invisible, whether thrones or dominions or rulers or authorities— all things have been created through Him and for Him. He is before all things, and by Him all things hold together. He is also the head of the body, the church; He is the beginning, the firstborn from the dead, so that He might come to have first place in everything. For God was pleased to have all His fullness dwell in Him, and through Him to reconcile everything to Himself by making peace through the blood of His cross—whether things on earth or things in heaven. Once you were alienated and hostile in your minds because of your evil actions. But now He has reconciled you by His physical body through His death, to present you holy, faultless, and blameless before Him— if indeed you remain grounded and steadfast in the faith and are not shifted away from the hope of the gospel that you heard. This gospel has been proclaimed in all creation under heaven, and I, Paul, have become a servant of it.
Colossians 1:13-23 HCSB

When Jesus came to the region of Caesarea Philippi, he asked his disciples, "Who do people say the Son of Man is?" They replied, "Some say John the Baptist; others say Elijah; and still others, Jeremiah or one of the prophets." "But what about you?" he asked. "Who do you say I am?" Simon Peter answered, "You are the Messiah, the Son of the living God." Jesus replied, "Blessed are you, Simon, son of Jonah, for this was not revealed to you by flesh and blood, but by my Father in heaven. *Matthew 16:13-17 NIV*

Behold, He is coming with the clouds, and every eye will see Him, even those who pierced Him; and all the tribes of the earth will mourn over Him. So it is to be. Amen. "I am the Alpha and the Omega," says the Lord God, "who is and who was and who is to come, the Almighty. *Revelation 1:7,8 NASB*

To fully enter into a deep, personal relationship with Jesus Christ, you need to recognize His numerous characteristics. These attributes set Him apart from anyone else as He came as the *Son of Man*. These traits also define Him as the only begotten *Son of God* who came as the *Sacrificial Lamb* of God. Let's take a moment to define those attributes according to the passage from Paul's letter to the church in Colossae in the first chapter.

> **The Son is the ...image of the invisible God, the firstborn over all creation. For in him all things were created: things in heaven and on earth, visible and invisible, whether thrones or powers or rulers or authorities; all things have been created through him and for him. He is before all things, and in him all things hold together. And he is the head of the body, the church; he is the beginning and the firstborn from among the dead, so that in everything he might have the supremacy. For God was pleased to have all his fullness dwell in him, and through him to reconcile to himself all things, whether things on earth or things in heaven, by making peace through his blood, shed on the cross,** *(Colossians 1:15-20 NIV).*

Jesus is not just a symbol of God; He is God incarnate. Jesus is the *visible image of the invisible, living God.* Jesus, the Son of God, is Emmanuel – God who is with us! He is the *Word that became Flesh and dwelt among us,* (John 1:14). As the visible image of the invisible God, and since Jesus is the Word that became flesh, it is essential to recognize the significance of Christ being the *Mediator* between us and the Father. Later on in John's Gospel, the words of Christ confirm this divine, relational attribute of Jesus when He replied to one of His disciples: **Don't you know me, Philip, even after I have been among you such a long time? Anyone who has seen me has seen the Father. How can you say, 'Show us the Father,'** *(John 14:9 NIV).*

The reference regarding the *first-born over-all creation*, isn't a means to define Jesus as being created. Rather, since He is the *Second Person* within the defining aspect of the *Triune God*, this scripture simply confirms His *pre-existence, preeminence*, and rightful *authority* over all creation. The first few verses of John's Gospel add clarification, while also providing verification to the third attribute of Jesus' divine nature as the One **in whom all things have been created.**

In the beginning was the Word, and the Word was with God, and the Word was God. He was with God in the beginning. Through him all things were made; without him nothing was made that has been made, *(John 1: 1-3 NIV).*

Jesus is before all things and *in Him all things hold together.* This reference details not only His *eternal, pre-existence*, but it also declares His *superiority* and *authority* over all things that were created through His Words, for His purpose and His pleasure. It also alludes to His all-sustaining power for all things natural as well as spiritual. What other explanation could address the New Testament accounts of Jesus walking on water, calming the raging storms, restoring sight to the blind, and even raising the dead to life. Simply stated, Jesus is the one who not only *spoke all things into existence*, but He is also the *means* that all things both natural and supernatural are *held together.* He is the *bond* that not only *gives life*, but *sustains life.* The significance of Christ being the Mediator between humanity and the Father adds credence to this consideration of Jesus being the One who holds all things together. Even our relationship, fellowship, and communing with the Father, is only available through Jesus.

So, the *preeminence of Christ*, becomes both the *qualifying* and *distinguishing* factor for Jesus being the only One who was righteously worthy to serve as mankind's *Redeemer.* As the *visible image of the invisible God* there could be no other option to carry out God's purpose of reconciling mankind back to Himself. Paul shares insight toward the end of the first chapter of his letter to the Colossians regarding God's purpose of reconciliation.

> Once you were alienated from God and were enemies in your minds because of your evil behavior. But now he has reconciled you by Christ's physical body through death to present you holy in his sight, without blemish and free from accusation— if you continue in your faith, established and firm, and do not move from the hope held out in the gospel. This is the gospel that you heard and that has been proclaimed to every creature under heaven, and of which I, Paul, have become a servant, *(Colossians 1:21-23 NIV).*

This text clearly defines humanity's need for a Savior. Mankind was *alienated* from God because of disobedience. One definition of *alienate* is *to estrange*. Without *grace*, everyone is not only estranged from God, but are considered to be His *enemy*. We were not just *alienated*; the Bible says that we were *actively hostile* to God because of our sinful nature. Consider what Paul declares in his epistle to the church in Rome: **The mind governed by the flesh is hostile to God; it does not submit to God's law, nor can it do so,** *(Romans 8:7 NIV)*.

The only thing that can change your *hostile status*, is to accept God's free gift of *redemption* through the life, death, and resurrection of Jesus the Christ. *Redemption*, or if you prefer the term *reconciliation*, required the *preeminent* Jesus to serve as the atonement for sin – Jesus paid the price for the sin of humanity. Jesus has already done the heavy lifting to offer God's mercy to you through His free gift, or rather, His grace is offered to you through the life, death, and resurrection of His Sacrificial Lamb.

During the days of the Apostle Paul and within the beginnings of the early church, false teachers at Colossae were insisting that people could get closer to God through angels and by observing certain rules and regulations. Such things will never allow you get close to God. In fact, they have the opposite effect; they create a wedge between you and the Lord. *Trying to be good enough, or attempting to do things on your own, minimizes the preeminence of Jesus!* It places Him in a box of your own secular making.

Jesus earned the title as the *Head of the body* or the church, when He conquered death as the resurrected Son of God. Make no mistake, He *is the firstborn of the dead!* In other words, He rose from the grave and offers eternal life to anyone who believes in Him as Lord and Savior. Various skeptics might try to deceive you by implying that those who Jesus' raised from the grave were the firstborn of the dead. You know, people like Lazarus, or Jairus' daughter. But these miracles were completely different from Christ's resurrection.

Lazarus and the daughter of Jairus were brought back to life in the same physical body. Sadly, for them, they had to eventually suffer through another physical death after they experienced Jesus' miraculous gift of being raised back to life in this world. They came back in the same exact body as they had left behind. They lived out the remainder of their earthly days in a *corruptible, earthly shell*. But

Jesus, was resurrected. He conquered death and received a resurrected body; one that radiated with God's power, glory, and perfection. Jesus' resurrection transformed His earthly body into a *holy, incorruptible vessel; worthy of honor, praise, and adoration*. Jesus' resurrection defined His supremacy over all creation and covered Him with the *complete fullness of God*, the Father. Through the Resurrected Christ, all things have been **reconciled back to God**.

Through these few short verses in Paul's letter to the Colossians, we are afforded an opportunity to reflect upon the true nature of the Lord, Jesus Christ. To enter into a deep, intimate relationship with Him, it's important to recognize Jesus for who He truly is and the purpose for which He first came into this world. Ultimately, that purpose was defined through the concept of *redeeming grace*. Just as it was in Paul's day, people are still trying to gain salvation by various means - through worldly pursuits or by their own works or merit. People often rely on astrology, good intentions; even being a good person, or turning to psychics, fortune tellers, engaging in false religions and worshipping godless idols. Jesus reminds us that there is only one way to find salvation as He said, *I am the way the truth and the life, no one comes to the Father, except through Me*, *(John 14:6 NLT)*.

For the past two-thousand years, there have been those who attempted to place Jesus in the box of something less than divine! They profess that Jesus is *a way* to heaven, but not the *Only Way* to enter into God's eternal promise. They will say Jesus was a great teacher, prophet, or Rabbi; but He was nothing more than a mere, mortal man who was better than most! But they are WRONG! It is only through Jesus Christ, who was with God in the beginning, and Who is God, that you can discover forgiveness of sin while being reconciled back to the One who created you! *Jesus is the way*, the *truth*, and the *life* for humanity. No one can gain access to the Father except through a personal relationship with Jesus! Period! **Jesus the Christ is both** ***"Supreme and Sufficient!"*** **He is all you need! God has made this Jesus, whom you crucified, both Lord and Christ,** *(Acts 2:36 NIV)*.

Jesus is Lord of all. John MacArthur nailed it when he said, "The biblical mandate for both sinners and saints is not to 'make' Christ Lord, but rather to bow to His lordship. He is ever and always Lord, whether or not anyone acknowledges His lordship or surrenders to His authority." *(The Gospel According to Jesus, 1988, page 203).*

To complete today's devotion, consider the following questions: *What have you learned regarding the preeminence of the Lord, Jesus Christ? Do you consider Him to be Supreme and Sufficient?* If so, do you live your life in such a way that others would agree with you? It is my prayer, that, the *preeminent Light of Jesus Christ* will shine out in your life like it never has before. I pray that wherever you go; whoever you meet; whatever you do; *your life will exemplify the reality* that the *Supreme* and *Sufficient* Jesus Christ is truly the Lord and Master of your soul! Take some time to consider the previous questions and write down your thoughts in the space below.

_____

_____

_____

_____

_____

_____

_____

_____

_____

_____

_____

_____

_____

_____

_____

_____

_____

_____

How Do You Know Him?

How do you know Him? Have you heard about His fame?
 Have you heard the many stories; the wonders of His Name?
 He's the Babe born in a manger, the Bright and Morning Star;
 The Word who dwelt among us, proclaimed both near and far.
He's the Holy One of Israel, the Gift from Heaven's Throne,
 The Living Word - Promised One - He is the Cornerstone.
He's the Alpha and Omega, the Beginning, and the End,
 Master, Teacher, Comforter; He is Prophet, Priest, and Friend.

King of kings and Lord of lords, the Spirit of Pure Love,
 The only begotten Son of God sent from heaven above.
The Lily of the Valley, He's the Name above all Names,
 The long-awaited Messiah, He bears your sin and shame.
He feeds the hungry masses, He heals the sick and lame,
 He bears all grief and sorrow; He takes on your sin and pain.
Prince of Peace, the Bread of Life, He is the Truth - the Way,
 The Gate that leads to heaven, and the never-ending day!

He came to earth, so long ago; He was born in Bethlehem,
 Immanuel - "God with us," - He is the great "I Am."
The sacrifice for all mankind, He died to set you free,
 He conquered death and lives again, to save both you and me!
As you contemplate this Jesus, God's Truth is what you'll find;
 With knowledge of redemptive love, for the sins of all mankind.
Now, do you really know Him, as your precious, saving Grace?
 Will you walk beside Him? Have you met Him face to face?

When you choose to lean upon Him, you will learn His many Names;
 His love is all sufficient; and His mercy is the same.
The Firstborn of the Living, and the Firstborn of the Dead.
 He sustains you with abundance, as God's sacred, Holy Bread.
His grace runs like a river- as an ever-flowing stream,
 He is the Living Water; and the Lord Who lives Supreme.

Lanny K. Cook

Day 36
Grace so Amazing

Scriptural Reflection

Now there was a Pharisee, a man named Nicodemus who was a member of the Jewish ruling council. He came to Jesus at night and said, "Rabbi, we know that you are a teacher who has come from God. For no one could perform the signs you are doing if God were not with him." Jesus replied, "Very truly I tell you, no one can see the kingdom of God unless they are born again." "How can someone be born when they are old?" Nicodemus asked. "Surely they cannot enter a second time into their mother's womb to be born!" Jesus answered, "Very truly I tell you, no one can enter the kingdom of God unless they are born of water and the Spirit. Flesh gives birth to flesh, but the Spirit gives birth to spirit. You should not be surprised at my saying, 'You must be born again.' The wind blows wherever it pleases. You hear its sound, but you cannot tell where it comes from or where it is going. So, it is with everyone born of the Spirit. [16] For God so loved the world that he gave his one and only Son, that whoever believes in him shall not perish but have eternal life. For God did not send his Son into the world to condemn the world, but to save the world through him.
John 3: 1-8, 16, 17 NIV

Therefore, if anyone is in Christ, the new creation has come: The old has gone, the new is here! All this is from God, who reconciled us to himself through Christ and gave us the ministry of reconciliation.
2 Corinthians 5: 17, 18 NIV

But God, who is rich in mercy, because of His great love with which He loved us, even when we were dead in trespasses, made us alive together with Christ (by grace you have been saved), and raised us up together, and made us sit together in the heavenly places in Christ Jesus, that in the ages to come He might show the exceeding riches of His grace in His kindness toward us in Christ Jesus. For by grace you have been saved through faith, and that not of yourselves; it is the gift of God, not of works, lest anyone should boast. For we are His workmanship, created in Christ Jesus for good works, which God prepared beforehand that we should walk in them. *Ephesians 2: 4-10 NKJV*

There is a *Prodigal Son parable* woven through the tapestry of each and every life. The only way to get through those prodigal moments, comes through the lessons learned within the process of making your own mistakes. But sadly, making a wrong turn is much easier than getting back onto the path that leads to life more abundant. Getting past the shame, guilt, and judgment associated with a bad choice is often the biggest obstacle to getting back on track. It's extremely difficult to make your way beyond those detours as the ridicule and pious condemnation from others makes you want to run away and hide. However, the judgement from others, pales in comparison to the burden you can place on yourself for the shameful decisions and mistakes of your own choosing or circumstance.

There is only one way to get past the many obstacles that we'd much rather forget – you have to *earnestly seek* God's strength through His **grace**. Sadly, you have no control if others choose to provide grace for your situation. The *grace* you need doesn't come from others, it *comes from above*. It's not in anyone else's job description to judge or convict you for being on the wrong path. That my friend, is the *role* of the *Holy Spirit*. In fact, it's not your job to condemn or convict yourself into repentance. The best you can do is *listen* and *respond* to that *still small voice* of the *Spirit*. He will guide you along the path, and urge you to get back on the right one if you've wandered off. That is the only way to find the freedom, peace, courage, and strength to move forward through life without constantly bearing the burden of personal guilt and regret.

Jesus' entire ministry is founded on the promise of grace. In fact, He is the *personification of God's grace*. His life radiated with the *application* of grace to those who were broken and lost; those who sought after Him with a *repentant heart* and a *desperate soul*. The Gospels are filled with a multitude of examples, sharing stories of how the Lord's grace and mercy was poured out over those who were hurting and lost. He reached out to touch the lepers, healed the blind, raised the dead back to life, and forgave those whose hearts were filled with regret and deep remorse. Jesus' ministry was truly the *perfect reflection of God's grace in action*. You see, ultimate or *divine grace* comes exclusively from the Father. Jesus is not only the personification of that grace, but He is the *conduit for the Father's unmerited favor* towards humanity. When you consider grace through such a lens, it provides a deeper insight into the parable Jesus shared in the Gospel of Luke, regarding the Prodigal Son.

> Then He said: "A certain man had two sons. And the younger of them said to his father, 'Father, give me the portion of goods that falls to me.' So, he divided to them his livelihood. And not many days after, the younger son gathered all together, journeyed to a far country, and there wasted his possessions with prodigal living. But when he had spent all, there arose a severe famine in that land, and he began to be in want. Then he went and joined himself to a citizen of that country, and he sent him into his fields to feed swine. And he would gladly have filled his stomach with the pods that the swine ate, and no one gave him anything.
>
> But when he came to himself, he said, "How many of my father's hired servants have bread enough and to spare, and I perish with hunger! I will arise and go to my father, and will say to him, 'Father, I have sinned against heaven and before you, and I am no longer worthy to be called your son. Make me like one of your hired servants.'"
>
> And he arose and came to his father. But when he was still a great way off, his father saw him and had compassion, and ran and fell on his neck and kissed him. And the son said to him, "Father, I have sinned against heaven and in your sight, and am no longer worthy to be called your son."
>
> But the father said to his servants, "Bring out the best robe and put it on him, and put a ring on his hand and sandals on his feet. And bring the fatted calf here and kill it, and let us eat and be merry; for this my son was dead and is alive again; he was lost and is found." And they began to be merry, *(Luke 15: 11-24 NKJV).*

There is no greater example of the grace of the Father depicted within any other lesson that Jesus spoke about during the days of His teaching. What is extremely intriguing about the dozens of parables shared by Jesus, most of them were prophetic depictions regarding *His Kingdom.* In fact, a majority of them share deep insight into the *End Times.* This particular parable does as well, even though every message

I've ever heard, simply presents it as a great moral lesson. If you are interested in the prophetic aspect of this parable, you'll discover profound insight from my book, *The Mystery of Zion, Israel and the Last Days - Second Edition Revised.* This particular study will strengthen your faith as you realize God's devotion, commitment, and intimate involvement within Israel's continuing role of redemptive promise. It's all contained within the eternal covenant God entered into with Israel that will culminate at the end of the ages.

The reality and the mystery of the Lord's parables involve the double perspective presentation within every lesson. Since *the word of God is living and powerful, and sharper than any two-edged sword, piercing even to the division of soul and spirit, and of joints and marrow, and is a discerner of the thoughts and intents of the heart,* (*Hebrews 12: 12 NKJV*). It's no wonder that the Word, reveals both a great moral subject, as well as providing significant prophetic revelation. Jesus' parables truly are a double-edged sword of literary and spiritual design.

Several years ago, I wrote a first-person narrative involving the possible thoughts of the ***prodigal son*** within Jesus' infamous parable of the wayward son returning home to the father. I understand that it's not necessarily accurate from a true historical perspective, but it does capture the possible considerations that the younger son experienced within the confines of his prodigal journey. It is presented from a reflective perspective after he returns home to his father. Regardless, it is worthy of contemplation as you take the time to ponder today's devotional topic.

> It's difficult to know where to begin. By looking at me now, you'd never be able to guess I have made some really bad choices in this life, which is why I would like to share this story. It's not a story of romantic adventure, glamorous travel or living a life of luxury. It is, however, the story of how a young man, who just happens to be me, chose to set out on a destructive path that nearly destroyed me. Even more important, it's also the story that exemplifies the true depth of a father's love and the grace that he offers because of that love.
>
> Growing up, I never liked anybody telling me what to do, where to go, or how to get there. It caused me to be mad at

the world, and I learned to carry a pretty big chip on my shoulder! It didn't help that I was the little brother in the family. And it really didn't help that my brother was arrogantly delusional. Then again, what big brother isn't? I'm convinced that he thought somebody had died and put him in charge of the entire world, especially my world! I'm sure most of you have had a sibling who was a big pain in the backside. My brother wasn't just a total pain, he was the boil of all boils, that somehow ended up deeply attached to my very own backside. To make things worse, he was the nastiest relational bully of all sibling bullies. However, I must admit that I'm really not being fair to boils or to bullies by comparing them to the first-born, entitled heir to my father's estate.

The worst part of my life was that my parents seemed to encourage him to treat me like a paramecium-sized piece of worthless slime. They always defended him and what really added to my ire was the fact that no one ever took the time to listen to my side of any story, which caused an emptiness inside of me that just wouldn't go away. Well, after spending my entire life playing second fiddle to my pompously, pontificating, pile of older sibling pooh, I finally had enough; I rebelled in every way imaginable. I rebelled against my brother! I rebelled against my mother. I rebelled against my father! I rebelled against my friends. I even rebelled against God Almighty! I decided it was time to turn my back on everyone and everything at that very moment in my life. I was going to do whatever was necessary for me to be totally independent and to discover my own personal happiness!

I approached my father and I demanded my inheritance. He owed me big time and I was entitled to it. I didn't want to wait around for the old man to die! After all, I had spent my entire life slaving away on his estate, so he could enjoy the "good life." I longed to be free of the oppression of a family that treated me with such denigrating disregard. I was determined to set out in search of my own destiny, in pursuit of my own dreams; a place where nobody could tell me what to do or where to go! I'd had my fill of being the younger sibling and I decided to wash my hands of the whole kit and caboodle of family servitude.

Do you know what my father did? He agreed! He gave me my portion of the inheritance and sent me out to experience life all on my own! He was extremely sad when he agreed, but I didn't care. He gave me what I wanted. Actually, he gave me what I deserved! At least, what I thought I deserved at the time. I went as far away from that place as possible and as fast as my two little legs would carry me. And boy howdy, did I ever experience the world. I lived like there was no God and like there was no tomorrow. I had a satchel full of silver and I began to live the wild life; chasing women, drinking myself into oblivion, then drinking even more, as I partied for days on end. Well, actually it was more like months on end. It really all was just a great big blur.

It was a wild adventure, and at the time, I thought I was having the ride of my life. Well, at least the parts of it that I could remember. I had friends coming out of the woodwork and everybody knew me my name! I was no longer John's boy or Steve's brother. My new friends loved me for who I was. They accepted me just the way I am! Or, so I thought.

Yeah, they loved me alright! That is until the money ran out, and I could no longer buy their friendship. After I'd squandered my entire inheritance, I had no place to turn! I had nothing to eat and no place to lay my head to even try to rest! The emptiness inside of me was unlike anything I had ever felt before in my life; it was literally all-consuming. Before long, I found myself wallowing in the muck and mire of the pigs. I had reached rock bottom. It caused me to take a serious look at the kind of a man I had become. There is something to be said about waking up in the filth of a pigsty. There's a kind of stench that can stay with you forever. It made me realize that maybe, just maybe I could have done things a bit different.

Finally, I came to my senses and realized that life was pretty good at home under my father's roof and I needed to go back to beg his forgiveness. Even his hired hands were better off than I was. I'd even work for free if he would just let me come back home. I had no idea if he would even hear me out, but when you're lying face down in pig poo and urine slop, you really don't have too many options available. I swallowed my pride and headed back home hoping I would get a chance to make things right. I've got to tell you, when my father saw me walking down the dirt road toward the house, he was so filled with joy that he ran toward me as fast as he could with his arms wide open. Not only did he accept my apology, but he slaughtered the fatted calf and invited all the neighbors in for a party to beat all parties. My father put his love for me into action by showing me grace. He didn't judge me, shame me, or even condemn me. He simply forgave me and welcomed me back into his presence and provision.

I found my way back home that day, but even more importantly, I was also able to find my way back into the arms of my heavenly Father. I learned the greatest lesson in my life through those terrible mistakes of my youth. You see, the Lord's love is the only thing that can truly satisfy the soul. Popularity, money, family, friends; none of those things can fill the emptiness within the deepest recesses of your heart. My emptiness was completely filled when I chose to humbly return to my father, and reconcile our relationship. While my earthly father graciously welcomed me back, I discovered that a relationship with my heavenly Father is the only way to meet the deepest longings of my heart and soul.

Yep, that's how a father shows his love to his children; by showing them grace and forgiving them for their mistakes. It doesn't matter how many bad choices you make in this life, your Father is always ready, willing, and able to welcome you back with open arms. That is, if you're willing to humble your heart and confess that you can't survive without him. I've got to tell you, it sure beats wallowing around in the pooh of a pigsty!

Nearly one-thousand-seven-hundred-fifty years later, a historical prodigal son realized the extreme depth of his depravity. He humbly repented of his horrific past in order to return back to his Father. In the process, he completely surrendered his life into a devoted ministry for His Master. His name was John Newton, a notorious slave trader and sea captain who transported innocent lives into a torturous hell of chains, bondage, and horrific suffering. The grotesque nature of his business dealings finally took their toll, breaking his back and spirit. The prolonged exposure to those inhumane missions, transporting enslaved human cargo; bound in chains, immersed in filth, contained in the belly of a sea-faring abyss, left his soul to die in a spiritual hell.

The horrendous enterprise in which he was involved finally brought him to his knees. The hell that he had created for thousands of innocent souls had returned to haunt his very spirit. But then, somehow, someway, he found the Father's mercy and grace. It was a benevolent gift that he had never offered to any of his suffering cargo, who were transported in shackles, and bound to live out their days in the dark despair of bondage. And yet, one day he finally realized that his soul too was bound in chains. He was finally moved to recognize that and he was destined to face a spiritual death that would forever separate him from the grace of the Father. At least it would if he didn't immediately change his course, and correct his heading to True North.

In 1772, after experiencing a profound come back to Jesus' meeting, John wrote probably one of the most prolific hymns of the Christian era, Amazing Grace. In spite of the serious mistakes of his past, and the extreme pain, suffering, and even death that he caused within the realm of the slave trade, he found forgiveness. He saw the error of his ways, and he chose to turn to the only One who could offer forgiveness through God's mercy and grace. This prodigal son repented of his ways, and returned to the Father. John Newton was welcomed back with open arms and he spent the remainder of his years serving the Lord with all of his heart, soul, and mind.

> And He said to me, "My grace is sufficient for you, for My strength is made perfect in weakness." Therefore, most gladly I will rather boast in my infirmities, that the power of Christ may rest upon me, *(2 Corinthians 12:9 NKJV).*

Take a moment to *ponder your moment of prodigal repentance;* when you finally realized your desperate need for a Savior. Use the space below to share those reflections.

_____

_____

_____

_____

_____

_____

_____

_____

_____

_____

*Amazing Grace how sweet the sound, that saved a wretch like me; I once was lost, but now I'm found, was blind but now I see... ***

The world that now surrounds us, is lacking in God's grace;
Political correctness consumes the human race.
Greedy-willful-sinful lust, destroys the hearts of men,
Pursuing life thru selfish gain, engulfed by reckless sin.
Hatred, anger, entitlement, in search of foolish gain--
Kindness, caring, righteousness; all held in sad disdain.

*Through many dangers, toils and snares I have already come, 'Tis grace that brought me safe thus far and grace will lead me home... ***

Division - malice – privilege; the news throughout the day;
The masses have rejected the *Straight & Narrow Way.*
Terror – riots- murder- crime; run rampant through the land,
A graceless heart cries for blood, pro-choice is on demand.
Caught within a downward spiral, sin consumes humanity;
The darkness of the human heart, laid bare for all to see.

*'Twas grace that taught my heart to fear, and grace my fears relieved, how precious did that grace appear, the hour I first believed...***

The world it seems, is doomed to die--"Grace" is hard to find;
The guilt and shame of wickedness, enslaves the human mind.
"Grace" - the only answer, for a world that's gone astray,
Battles rage in hearts of men to always have their way.
God's love endures forever, true "Grace" is in His plan;
Redemption from a sin-filled plight—it saves the soul of man.

*The Lord has promised good to me, His word my hope secures; He will my shield and portion be, as long as life endures... ***

In a dusty, lowly stable, a child was born one night,
The Promise of the Ages, the Way, the Truth, the Light –
Jesus came to save the masses, the Atonement for our sins;
Shed His blood, the Sacrifice – 'the place where "Grace" begins.
The baby born so long ago, provides the only choice -
"Grace" is freely offered when you listen to His voice...

*Yea, when this flesh and heart shall fail, and mortal life shall cease, I shall possess, within the veil, a life of Joy and Peace... ***

God offers true forgiveness, if you turn from sinful ways;
Accept His Gift of saving "*Grace*" before your final days!
When you trust in Jesus Name, God's "*Grace*" will be revealed,
Grace has taught the heart to sing, behold your heart is healed.
Amazing Grace how sweet the sound, it saved a wretch like me...
This prodigal is welcomed home, God's grace has set me free.

Lanny K Cook

*The earth shall soon dissolve like snow, the sun forbear to shine; but God, who called me here below, will be forever mine. *Amazing Grace -*
John Newton

Day 37
Glory and Praise
Scriptural Reflection

Praise the Lord!
Praise God in His sanctuary;
Praise Him in His mighty firmament!
Praise Him for His mighty acts;
Praise Him according to His excellent greatness!
Praise Him with the sound of the trumpet;
Praise Him with the lute and harp!
Praise Him with the timbrel and dance;
Praise Him with stringed instruments and flutes!
Praise Him with loud cymbals;
Praise Him with clashing cymbals!
Let everything that has breath praise the Lord.
Praise the Lord!
Psalm 150:1-6 NKJV

Sing to the Lord a new song;
sing to the Lord, all the earth.
Sing to the Lord, praise his name;
proclaim his salvation day after day.
Declare his glory among the nations,
his marvelous deeds among all peoples.
Psalm 96:1-3 NIV

May the Lord God, the God of Israel,
who alone does wonders, be praised.
May His glorious name be praised forever;
the whole earth is filled with His glory.
Amen and amen.
Psalm 72:18, 19 HCSB

Through the years I've had numerous opportunities to serve as the Host for a gospel sing-along at my local church. At one of those memorable nights of good ole fashioned gospel music, I realized the difference between the music of my faith and the secular music that brought me endless moments of enjoyment throughout more than sixty years of life. It's not the difference in the notes, the melodies, the harmonies, the discord or even the lyrics that makes gospel music different from all other genres. The difference lies in the *inspiration* from the *Composer* of all *creation*. Gospel music isn't born through inspiration, meditation, perspiration, education, or self-reflection. *Gospel music* is born through a *personal encounter* with the *Creator Himself.*

Music has always been a special gift; one that I believe comes directly from the Lord. Music is like a sweet aroma that rises to the nostrils of the Creator. It is a reflective reminder of the mystery involving the *invisible God whose glory* is pronounced through the invisible notes that audibly echo from within the power of His grace. Music is the *conduit of worship*. It rises out of a gracious heart, anointing the Lord with the praise and adoration that only He deserves. But it's not merely a one-way street. While the melodies of praise rise as a blessing to the Father, He reflects His blessing back to the ones who engage in the act of heartfelt worship. As you lift your heart in praise to God, He in turn showers you with His grace, mercy, love. Songs that focus our attention back to the Lord, *soothe* the savage heart, *calm* an anxious mind, *water* a thirsting soul, *sustain* your very faith, *feed* your hungering spirit; while *drawing* you into the very presence of your Maker and the Creator of all things.

...and the Levites who were the singers, all those of Asaph and Heman and Jeduthun, with their sons and their brethren, stood at the east end of the altar, clothed in white linen, having cymbals, stringed instruments and harps, and with them one hundred and twenty priests sounding with trumpets— indeed it came to pass, when the trumpeters and singers were as one, to make one sound to be heard in praising and thanking the Lord, and when they lifted up their voice with the trumpets and cymbals and instruments of music, and praised the Lord, saying: "For He is good, For His mercy endures forever," that the house, the house of the Lord, was filled with a cloud, so that the priests could not continue ministering because of the cloud; for the glory of the Lord filled the house of God, *(2 Chronicles 5:12-14 NKJV).*

Do you know that there was no such thing as gospel music until after Jesus arrived? When Jesus began His ministry nearly two-thousand years ago, the gospel music scene exploded. Even without a radio station, gospel music filled the hearts and minds of the multitudes within the Promised Land. The melodious hope of the Good News, was born through personal encounters with Jesus - like the woman with the issue of blood, who reached out in faith to touch the hem of His garment, or the blind man who cried out to Jesus and his vision was restored by the Savior's touch. The woman at the well; the lepers who were healed from their affliction, and the dead who were raised from the grave; were all miraculous wonders performed by Jesus so the world would recognize Him as the long-awaited Messiah. Those personal encounters with the *Man of Miracles* transformed the lives of countless individuals. When Jesus reached out to touch someone, it wasn't just a physical condition that was healed, it was also their heart, mind, and soul. They were filled with the radiant glory of the Master as well as a joy that they couldn't contain within themselves.

It was a personal encounter with Jesus that turned John Newton's life around, causing him to surrender his eternal destiny into the hands of the Lord. He spent the rest of his life sharing the Gospel to a lost and hurting world. But the crowning achievement of his ministry came when he penned the lyrics to one of the greatest hymns of all-time, *Amazing Grace.* Then of course there is Horatio Spafford, who is credited with penning the lyrics to *It is Well with My Soul,* after the tragic loss of four daughters who drowned at sea. Gospel music is born in the valleys of life, within the tragedies of our existence, and on the mountain top experiences that proclaim victory by faith.

At the darkest moments in life, when a soul cries out in desperation to the Savior, a melodious measure of mercy fills the heart, mind, and soul of the one in anguish. God's *grace resonates* through anyone humble enough to admit they are too hurting, sick, weak, broken, sinful or lost to make it on their own. When anyone cries out to Jesus, *miracles happen.* When they occur, the resulting excitement can't be contained; it has to be shared. That's what gospel music is all about – *Jesus' response* to your cries, your hopes, your failures, and your dreams.

I grew up enjoying a wide variety of musical genres, from Country to Rock and Roll, and from Classic Instrumental to Jazz. I guess you could say that I have a rather eclectic taste for music. As a baby boomer, I grew up with some of the greatest classics composed and better yet, some of the most legendary performers the world has ever been blessed to hear. Of course, everybody loved the music of Glenn Miller, Mitch Miller, and Lawrence Welk back in the big band era. I still remember sitting around with the folks and the grandparents watching Mitch's bouncing ball and Lawrence Welk's champagne music aired on television, every Saturday evening.

There were extremely talented singers back in my formative years, who really knew how to sing. They also had the talent to put their heart and soul into every song they performed. I was raised on the sounds of country legends; when it was truly Country Western music. As a teenager and then into adulthood, I grew to love the sounds of so many amazing artists and bands. There are far too many to mention.

However, my love for a wide variety of music was instilled in me as I participated in school bands beginning in the fifth grade, including concert bands, marching bands, and jazz bands. So, of course, I was exposed to all sorts of music during those days. I loved Jazz, I loved the 1812 Overture, Fanfare for Trumpets, Tuff Sax, the Big Band sounds, and when I hear a John Phillip Sousa march, I'm taken back to my days of marching in parades, with our 150-piece high school marching band. As a trumpet player, I was inspired by the likes of Herb Albert and the Tijuana Brass, Doc Severinsen, Louie Armstrong, Maynard Ferguson, Chuck Mangione, Chicago, the Doobie Brothers, and even Santana. The brass sections of those amazingly talented entertainers still send goosebumps down my spine, as the symphony of greatness resonates from the brass bells of a horn section through the talented lips of gifted performers.

Looking back on the wide variety of musical styles that have touched my heart, I feel extremely blessed. But I have to say that it is gospel music that I most often return to in order to find encouragement, peace, and a sense of tranquility. Specifically, it's Southern Gospel that continues to have the biggest and most consistent impact on my life. Secular music *lifts my spirit*, but Gospel music *fills my soul*. I

291

remember so many Sunday evenings at the small community church where I grew up, singing the old gospel hymns for the entire service, allowing me to mindfully enter into the presence of the Lord in a profound way. That ole-time gospel somehow still manages to penetrate deeper than any other music. It doesn't just inspire, or encourage, or even just touch my heart and mind; it speaks directly to my soul. Gospel music doesn't just add to life! *Through an encounter with Jesus, you are given life.* Gospel music is all about the gift of *Life.* That is only available through a personal relationship with the *Truth* and the *Way.*

The first historical reference to gospel music came through Jesus' Triumphal Entry into Jerusalem. It erupted like a flash mob, singing and giving praise to God – the Messiah had officially arrived. All the personal encounters people had experienced with Jesus culminated at this most significant moment. As the throngs *sang new songs to their Redeemer,* the mob was so exuberant, the religious leaders told Jesus to shut them up because the music was too loud. It was hurting their ears. It was annoying their self-righteous piety! It was too much of a distraction to their contrived religious propaganda! But Jesus told them, if He was to *silence the crowds, the stones would cry out in praise,* (Luke 19:40).

Take a moment to consider the prophetic words found in the book of Ezekiel, declaring Jesus *would remove hearts of stone and replace them with new hearts of flesh,* (Ezekiel 36:26). Jesus was telling the religious leaders that their spiritual hearts were stone cold. They needed to repent of their legalistic view of God. They could hang on to their heart of stone, or they could accept Jesus for Who He is and receive a new heart of flesh. The *Good News had arrived* - the time had come for hearts and lives to be forever changed. It was time to let *hearts sing to the Lord.*

> Do not get drunk on wine, which leads to debauchery. Instead, be filled with the Spirit, speaking to one another with psalms, hymns, and songs from the Spirit. Sing and make music from your heart to the Lord, always giving thanks to God the Father for everything, in the name of our Lord Jesus Christ, (Ephesians 5:18-20 NIV).

As I reflect back on my life, I gratefully acknowledge that the difference between gospel music and every form of secular music, lies within my personal encounter with Jesus. What do all gospel songs have in common? True inspiration comes not through human means or secular inspiration. Rather, it comes through the ultimate lyricist and composer of the faith. Hebrews shares this thought of encouragement:

> Fixing our eyes on Jesus, the author and perfecter of faith, who for the joy set before Him endured the cross, despising the shame, and has sat down at the right hand of the throne of God, *(Hebrews 12: 2 NASB)*.

Gospel music fills the soul with a deep sense of the spiritual- a *personal verse from the divine*. Every gospel song ever written, possesses this same common thread – it flows from the Lord, into the heart of *a sinner saved by grace*. To me, gospel music provides encouragement as a chorus rises out of the throngs from a great cloud of witnesses; all of which, have had personal encounters with Jesus. Gospel music is a reminder that if you *fix your eyes on Jesus, the author and perfecter of your faith,* you will be able to make it through this world with a song in your heart, a bounce in your step and the melody of grace flowing lyrically out of your life. You just have to always remember to say, *'tis so sweet to trust in Jesus!* So, what about you? What kind of music moves your soul, lifts your spirit, and fills your heart with peace? How often do you immerse your soul with the comfort, peace, and assurance through some form of Gospel music?

Take a moment to turn your radio on, and praise the Lord for His grace. *What song carries you out of the worry and frustration on any given day, allowing you a personal moment of worship and praise to the One from which all gospel flows? What are the lyrics to that song?* Write them out on the space below.

_____

_____

_____

_____

_____

_____

Praise the Lord!

Praise God in His sanctuary –
>*Praise Him in His mighty heavens* *
>As the heavens declare God's glory, His creation on display...
>The baby Jesus was born of flesh, in a stable strewn with hay!
>The Savior of the world has come, the Truth - the Life - the Way;
>He is the Gate that leads to heaven, and God's never-ending day!

Praise Him for his acts of power;
>*Praise Him for his surpassing greatness.* *
>Now lift your eyes toward heaven, to stand upon God's Word,
>'Twas God Who gave His only Son – the blessed, holy Lord!
>"Glory to God in the highest," sang the angels in one accord;
>"Peace on earth, goodwill to all" goes out from this day forward!

Praise him with the sounding of the trumpet,
>*Praise him with the harp and lyre,* *
>God's love endures forever, through the Son He had a plan–
>Redemption from this sinful plight, to save the souls of man.
>"For unto us a child is born," that's how God's grace began...
>"And to us a Son is given, to save the fallen human clan!

Praise him with timbrel and dancing,
>*Praise him with the strings and pipe,* *
>The promise of salvation whispers deep within each heart–
>As seasons pass, time moves on, and moments quickly part...
>If you choose to take God's Promise, redemption will impart;
>His peace, His joy, His presence - His love will never part!

Praise him with the clash of cymbals,
>*Praise him with resounding cymbals.* *
>The sacrificial Lamb of God –– He died upon a tree,
>Born to be the sacrifice – He will set the sinner free!
>King of kings and Lord of lords, He holds your destiny;
>He conquered death, defeated sin, and now lives eternally.

Let everything that has breath praise the LORD. *
>As you celebrate the Savior, may you Praise His Holy Name;
>Accept His gift of "amazing grace," then you'll never be the same!
>May you sing throughout each day; sing without refrain,
>Lift your eyes toward heaven, may you praise His holy Name!

Lanny K. Cook

Praise the Lord! - Psalm 150

Day 38
The Humble Gospel Message
Scriptural Reflection

Jesus Christ is the same yesterday and today and forever. *Hebrews 13:8 NIV*

"The Spirit of the Lord God is upon Me,
Because the Lord has anointed Me
To preach good tidings to the poor;
He has sent Me to heal the brokenhearted,
To proclaim liberty to the captives,
And the opening of the prison to those who are bound;
To proclaim the acceptable year of the Lord,
And the day of vengeance of our God;
To comfort all who mourn,
To console those who mourn in Zion,
To give them beauty for ashes,
The oil of joy for mourning,
The garment of praise for the spirit of heaviness;
That they may be called trees of righteousness,
The planting of the Lord, that He may be glorified."
Isaiah 61: 1-3 NKJV

How beautiful upon the mountains
Are the feet of him who brings good news,
Who proclaims peace,
Who brings glad tidings of good things,
Who proclaims salvation,
Who says to Zion,
"Your God reigns!"
Isaiah 52: 7 NKJV

Sing to the Lord, all the earth;
Proclaim the good news of His salvation from day to day.
Declare His glory among the nations,
His wonders among all peoples.
I Chronicles 16: 23, 24 NKJV

Before you can effectively share the *light of Jesus*, you need to fully realize that He is the most important relationship that anybody can have in life. You need to understand that *Jesus is Supreme* and that He alone is all-*Sufficient*. You not only need to believe that, but live your life accordingly! You can't be a follower of Jesus and dabble in the occult, astrology, fortune telling, or only accept the part of the Scripture that fits into your spiritual determination and lifestyle. Paul's letter to the Christians in Colossians is going to help understand the importance of staying focused on the *righteous integrity* of the *humble Gospel* message. You can't let the world distract you from the veracity of Jesus' ministry and purpose.

Let's start today's devotion by taking a look at the historical context of the book of Colossians. Colossae is located on a hill overlooking Turkey's Lycos River Valley approximately one hundred miles east of Ephesus. This is the region where the seven Asian Churches are located; the ones spoken of in the Book of Revelation chapters one through three. Of all the churches that Paul wrote to, this was the smallest assembly of believers. In fact, Paul never visited the church and we don't even have a biblical record of how it started.

The church in Colossae probably began sometime during the time of Paul's three-year ministry in Ephesus. The founders of this small congregation were either Timothy, Paul's close companion; Epaphras, who was the pastor of the church at the time; or possibly Nymphas and/or Philemon who owned homes where the church of mostly Gentile believers met. Paul wrote this letter during his first imprisonment in a Roman jail. It has been called the *twin Epistle* of Ephesians, as both were written around the same time, approximately 61 AD. Keep in mind that this letter was written approximately thirty years after Jesus' resurrection and ascension into heaven.

Paul's book to the Ephesians magnifies the church of Christ while focusing on the body of Christ; while Colossians magnifies the Christ of the Church, or the *Head*, focusing on the *Supremacy* of Jesus Christ. Colossians is the most *Christ-centered book* in all of the Bible. If you want to build a strong foundation of faith, it has to be constructed on the *humble Gospel message*. It can't be sugar-coated. It can't be watered down, and it can't be fortified with any religious distractions.

The Gospel has to remain pure, spotless, and unblemished; just like Jesus, as He became the Sacrificial Lamb of God.

If you didn't know better, you would think that Paul was writing it to the church in America today! Which is understandable because humanity hasn't changed a whole lot over the past two-thousand years. The good news is that neither has Jesus Christ, according to Hebrews 13:8 NIV *Jesus Christ is the same yesterday and today and forever.*

The Colossian Church was experiencing a worldly influence that was threatening the very foundation of the believer's faith in Jesus Christ. Paul shares a reference to these influences in the second chapter of his letter. Apparently, the church was being pressured to combine elements of *Greek philosophy, Jewish legalism*, as well as a form of *mysticism* into their doctrinal beliefs and rituals of worship, as well including it throughout their teachings. Does that sound familiar to you? It sounds a lot like the battles Israel had during her years of exile, living in foreign lands where they continually embraced the gods of neighboring nations. Things really aren't any different today for any Christian believer. The challenge to remain true to the course of Christ's Gospel is extremely difficult with all the worldly distractions you face.

Many people in the church practiced *asceticism*, which is a strict form of *self-restriction*, focusing on avoiding all types of *worldly indulgence.* From that perspective, everything in life had to be pursued in a disciplined manner for religious acceptance. In other words, faith was linked to *works*, rather than *grace*. This wasn't the only distraction in the church body, as others actively *worshipped angels*, claiming they were the intermediaries between humanity and God. Many individuals in the church also pursued mystical experiences out of the spiritual realm, claiming they were an essential part of the Christian faith. Simply stated, they took the teachings of Jesus, added their own flavor and an acceptable social flair to make the *gospel palatable to everyone.* Once again, does that sound familiar? All of these pagan rituals and pursuits were not only a distraction to the true person and purpose of Christ, but they were also an *abomination to God*.

However, it's important to remember, at this time in the early Church history, they didn't have the New Testament to refer to or study. They had the Torah and the words of the Prophets. Other than that, they had the *oral traditions* passed down for three decades that often shared a tainted version of Jesus' teachings. Of course, that's why Paul wrote this letter to the Colossians.

I heard a story many years ago that illustrates the people-pleasing tolerance that had infested the church in Colossae. Maybe you've heard it before, but here goes.

> Did you hear about the accountant who applied for a top-level position with a fortune 500 Company? He had already made it through an extremely meticulous screening process, and proceeded through several rounds of exhaustive interviews. When he was called back for a final, one-on-one meeting with the CFO of the company, he was ecstatic. After a rather long and grueling interview that lasted for several hours, the Executive asked him one final, rather odd question: "What is 2+2?" The applicant thought for just a minute, realizing the intense gravity of this profoundly simple question. After some rather serious contemplation he finally replied, "Whatever you want it to be!"

Sadly, in today's society, many Christians take this same approach toward their faith. They make the teachings of Christ fit into something that meets their own personal agenda. They water it down so badly that it doesn't bear any semblance to the Truth of the Gospel in the name of *tolerance* and *political correctness!* Scripture is taken *out of context*, not considering the *cultural considerations of the time*, while attempting to pound a round peg of *truth* into a square hole of *personal preference*. That's exactly what was happening to the church in Colossae! There were those who were twisting and contorting the Gospel message of Jesus to make it conform to their pleasure. They placed Jesus in a box that suited their needs; integrating cultural rituals in order to present a socially acceptable religious experience, while claiming it to be the Gospel of Christ.

As you study the Gospels you quickly realize that Jesus doesn't *conform to any man-made standard, interpretation, or practice*. Never once did He meet the expectations of the majority of people or religious leaders of His day! They were looking for an all-powerful military leader who would whip the tail of Rome and anyone else who got in the way of Israel! They were looking for a conquering king to save them from the tyranny of Rome and deliver them from oppression that had ruled over them for much of their history!

Israel wasn't looking for a Messiah who would serve as the *Sacrificial Lamb* of God. Instead, they were looking for the *Lion of Judah* who would come to devour all of Israel's enemies and destroy those who stood against her. They were looking for an earthly king, rising victorious to set up a worldly kingdom! You see Jesus never fit into their man-made box of expectations! Actually, Israel wanted so badly to jump to the end of the story, they skipped over the middle pages of God's prophetic Word.

Thirty years after the resurrection of Jesus and His ascension into heaven, the new Christian body was picking up momentum and many of the new converts were trying to mix the truth of the Gospel of Jesus with their *interpretive* and *pagan* pursuit of religious *conformity*. That's why this short, powerful letter from Paul is so important. It brings the Truth, Way, and Life of *Jesus the Christ* back into focus proclaiming His supreme *Power, Glory, and Preeminence*.

Jesus is the embodiment of the *full deity of God* - the *Creator* and *Sustainer* of all life, the *Head of the church*, the *Resurrected Son of God*- *fully man* yet *fully God*. He is the *all-sufficient Savior* and the *Author* and the *Finisher of the faith*. He is the *Alpha* and *Omega*, the *Beginning* and the *End* - *the First* and the *Last*. He is the *Living Word of God* who spoke creation into existence: *Who was*, and *Is* and *Is to come!*

Jesus is the *King of kings* and *Lord of lords*, the *Lion of Judah*, the *Holy One of Israel*, and the *Promise of the Ages*. He is the *Sacrificial Lamb*, the *Atonement* for your sin, the *Redeemer* of your soul, the Long-Awaited *Messiah!* He is *Wonderful Counselor, Prince of Peace*, and the everlasting **Father!** He is the *Bread of Life*, the *Living Water*, the *Life*, the *Truth*, and the *Way*. And that is just the tip of the iceberg when it comes to the *preeminence* of Jesus the Christ!

That is what Paul clarifies as the false teachers in Colossae were doing their best to minimize Jesus. Many people thought He was important but not essential. They had given Him a place in their lives, without recognizing that He deserved to be first in their lives. Jesus was *prominent* to them, but certainly not *preeminent* in their eyes. Jesus is before all things, as well as above all things! Many believers today hold on to this same perspective. What about you?

The very essence of the humble Gospel message is contained within the truth and the *accuracy of Jesus' teachings.* That truth is dependent upon the *supremacy* of Christ. So, the challenge for you, as you reflect on today's devotion is to focus on the divine nature of Jesus. Do you believe the truth of the Gospel of Jesus Christ? Do you recognize the *person,* the *power,* and the *preeminence* of Jesus the Christ? Do you recognize Him as the only begotten Son of God? *Do you accept Him at His Word? Have you surrendered your life into His will, and His ways?* If so, take some time to give Him the glory and praise His holy name!

> To him who is able to keep you from stumbling and to present you before his glorious presence without fault and with great joy— to the only God our Savior be glory, majesty, power, and authority, through Jesus Christ our Lord, before all ages, now and forevermore! Amen, *(Jude 24, 25 NIV).*

As you ponder today's devotion, share your thoughts about the *supremacy of Jesus Christ and why that's important for your faith.*

_____

_____

_____

_____

_____

_____

_____

_____

_____

_____

_____

_____

The Humble Gospel Message

Jesus left the splendor of heaven; in tender humility He came,
      To a family with little to offer - no wealth, no power - no fame.
The Word became flesh among us, on a cold and star-filled night;
      A Savior born unnoticed, within a manger's modest light.

No crowds were there to greet Him, No one seemed to care,
      Even the stables' beastly tenants; were not noticeably aware;
There were no trumpets blaring, no headlines would declare;
      Immanuel, yes, God with us; Salvation He'd come to share.

The lowly, paltry shepherds, the outcasts of their day;
      Were filled with fear and trembling, as they heard the Angel say:
"Fear Not, I bring good tidings, Good News for all the earth -
      For unto you a Child is born... Now go celebrate His birth."

Angels proclaimed the wonder, as they sang the Gospel hymn:
      "Glory to God in the highest, on earth peace, goodwill to men!"
Yet, no one seemed to notice, Mankind continued as before...
      Going about their routine business, tending to the daily chore.

Unpretentious, Unassuming, Unobtrusive, Son of God,
      He lived His life in humility, while on this earth He trod,
He lived a life of service – it was a ministry of grace;
      Selfless, caring, giving --- for all the human race.

God so loved His children, that He chose to share His plan;
      He sent Salvation to this world – to save the souls of man.
The gift He freely offers – a humble, sacrificial love,
      The atoning price was paid for sin, sent from heav'n above.

Jesus is quietly waiting, as He softly calls your name;
      And when you choose to listen, you will never be the same.
He will never force the issue--won't demand you make a choice;
      In humility He's waiting -- Do you hear His loving voice?

With your humble adoration - He will save you from your sin;
      Thru humility - forgiveness flows - If you choose to let him in.
As you celebrate redemption, may you embrace Humility,
      With the humble, gospel message: His Grace, will set you free.

Lanny K. Cook

Day 39
Shout it From the Mountain Top
Scriptural Reflection

I, Jesus, have sent my angel to give you this testimony for the churches. I am the Root and the Offspring of David, and the bright Morning Star." The Spirit and the bride say, "Come!" And let the one who hears say, "Come!" Let the one who is thirsty come; and let the one who wishes take the free gift of the water of life. *Revelation 22: 16, 17 NIV*

> The people walking in darkness
> have seen a great light;
> on those living in the land of deep darkness
> a light has dawned.
> *Isaiah 9:2 NIV*

But Moses said to God, "Who *am* I that I should go to Pharaoh, and that I should bring the children of Israel out of Egypt?" So He said, "I will certainly be with you. And this *shall be* a sign to you that I have sent you: When you have brought the people out of Egypt, you shall serve God on this mountain." *Exodus 3:11, 12 NKJV*

The sight of the glory of the Lord *was* like a consuming fire on the top of the mountain in the eyes of the children of Israel. So Moses went into the midst of the cloud and went up into the mountain. And Moses was on the mountain forty days and forty nights. *Exodus 24:17, 18 NKJV*

Now after six days Jesus took Peter, James, and John his brother, led them up on a high mountain by themselves; and He was transfigured before them. His face shone like the sun, and His clothes became as white as the light. And behold, Moses and Elijah appeared to them, talking with Him. *Matthew 17:1-3 NKJV*

Everybody trusts in something or someone for answers to big issues. Throughout life we ponder questions such as *Why am I here? What is my purpose? What happens after I die? Is there life after death? Where will I spend eternity?* Humanity has an innate desire for eternal significance. We are created in the image of God and He placed that desire in each of us. It's like a compass that points us back to spiritual north - back to God.

> He has made everything beautiful in its time. He has also set <u>eternity</u> in the human heart; yet no one can fathom what God has done from beginning to end, *(Ecclesiastes 3:11 NIV).*

From the beginning of creation, man has pondered the possibilities as to *what lies beyond this life*. The Egyptians and the Romans provide examples of cultures that had a preoccupation with life after death. All the Pharaohs of Egypt and the many Caesars of Rome proclaimed themselves to be gods while they were still alive. Caesar Augustus of the Roman Empire during Jesus' day was a perfect example. Augustus actually used the Greek word gospel to describe his new world order. The empire declared him a god and established rites of worship proclaiming that his reign would last forever. Sadly, for him, and the multitude of demented rulers declaring their own immortality, that wasn't the case. *Immortality is only available through a personal relationship with Jesus.*

There are those today, who believe that all roads lead to their personally, contrived version of heaven. Some religions proclaim that certain members can become *a god* of their own little planet, somewhere in a galaxy far away. Their defined status of personal deification, lays promise to a whole gaggle of virgins, guaranteed to make their planetary reign one of intimate pleasure and personal contentment. Nearly all religions attempt to provide answers to what lies beyond this world and most contain some form of works-based access for redemption. In other words, you can earn your way to a personally contrived dream of paradise. The only exception to this view is *contained within the truth of Christ's teaching*. It is only through Jesus Christ that a soul can find redemption. It's only by God's grace! Only through Jesus can sins be forgiven and salvation secured. You can't earn it through good works, buy it, or even be born into it. There is no feat that can be accomplished; nothing that you can ever inherit that will make you worthy enough to deserve God's grace! Redemption is only available through the life, death, and resurrection of the Lord, Jesus Christ.

No single life in the history of humanity has had a more significant impact, than that of the Lord Jesus Christ. I think it's important, as we come to the end of this forty-day devotional, to once again reflect on the divine nature of Jesus.

> I am the way, and the truth, and the life; no one comes to the Father but through Me, (John 14:6). Jesus said to them, I am the bread of life; he who comes to Me will not hunger, and he who believes in Me will never thirst, (John 6:35). Then Jesus again spoke to them, saying, "I am the Light of the world; he who follows Me will not walk in the darkness, but will have the Light of life," (John 8:12).

Jesus, is not an *expression of exasperation*, a word of *profanity*, or a form of revolting *vulgarity*, Just the opposite. Jesus, is the *Name above all names*. He is the *King* of kings and the *Lord* of lords. He is the *Alpha* and the *Omega*, the *Beginning*, and the *End!* Jesus is more than just some historical figure. He has inspired more songs, been the subject of more books, has stirred the hearts of more poets, and roused the talents of more artists than any other person in the history of the world. Why? It's because of Who He Is! *Jesus is the Author and the Finisher of our faith!* (Hebrews 12:1, 2 NIV).

The earliest memories of my life are intertwined with going to church and *learning about Jesus.* I was blessed to have been raised in a home that placed Christ at its center and made church an active part of my formative years. Growing up, I never had a doubt in my mind about Who Jesus is. I knew beyond a shadow of a doubt that Jesus is real, that He is the Son of God, who was born of a virgin. He lived a sinless life and died an excruciating death on the cross for my sins and that on the third day, He rose from the grave and lives forever more. In our home, Jesus was significant. He was placed at the center of our little family world. We prayed before every meal, and around the dinner table we discussed the Bible, as well as our faith. We attended church services every week.

As a teenager, after being immersed in the the true evidence that supports the Christian faith, I accepted Jesus into my heart. At a little church camp in the Rocky Mountains named Id-Ra-Ha-Je, I made the decision to *follow after Him* all the days of my life. My life was changed forever! What I learned through my childhood is that *experiencing Jesus isn't an event that happens at church on Sundays, or even at church camp for a week in the summer; it truly is a lifestyle. It's a way to live life to the fullest.* People sometimes imply that the only reason I'm a Christian is because I was brainwashed from my youth. There is nothing further from the truth! I follow Jesus, because I have personally experienced His love and throughout my life, I have seen His faithfulness and grace in action.

Nobody has changed the world like Jesus. His birth is so significant that it *split recorded history into two timelines* – AD - Anno Domini (Nostri Jesu Christi) and BC - Before Christ. Philip Yancey in his book, "The Jesus I never Knew," summarizes the true essence of Jesus; "I am drawn to Jesus, irresistibly, because He positioned himself as the dividing point of life – my life" For 2000 years, the influence Jesus had on the lives of people has never been surpassed. People who encounter the risen Christ are totally transformed. No one who meets Jesus ever stays the same.

> Do not let your hearts be troubled. You believe in God; believe also in me. My Father's house has many rooms; if that were not so, would I have told you that I am going there to prepare a place for you? And if I go and prepare a place for you, I will come back and take you to be with me that you also may be where I am, (John 14:1-3 NIV).

Only through Jesus, can your sins be forgiven and your life filled with hope. Once you open your heart to let Jesus in, you will be forever changed---transformed---and your eternal destiny sealed. Eye has not seen, nor ear heard, nor have entered into the heart of man the things which God has prepared for those who love Him, *(I Corinthians 2:9 NKJV).*

> For the wages of sin is death, but the gift of God is eternal life in Christ Jesus our Lord, *(Romans 6:23 NIV).*

> This is how God showed his love among us: He sent his one and only Son into the world that we might live through him. This is love: not that we loved God, but that he loved us and sent his Son as an atoning sacrifice for our sins. Dear friends,

since God so loved us, we also ought to love one another, *(I John 4:9-10 NIV).*

I have been privileged over the years, to be mentored by two devoted, men of God. These men spoke into my life, helping me focus on the goal to desperately follow the Lord, Jesus Christ. Pastor Bob Serrao was the pastor of my youth who invested a lot of time into our teen group. He was the one who instilled into my heart a deep devotion to follow after Jesus. It was the messages shared by him at that little church camp when I was a teenager, that caused me to respond to the voice of my Master. It was Pastor Bob who encouraged me to make a commitment to follow Christ. On the side of a beautiful mountain meadow, sitting beneath the canopy of God's heavenly splendor, my life was forever changed. I chose to surrender my life into the Lord's hands. It was at that very moment when my soul took flight on a personal journey of intimacy with Jesus.

Nearly forty years later, I was blessed once again to have another man of God speak into my life, helping my faith persevere through some extremely difficult challenges. His name was Vince and he was an avid hiker and mountaineer. Pastor Vince was an amazing man of God, who was always focused on his ministry. Nothing seemed to ever slow him down. He was like an energizer bunny who would just keep going when everybody else was drained. I went on a short-term mission trip to Alaska with Vince as the leader. It was two weeks of exhaustive labor at a radio station in the little village called North Pole. I was a last-minute replacement on the team, joining them just weeks before departing out of Denver.

During that trip, I got to know Vince. He was a man after God's own heart. Our days were filled with lots of hard work. It involved a whole lot of sweat, a few tears by some of the ladies in the group, along with a bit of blood from the hazards of our labor, I began to develop an admiration for Vince. A friendship developed during the long, twenty-hours of sunlight, as we didn't dare, waste too much time on sleep.

Vince shared that God seemed to be leading him to a mission. He felt called to place the Word of God upon the highest mountain peak on each of the seven continents. To prepare for his quest, he chose to climb all fifty-three of the fourteeners in the state of Colorado. A fourteener is a mountain that is at least 14,000 feet above sea level. On each of those Colorado peaks He successfully placed a Bible. It was his undying belief that the word of God needed to be proclaimed from the highest mountains throughout the world.

Pastor Vince completed his initial goal of placing God's Word on the highest peak of each of the world's seven continents, including Mt. Everest. Vince attempted to climb Everest twice, but due to altitude sickness, which resulted in a serious medical condition called pulmonary edema, he had to abandon his quest. However, on his second attempt at Everest, he handed his dream off to a fellow climber. This man successfully reached the summit, placing the Bible on the highest peak in all the world. The irony of this tag-team effort on the highest and most deadly mountain in all the earth, involved the colleague Vince chose to complete his mission. The man who ascended the summit of Everest to place God's Word on the earth's highest peak, was a Jew. It was a descendent of Abraham that completed God's assigned task.

Not too long after the success on Everest, Vince continued his mission by making a trip to Switzerland. His objective had taken on a broader scope. Now he felt called to place a Bible on the highest peak of various nations. In this case, it would be the Matterhorn, a mountain that borders Italy and Switzerland. Just a week before Vince left for this final mission trip, he had shown me pictures he had taken during a training climb on a local fourteener called Longs Peak.

One particular image provided a daunting perspective on a piece of the trail that is referred to as the chute. It is a treacherous passage on a short section of the trail that requires hikers to trek across a very narrow gap. The chute requires a precarious, acrobatic tight-rope act to continue on to the other side of the trail. Both sides of the chute fall off abruptly, but the one side drops straight down for a thousand feet. To slip and fall on this section of the trail is certain death for any climber. Through the years, numerous hikers have met their demise at this particular spot of this mountain trail.

My friend, mentioned in passing, as I was closely studying this particular picture, how eerie it would be to lose footing, and plummet a thousand feet to your death. I solemnly agreed as I moved on to a more scenic image in his majestic collage and I never gave it a second thought as he continued to share photos of his latest adventure. A few days after our visit, Vince headed out to Switzerland.

Vince reached the summit of this majestic piece of real estate and placed a Bible, securely wrapped in plastic at the pinnacle of this magnificent peak of God's creation. As the team made its descent from the summit, Vince and another climber were descending over a non-technical part of the mountain. This meant that none of the climbers were tethered with safety ropes. Suddenly, without warning a horrendous gust of wind caught Vince and a fellow climber, blowing them over the edge of a cliff. The thousand-foot free-fall claimed the precious life of Vince, along with that of his companion. Ironically, his simple words, shared in passing just a few weeks earlier, became a prophetic declaration regarding, what turned out to be, his final climb.

Vince's death was tragic. It was heartbreaking. It was shocking for everyone who knew him. But for me, it went beyond that as I had etched within the recesses of my memory a picture of the chute, and my imagination created a haunting image of Vince free-falling down that passage. However, in my mind, I never saw Vince hit bottom. Thank goodness! I honestly believe in my heart that it's because Vince's Lord and Master opened the window of heaven during his final descent to allow his soul entrance to eternal peace.

I am confident, that my friend, Vince, didn't make that final, earthly journey alone. His Lord was with him all the way. Jesus was there to carry his faithful servant home at that very moment, when at his appointed time, Vince took his final breath. At that instant, he took the ***wings of the dawn*** and entered into his eternal reward, all because of the faith he had in his Lord and Master.

> Now faith is the substance of things hoped for, the evidence of things not seen. For by it the elders obtained a good testimony. By faith we understand that the worlds were framed by the word of God, so that the things which are seen were not made of things which are visible. By faith Abel offered to God a more excellent sacrifice than Cain, through which he obtained witness that he was righteous, God testifying of his gifts; and through it he being dead still speaks. By faith Enoch was taken away so that he did not see death, "and was not found, because God had taken him;" for before he was taken, he had this testimony,

that he pleased God. But without faith it is impossible to please Him, for he who comes to God must believe that He is, and that He is a rewarder of those who diligently seek Him. By faith Noah, being divinely warned of things not yet seen, moved with godly fear, prepared an ark for the saving of his household, by which he condemned the world and became heir of the righteousness which is according to faith.

By faith Abraham obeyed when he was called to go out to the place which he would receive as an inheritance. And he went out, not knowing where he was going. By faith he dwelt in the land of promise as in a foreign country, dwelling in tents with Isaac and Jacob, the heirs with him of the same promise; for he waited for the city which has foundations, whose builder and maker is God. By faith Sarah herself also received strength to conceive seed, and she bore a child when she was past the age, because she judged Him faithful who had promised. Therefore, from one man, and him as good as dead, were born as many as the stars of the sky in multitude—innumerable as the sand which is by the seashore. These all died in faith, not having received the promises, but having seen them afar off were assured of them, embraced them, and confessed that they were strangers and pilgrims on the earth. For, those who say such things declare plainly that they seek a homeland. And truly if they had called to mind that country from which they had come out, they would have had opportunity to return. But now they desire a better, that is, a heavenly country. Therefore, God is not ashamed to be called their God, for He has prepared a city for them, *(Hebrews 11:1-16 NKJV).*

Faith *requires action* on your part. You can't wait around hoping for faith to drop into your lap. It doesn't just appear through the wave of some magic wand, or by some cosmic wonder. You have to seek after it before opening your heart to receive it into your life. Faith will only develop as you actively pursue the answers to the spiritual questions, challenges, and circumstance of life. Faith is defined by your personal search for God's promise of significance. It is only available as you reach out to Him and allow His *power of promise* to transform your life. As we close today's devotion, consider what Peter shared regarding the *Lord's promise.*

The Lord isn't really being slow about his promise, as some people think. No, he is being patient for your sake. He does not want anyone to be destroyed, but wants everyone to repent. But the day of the Lord will come as unexpectedly as a thief. Then the heavens will pass away with a terrible noise, and the very elements themselves will disappear in fire, and the earth and everything on it will be found to deserve judgment. Since everything around us is going to be destroyed like this, what holy and godly lives you should live, looking forward to the day of God and hurrying it along. On that day, he will set the heavens on fire, and the elements will melt away in the flames. But we are looking forward to the new heavens and new earth he has promised, a world filled with God's righteousness. And so, dear friends, while you are waiting for these things to happen, make every effort to be found living peaceful lives that are pure and blameless in his sight, *(2 Peter 3:9 - 14 NLT).*

As you silence your heart to come before the Lord today; *ask Him to quicken your heart to His promise.* Take time to consider what you hear Him say. Then, come back to this page and share what His voice is calling you to share for *His radiant glory.*

_____

_____

_____

_____

_____

_____

_____

_____

_____

_____

_____

_____

_____

_____

From the Highest Mountain Peak

In silent meditation, I heard His still small voice,
      Calling me to action, to make a daring choice;
To follow in His footsteps - devoted to His plan,
      To share the gospel message, that saves the souls of man.

I heard His voice and answered, "I chose the narrow way,
      That leads to life eternal and the never-ending day!"
I gave my life to Jesus, and I offered him my all,
      Devoted to the mission - I answered His sweet call!

No matter what the challenge, I'll give my very best,
      I'll stand for Christ and run the race, until the final test.
No matter what the mission, I will give my all in all,
      I will humbly serve my Master, 'til the final trumpet call!

In silent meditation, again I heard His voice,
      "Go forth to all the nations, and offer them a choice.
Tell them that I love them! Tell them of the price;
      I paid for their salvation through My loving sacrifice."

Shout forth the gospel message from the highest mountain peak;
      Share God's love with all the world – the lost, the hurt, the weak!
Place His Word upon the mountain, so all the world may find;
      The path that leads to heaven, thru God's grace for all mankind.

Yes, I've climbed the highest mountains and I've seen God's majesty;
      I've shared His Word that brings new life to sinners just like me!
Again, I hear Him beckon. "My son, come find your rest......"
      "My good and faithful servant, you've given Me your best!"

Lanny K. Cook

Day 40
Wings of the Dawn
Scriptural Reflection

Lord, You have searched me and known me. You know when I sit down and when I get up; You understand my thought from far away. You scrutinize my path and my lying down, and are acquainted with all my ways. Even before there is a word on my tongue, Behold, Lord, You know it all. You have encircled me behind and in front, and placed Your hand upon me. Such knowledge is too wonderful for me; It is too high; I cannot comprehend it. Where can I go from Your Spirit? Or where can I flee from Your presence? If I ascend to heaven, You are there; If I make my bed in Sheol, behold, You are there.

If I take up the wings of the dawn, If I dwell in the remotest part of the sea, even there Your hand will lead me, And Your right hand will take hold of me. If I say, "Surely the darkness will overwhelm me, And the light around me will be night," Even darkness is not dark to You, And the night is as bright as the day. Darkness and light are alike to You. For You created my innermost parts; You wove me in my mother's womb. I will give thanks to You, because I am awesomely and wonderfully made; Wonderful are Your works, and my soul knows it very well.

My frame was not hidden from You When I was made in secret, and skillfully formed in the depths of the earth; Your eyes have seen my formless substance; and in Your book were written All the days that were ordained for me, when as yet there was not one of them. How precious also are Your thoughts for me, God! How vast is the sum of them! Were I to count them, they would outnumber the sand. When I awake, I am still with You. Search me, God, and know my heart; Put me to the test and know my anxious thoughts; and see if there is any hurtful way in me, and lead me in the everlasting way.
Psalm 139: 1-18, 23-24, NASB

Therefore, God exalted him to the highest place and gave him the name that is above every name, that at the name of Jesus every knee should bow, in heaven and on earth and under the earth, and every tongue acknowledge that Jesus Christ is Lord, to the glory of God the Father. *Philippians 2:9-11 NIV*

315

As our forty-day journey together draws to a close, I would be remiss to not end with a few simple questions. *How is your relationship with Jesus?* I pray that your connection to Him is stronger, deeper, and more intimate now than it has ever been. It's important throughout the next few days, weeks, and even months, to take time to reflect on the insight you've gained through this journey regarding the truth of the *life, death,* and *resurrection* of Jesus Christ. He not only came to save you from the chains of sin and shame, but He also came to *save you from yourself.* You will never be able to enter into His presence on your own accord. Thinking you can, is arrogant folly.

> For the message of the cross is foolishness to those who are perishing, but to us who are being saved it is the power of God, *(1 Corinthians 1:18 NIV).*

The truth for each of us is that we are often our own, worst enemy. The voice that often consumes your thoughts and mind, is a natural byproduct of an inherited, fallen, sinful nature. You can't listen to any of those negative voices, trying to cripple the reality of who you are in Christ! They are all lies. They come from an enemy intent on turning you away from the Lord. Don't listen to them. Rather, turn your eyes toward the Master, as you still your heart to hear the truth of His love for you. You need to listen, believe, and trust the Word of God. After all, it is the *Word* who is the **visible image of the invisible God.** It is the Word who became flesh, and died on the cross so that you have a choice.

If God loved you so much that He *willingly* sent *His Son* to give you a chance to live with Him for eternity, why would you listen to any voices that try to convince you otherwise? If *God values you that much*, you should *never believe the lies* that this world throws against you. Because of Jesus Christ, you have been given the *opportunity to choose for yourself.* It's a simple choice; between *life* and *death.* Never forget God's words to Israel found in the Old Testament book of Deuteronomy.

> Today I have given you the choice between life and death, between *blessings* and *curses.* Now I call on heaven and earth to witness the choice you make. Oh, that you would *choose life,* so that you and your descendants might

live! *(Deuteronomy 30:19 NLT)*.

Congratulations on completing this journey of divine preparation. My second question to you is intended to keep you moving forward from this point on as you commit to deepen your relationship with Jesus. *What are your plans from this point forward to stay connected with Christ?* Those plans might include setting aside a time to pray on a more regular basis, or to do the same for reading through a specific book of the Bible. If that happens to be your goal, I would highly suggest you start with something in the New Testament. The Gospels are a great place to begin, reading from the first verse in Matthew, through the last verse in John. From that point forward, you can continue to read straight through to the last word in John's Book of Revelation. But just reading through these scriptures will raise all sorts of questions, so I highly recommend finding *a study Bible* to help you through your daily time of devotion. Also, make sure to access *a translation* that lends itself to your understanding of the message shared by the author of each book. The King James Version, might not be the best translation of the Bible for you to get the most of out of your study. Although that is the version that I grew up with, and I still enjoy the old-English flow of scripture from that particular translation.

But, speaking of studies, be sure to make your reading time, one that is focused on *digging deep into the Word* as a study. To get the most out of your time, don't just skim through the passages, but *refer to the annotation* and *notes* contained within your study Bible. Read the passage, then re-read the passage. *Pray* about it while you reflect on the scriptural intent of each section. Examine each passage through the *lens of context*, don't just take a specific verse and interpret it in a *literal sense*. Research to whom it was written; seek to understand the *culture*, the *situation*, and then search for *validating scripture* from other sources in the Bible. That is how you find clarity to the purpose of each particular passage. And then, tuck these divinely inspired words from God, deep into your heart.

Finally, the last question that I need to ask is this: *When your time to leave this world arrives, are you prepared to take the wings of the dawn, and meet your Redeemer, face to face?* The only guarantee that you have in this world is that one day you will leave it forever. There are only two paths available to you when your final day arrives, as you exhale your last, earthly breath. You will either escape on the *wings of the dawn* to meet Jesus, face to face, or you will be snatched away on the *wings of darkened despair,* to a place where you will be forever separated from your Maker and Creator. Which simply means that you will never rest in peace for all of eternity. Anguish and suffering will be your only companion if you choose to cling tight to the *unforgivable sin* of rejecting Jesus as your Lord and Savior. The choice is yours. It's essential that you choose wisely right now, as tomorrow is never guaranteed.

If you've never accepted Jesus into your life, it's simply a matter of *believing* that *He is Who the Bible says He is.* You've just completed a forty-day journey of discovery verifying the *unlimited mercy, grace,* and *love* that *Jesus freely offers* to you. As you believe; you will receive, by simply asking Him into your life. But you must choose to open the door and let Him in. I promise, your life will be *forever changed.* You will become a child of the living, Holy God. Your eternal destiny will be secured as your name is now written in the *Lamb's, Book of Life.* Then, when your final moment on earth arrives, you will take the *wings of the dawn,* and you will forever be with your Lord and Master, Jesus Christ.

The Lord bless you and keep you;
the Lord make his face shine on you
and be gracious to you;
the Lord turn his face toward you
and give you peace. Numbers 6:24-26 NIV

The Wings of the Dawn ~ Psalm 139

The "Wings of the Dawn," what a beautiful phrase,
      Evoking an image, 'midst the sweetest of days.
Like an eagle in flight, upon outstretched wings,
      Soaring high in the sky, above pastoral scenes.
Beyond the clouds, not hampered by weather,
      The wind of my spirit will rise up forever.
The horizon is tranquil, engulfed in the Light,
      It draws my attention - what a beautiful sight.

The future I see.... it's almost within reach,
      Like waves gently lapping on the sand of a beach.
Scenes that appear as I've soared through this life,
      Are sprinkled with joy and some trials and strife.
The wind shares with me a message so clear,
      As I silence my heart, in an effort to hear;
Each verse is quite different, as the seasons fly by,
      I hear a new meaning, as the midnight draws nigh.
For the time fast approaches, when I can sail no more,
      To another adventure, toward a beckoning shore;
So, I lift up my eyes toward the Glory above,
      Where lives are united in God's boundless love!

A hand lifts me up with His wind under wing,
      Sweet rhapsodies ring out as a fresh gentle spring.
Salvation has found me - I will wander no more,
      I glide through the heavens, His Way to explore.
I fly toward the entrance - to the door high above,
      That beckons my presence to abide in His love.
And there I will enter on the "Wings of the Dawn,"
      Within the Glory of Jesus, my soul will live on!

                                    Lanny K. Cook

Notes of Personal Reflection

ABOUT THE AUTHOR

Lanny's creativity allows him to write about a myriad of life topics which is why he refers to his efforts as *"life journaling."* Through his eighteen years as a single dad, working in a public high school for nearly thirty years, serving in volunteer ministry for most of his adult life - along with being a pastor and chaplain for more than a decade, Lanny possesses an eclectic array of experience from which his repertoire of informative and inspirational writing originates.

Lanny retired after decades of service in the public education system as a teacher and as an administrator. He completed his Bachelor and Master of Education Degrees from Colorado State University and a Master of Arts in Public School Administration from the University of Phoenix. In 2007 he completed a Doctor of Ministry degree from Newburgh Theological Seminary and a PhD in Biblical Studies in 2014. This academic preparation provided him the credentials to serve as an ordained pastor at several churches for more than a decade, as well as finally retiring from ministry with several years of chaplain service with Market Place Chaplains in Denver. In 2006 Lanny was recognized by Goodwill Industries of Denver as the "Educator of the Year." In July, 2023 he was recognized as a "Legendary Local" by the Commerce City Historical Society for his contributions to the students and programs of the local school district.

Lanny has published numerous titles that include a historical fiction piece, entitled, "*Unforgiven Destiny,* The Life and Times of John Frederick Williams." His other published works include; "*Destiny Defined* - Sons of the Eastern Plains;" "*Fingernails on the Chalkboard* - An Insider's Look into the Public Education System;" "*The Mystery of Zion* - Israel and the Last Days;" and "*Amazon Culture* – Exploring the Jungle of Narcissism."

Find Lanny's website at www.LannyCook.com where you can discover more about him and his published works, or you can simply scan the QR code below:

To check out all of Lanny's books available for order through Amazon or to leave a review for Radiance of Glory, scan the QR code below to go directly to Amazon.

www.ingramcontent.com/pod-product-compliance
Lightning Source LLC
Chambersburg PA
CBHW051413090426
42737CB00014B/2637